A WORLD in CHANGE

Searching for Stability

Timely Reports to Keep
Journalists, Scholars and the Public
Abreast of Developing Issues, Events and Trends

Editorial Research Reports
Published by Congressional Quarterly Inc.
1414 22nd Street, N.W.
Washington, D.C. 20037

About the Cover

The cover was designed by Assistant Art Director Robert Redding

PRINTED IN THE UNITED STATES OF AMERICA

Editor, Hoyt Gimlin
Associate Editor, Martha V. Gottron
Editorial Assistants, Leah Klumph, Elizabeth Furbush
Production Manager, I. D. Fuller
Assistant Production Manager, Maceo Mayo

Library of Congress Cataloging in Publication Data

Main entry under title:

A World in change.

Reports originally appeared in Editorial research reports.
Bibliography: p.
Includes index.
1. World Politics — 1975-1985 — Addresses, essays, lectures. I. Congressional Quarterly, inc. II. Editorial research reports.

D849.W68 1985	909.82′7	85-7766

ISBN 0-87187-359-1

Contents

Foreword

"If we are to change the world we must first understand it," Secretary of State George P. Shultz once told the United Nations General Assembly. No one pretends that bringing about either change or understanding is easy. All too often, change is perceived and understanding is achieved long after a series of events, the work of historians rather than politicians. But sometimes trends in international affairs are detected in their current state, even if their full meaning is not always apparent.

Some of the subjects explored in this book belong in the category of trend-tracking. Take Europe, with its retreat from the advanced welfare state. This retreat extends even to southern European democracies that have socialist governments. Or look at China, trying to break out of an ideological mold to sample the wares of the West. It is following a course charted by some of the communist countries in eastern Europe. In Germany, the theme of reconciliation did not suddenly surface as countries on both sides of the Atlantic struggled to find the proper way of observing the 40th anniversary of the end of World War II in Europe. Throughout the postwar years, West Germany has sought to create loyal ties with former enemies in the West, and later to extend the hand of friendship to separated brethren in communist-controlled East Germany.

East-West relations will continue to create global anxieties as long as the world lies under the potential threat of nuclear annihilation. After a 13-month hiatus, the United States and Russia resumed arms control talks in March on issues that are discussed in the first of this book's 10 reports. These reports look not just to the great nuclear powers and centers of conflict, but also to America's neighbors north and south, examining significant changes occurring in those lands. Other reports study the chronic racial unrest in South Africa, and the desperate food shortages elsewhere on that continent. We hope they all will contribute, however modestly, to our understanding of the world.

Hoyt Gimlin
Editor

May 1985
Washington, D.C.

ARMS CONTROL NEGOTIATIONS

by

Mary H. Cooper

Feb. 22
1 9 8 5

Editor's Note: The opening round of the three-part Geneva arms control talks ended in stalemate April 23. At issue throughout the six-week session was the Strategic Defense Initiative, the Reagan administration's program of research into the feasibility of creating a land- and space-based weapons system to defend the United States from nuclear attack. Soviet negotiators held fast to their position that SDI be banned before discussing proposals to limit offensive nuclear weapons. The Americans rejected this view, saying that a ban on research cannot be verified and is thus not an acceptable issue for negotiation.

The negotiators in Geneva did not work in isolation. On March 10, just two days before the talks began, Soviet leader Konstantin Chernenko died after a long illness and was succeeded — as had been widely predicted — by Mikhail Gorbachev. While the transition in leadership brought no appreciable change in the Kremlin's stance at Geneva, Gorbachev announced April 7 that the Soviet Union would unilaterally halt deployment until November of SS-20 intermediate-range nuclear missiles aimed at Western Europe and challenged the United States to impose a similar freeze on its deployment of Pershing II and cruise missiles in Europe. The White House denounced Gorbachev's proposal as a propaganda ploy designed to foment dissent among the NATO allies and weaken the Americans' hand in Geneva. The Pentagon, meanwhile, released its fourth edition of "Soviet Military Power," claiming the Soviet Union is conducting similar strategic-defense research and citing several instances of alleged Soviet non-compliance with existing arms limitation agreements.

Despite the lack of progress at the negotiating table, the two sides did appear to offer hope of future accommodation after talks resume May 30. Not only did they cautiously welcome the possibility of a Reagan-Gorbachev summit this fall — the first such meeting since Reagan became president in 1981 — but they acted quickly to prevent a potentially explosive incident — the March killing by Soviet guards of an American military liaison officer on duty in East Germany — from jeopardizing the outcome of the talks.

ARMS CONTROL NEGOTIATIONS

A FTER a 13-month hiatus, the United States and the Soviet Union are about to return to the bargaining table in Geneva, Switzerland, to resume arms control negotiations. The talks, scheduled to begin March 12, will for the first time encompass three separate categories of arms: strategic nuclear weapons, intermediate-range nuclear weapons and — a category never before given special consideration — space weapons.

But no sooner was the agreement to resume negotiations announced than the prospects for their successful outcome were clouded by conflicting interpretations of the ambiguously worded announcement itself. The document to which both delegations agreed Jan. 8 specified that all three areas be "considered and resolved in their interrelationship." Subsequent statements by Soviet Foreign Minister Andrei A. Gromyko made clear the Soviet position that no agreement can be reached in any one area unless agreement is also reached in the other two. "If no progress were made in space," he said Jan. 13 in a television interview with Soviet journalists, "then none could be made in the question of strategic weapons." American spokesmen denied such iron-clad "linkage" was intended. "Interrelationships, yes," explained White House spokesman Larry Speakes, "but as far as linkage where one doesn't proceed without the other, no, that's not our position."

Another potential conflict that became immediately apparent centered around President Reagan's Strategic Defense Initiative, popularly known as SDI or, to its critics, "Star Wars." Now in the research stage, SDI envisions a new type of non-nuclear, space-based defense against nuclear attack that its supporters say would remove the enemy's incentive to use nuclear weapons. Advocates say the research program does not violate the terms of the 1972 Anti-Ballistic Missile (ABM) Treaty, which forbids the deployment of weapons in space, and say it should not be used as a "bargaining chip" in Geneva. Only if the program passes from the research stage to the development and deployment of weapons, they say, should SDI be a subject of negotiation. President Reagan reiterated this position in a recent interview. Asked if he would halt SDI research in return for Soviet concessions on offensive weapons, he replied: "No, I would want to proceed with what we're doing...." [1]

[1] Interview with *The New York Times*, Feb. 13, 1985.

The Soviet Union is adamantly opposed to SDI and clearly intends to place the program at the top of its agenda in March. Far from being a benign defensive system, they say, SDI would guarantee the success of an American first strike against the Soviet Union. As such, it can only be interpreted as a destabilizing offensive weapons system and must be banned before it ever gets off the ground.

The selection of the negotiating teams is also an indication of each side's opening positions. On the U.S. side, the delegation will be headed by a newcomer to nuclear arms talks, Max M. Kampelman. On record as a hard-liner toward the Soviet Union and supporter of SDI, he will also lead the American team dealing with space weapons. John Tower, a former senator (R-Texas, 1961-85) and chairman of the Senate Armed Services Committee who supports Reagan's military buildup, will be the chief negotiator on strategic, or long-range, weapons *(see glossary, p. 13)*. The only delegation head with negotiating experience in the area to which he has been assigned is Maynard W. Glitman, a career diplomat who was deputy head of the delegation in previous talks on the intermediate-range nuclear force (INF).[2] He will lead the delegation on INF talks in Geneva.

Veteran arms negotiator Paul H. Nitze will play an important behind-the-scenes role. By far the most experienced arms control expert connected with the new talks, Nitze will be a "special adviser" to the proceedings. Hard-liners were encouraged by the selection of Kampelman and Tower. At the same time, however, supporters of arms control were encouraged by the surprise replacement of Edward L. Rowny, chief negotiator in the stalemated strategic arms reductions talks (START), and his relegation to a less visible advisory position.[3] Rowny, a retired general with strong conservative backing, has criticized past arms control efforts.

The Soviet delegation has greater experience in arms control negotiations. Delegation head and chief negotiator on strategic arms will be Viktor Karpov, who also led his party to the START talks. The space weapons team will be led by Yuli Kvitsinsky, former INF negotiator and co-author, with Nitze, of the ill-fated "walk-in-the-woods" proposal before those talks collapsed *(see p. 18)*. His place as chief negotiator for the INF

---

[2] The United States and the Soviet Union opened talks in Geneva in November 1981 aimed at limiting INF missiles based in Europe. Moscow broke off these talks two years later when the first American-made Pershing II and cruise missiles were deployed in Western Europe in accordance with a 1979 NATO decision *(see p. 16)*.

[3] The Reagan administration, critical of the strategic arms limitation talks (SALT) begun in 1969, proposed instead reducing the levels of these long-range nuclear weapons. START talks began in June 1982 but were suspended in December 1983 when Moscow refused to set a date for their resumption *(see p. 19)*.

Chernenko's Health

While official Soviet statements offer conflicting accounts of Konstantin U. Chernenko's state of health, the 73-year-old Soviet leader was last seen in public Dec. 27 and is reportedly suffering from emphysema and heart disease. Speculation on the eventual succession of a younger Kremlin leader has focused on 53-year-old Mikhail Gorbachev, the youngest member of the ruling Politburo. Gorbachev would be the first Soviet leader whose political formation was not directly shaped by World War II and the rule of Josef Stalin.

Whoever Chernenko's successor may be, however, the transition's impact on the Geneva talks may be minimal. Continuity in the Soviet position on arms control appears to be assured not only by the Politburo's final say in the matter but also by the active role that veteran negotiator Andrei A. Gromyko continues to play in the arms control process.

Should Chernenko die, his successor would be the fourth Soviet leader since Ronald Reagan was first elected to the White House. Leonid I. Breznev died in 1982 and was succeeded by Yuri V. Andropov, who died in February 1984. He was succeeded by Chernenko.

talks will be taken by Aleksei Obukhov, another experienced arms control negotiator.

President Reagan's Call for a 'New Dialogue'

In contrast to the skepticism with which he regarded arms control during his first term, Reagan welcomed the Geneva talks, saying he had "no more important goal" in his second term than to "achieve a good agreement — an agreement which meets the interests of both countries, which increases the security of our allies and which enhances international stability." [4]

At the same time, Reagan sought significant increases in defense spending for fiscal 1986, reinforcing his position that the United States should only enter into negotiations with the Soviet Union from a position of strength (see p. 6). In addition, the administration has stepped up its campaign calling into question Soviet compliance with the terms of past arms control agreements. In a report to Congress, the administration cited 13 areas of "concern," but focused its attention on one "clear violation" of the 1972 ABM Treaty, a phased-array, early warning radar system now under construction near the Siberian city of Krasnoyarsk.[5] Calling the provision controlling deployment of phased-array radar "the linchpin of the ABM Treaty,"

---

[4] Statement issued Jan. 22, 1985.
[5] The unclassified version of the non-compliance report, required by the fiscal 1985 Defense Authorization Act, was released Feb. 1.

a senior administration official, who briefed reporters on condition he not be identified, termed Soviet non-compliance "a dagger pointed at the whole arms control process in the future."

With public opinion apparently solidly behind him and such misgivings about Soviet trustworthiness, why is Reagan embarking on new arms control negotiations? Kenneth Adelman, director of the U.S. Arms Control and Disarmament Agency, gave three reasons: "New arms control agreements, if soundly formulated, can serve U.S. security interests; entering into new negotiations does not in any way condone past Soviet behavior; and arms control gives us leverage and another way to get the Soviets to abide by existing agreements." [6]

Such an agreement would have to take account of changed expectations, as reflected in the administration's new "strategic concept," which couples the traditional aims of arms control negotiations in the short term with a longer-term vision of strategic defense. Deputy Secretary of State Kenneth W. Dam first presented the strategy, which other officials have since restated verbatim: "For the next 10 years, we should seek a radical reduction in the number and power of existing and planned offensive and defensive nuclear arms, whether land-based, space-based or otherwise. We should even now be looking forward to a period of transition, beginning possibly 10 years from now, to effective non-nuclear defensive forces, including defenses against offensive nuclear arms. This period of transition should lead to the eventual elimination of nuclear arms, both offensive and defensive. A nuclear-free world is an ultimate objective to which we, the Soviet Union and all other nations can agree." [7]

Continuing Push to Build Up U.S. Defenses

Even as the administration was elaborating its negotiating position for the coming talks, it was trying to build support in the United States and Europe for its defense modernization program, including SDI. This program, it argues, is necessary to persuade the Soviet Union to bargain in good faith. The administration requested that Congress approve a $2 trillion military budget over the next five years, beginning with $313.7 billion for fiscal 1986, which starts Oct. 1, 1985. Part of the money would be used to reinforce the arsenal of strategic nuclear weapons: the budget includes $3.2 billion for 48 land-based MX missiles,

---

[6] Adelman spoke at a State Department briefing Feb. 1. The arms control agency was set up in 1960 to advise the president and secretary of state on arms control.

[7] Dam spoke Jan. 14 before the Foreign Policy Association in New York. The new strategic concept was reportedly drafted by Paul Nitze and presented to Gromyko by Secretary of State Shultz at a meeting of the two in Geneva, Jan. 7-8. Nitze later reiterated the concept in a meeting Jan. 25 with reporters. See *The Washington Post*, Jan. 26, 1985.

President Reagan and Vice President Bush with the U.S. negotiating team; from left, chief Max M. Kampelman, John Tower and Maynard W. Glitman

$5.6 billion for 48 B1 bombers and $5 billion for a Trident submarine and Trident missiles.

Administration spokesmen, led by Defense Secretary Caspar W. Weinberger, maintain that Reagan's four-year-old program to "rearm America" is what led the Soviet Union back to the bargaining table and that efforts to reduce the Pentagon's budget will only undermine the American position in Geneva. Because of widespread bipartisan concern over the $200 billion federal budget deficit, however, the administration's defense budget request will undoubtedly be pared.[8] Reflecting this sentiment, Sen. Sam Nunn, D-Ga., told Weinberger during hearings before the Senate Armed Services Committee: "It's not a question of whether it will be cut, it's a question of how much it will be reduced."

Another subject of concern to the administration is the ongoing debate over the controversial MX missile. Dubbed the "peacekeeper" by Reagan because of its purported contribution to nuclear deterrence, the MX is a new, more accurate intercontinental ballistic missile (ICBM) armed with 10 nuclear warheads whose production has been delayed by congressional opposition.[9] The administration is trying to increase support for the program in Congress before it comes to a vote, possibly in March just as the Geneva talks are to open: "I must tell you, frankly," Weinberger told the Senate Foreign Relations Committee Jan. 31, "that cancellation of key programs, such as MX, will prolong negotiations, not facilitate them, and will reduce our ability to achieve arms reductions."

---

[8] For background, see "Federal Budget Deficit," *E.R.R.*, 1984 Vol. I, pp. 45-64; "Reagan's Defense Buildup," *E.R.R.*, 1984 Vol. I, pp. 309-328.

[9] Of the 100 missiles called for in the MX program, 21 are already under production. Under a complex formula agreed to in 1984, $1.5 billion earmarked for the production of 21 more MX missiles cannot be released until after March 1. Even then, the money cannot be spent until both the House of Representatives and the Senate vote their approval.

Further complicating the administration's effort to boost defense spending on Capitol Hill is the recent change in leadership on several key congressional committees. In particular, Rep. Les Aspin, D-Wis., newly elected chairman of the House Armed Services Committee, has suggested he may drop his support for the MX, a weapon he said may be unnecessary if Reagan's strategic defense initiative proves feasible.[10]

"Star Wars" itself has now overtaken the MX as the most controversial element of the administration's defense modernization program. In its preliminary research phase alone, SDI is expected to cost $26 billion, while some estimates of its final figure reach $1 trillion.[11] But budget concerns are only a small element of the growing criticism over SDI. While supporting the current research effort, former Secretary of State Cyrus R. Vance said he was "strongly opposed" to pursuing strategic defense beyond the research stage. "Once we cross the line from basic research to deployment," he told the Senate Foreign Relations Committee Feb. 4, "we have very radically changed the basic strategic doctrine." [12] He voiced the concern of many arms control advocates in Congress that the deployment of a strategic defense system in space would set off a new arms race. They fear that the Soviet Union would try to penetrate the defense with new offensive weapons and the United States would then be compelled to build even more elaborate defenses.

Up to now, the debate over SDI has been largely confined to the scientific community, where technical considerations are called into play either to boost or to debunk the program. Some of its supporters are physicists working in arms research facilities.[13] Others, however, oppose SDI as technically unfeasible. Some say that even if it were possible to extend a nuclear umbrella over the United States, SDI would pose grave dangers. According to a study conducted by the Union of Concerned Scientists: "If the president's vision is pursued, outer space could become a battlefield. An effective defense against a missile attack must employ weapons operating in space. This now peaceful sanctuary, so long a symbol of cooperation, would be violated. And the arduous process of arms control, which has scored so few genuine successes in the nuclear era, would also be imperiled — perhaps terminated — by the deployment of weapons in space." [14]

---

[10] Aspin has long supported the renegotiation of the ABM Treaty. See Les Aspin, "Missiles Become Protected," *The New Republic,* February 1981.

[11] The fiscal 1985 budget includes $1.4 billion for SDI; the administration has asked for $3.7 billion in fiscal 1986.

[12] Vance served under President Carter from 1977 to 1980.

[13] See, for example, letters to the editor in support of SDI published in *The Wall Street Journal,* Jan. 17, 1985.

[14] Union of Concerned Scientists, *The Fallacy of Star Wars* (1984), pp. 5-6. UCS is a nonprofit organization of 100,000 scientists and citizens concerned about the impact of advanced technology on society.

NATO, Soviet Concerns

THE DEBATE over SDI may be reawakening anti-nuclear sentiment in other countries, a worrisome prospect to administration supporters. The opposition Liberal Party in Canada in early February challenged the Conservative government of Prime Minister Brian Mulroney over its current negotiations with the U.S. government to modernize an early warning system in northern Canada. The Liberals said that the modernization would draw Canada into participation in SDI. Defense Minister Robert Coates denied that the new $1 billion North Warning System would be a part of SDI.[15]

Far more troubling to the administration is the effect an anti-SDI campaign among NATO's European members might have on the American position in Geneva.[16] So far the initiative has elicited no official opposition from the allied governments. Lord Carrington, NATO's secretary general, went so far as to say that it would be "the height of imprudence" for the United States to interrupt research on SDI.[17]

But SDI alarms many European observers who fear that the creation of an anti-ballistic defense over North America would encourage the United States to withdraw into a "Fortress America," abandoning Western Europe to its own defenses. With the United States safely protected behind its space-based shield, they say, Europe would become an attractive battlefield for a nuclear exchange. The governments of allied nations — West Germany, Britain, Italy, Belgium and the Netherlands — that supported a 1979 NATO decision to deploy 572 new intermediate-range nuclear weapons on their soil may have special cause for alarm.[18] The deployment began on schedule in December 1983, but it fueled a widespread anti-nuclear movement that undermined the ruling governments' political strength. The

[15] The United States and Canada are now negotiating an agreement to modernize the Distant Early Warning system — or DEW line — originally built to detect low-flying, strategic bombers that the Earth's curvature prevented U.S.-based radar from picking up from far away. It was allowed to deteriorate as the Soviet Union based its strategic arsenal ever more heavily on land-based ICBMs.

[16] NATO was formed in April 1949 as a military alliance against Soviet aggression in Europe in the wake of the Berlin blockade. It is made up of 16 countries: Belgium, Britain, Canada, Denmark, France, West Germany, Greece, Iceland, Italy, Luxembourg, the Netherlands, Norway, Portugal, Spain, Turkey and the United States.

[17] Lord Carrington, who served as foreign minister in the conservative government of British Prime Minister Margaret Thatcher, spoke Jan. 22 while visiting Ottawa.

[18] NATO's December 1979 "dual-track" decision called for U.S.-Soviet negotiations on intermediate-range nuclear forces. If negotiations were not successful, the decision called for the deployment in Europe of 464 ground-launched cruise missiles and 108 Pershing II missiles — each with a single nuclear warhead — beginning in December 1983. All 108 Pershings are to be deployed in West Germany, and 54 are reportedly in place now. Deployment of the cruise missiles has already begun in Britain, West Germany and Italy, and is scheduled to begin this year in Belgium and the Netherlands.

9

conservative government of West German Chancellor Helmut Kohl is particularly vulnerable. Already weakened by economic stagnation, the government faces elections in two years and can expect strong opposition from the country's peace movement.[19]

Only days after it was announced that U.S.-Soviet arms talks would resume, Belgian Prime Minister Wilfried Martens dismayed the Reagan administration by refusing to permit the cruise missile deployment scheduled in March. He said his government would decide by the end of that month when to begin deployment, but observers predicted that Martens, who is under pressure from anti-nuclear forces, would delay such a decision until after national elections are held in December. The Netherlands is exhibiting similar sensitivity to domestic anti-nuclear sentiment. The government there has delayed deployment of 48 cruise missiles until November.

As if NATO's jitters were not enough to jeopardize Reagan's plan to arrive in Geneva with a strong hand, U.S. allies in the southern Pacific dealt the administration an unexpected blow. First, New Zealand's Prime Minister David Lange, following up on a campaign promise to prohibit nuclear weapons in the country, announced his government would deny port access to a U.S. warship scheduled to arrive for joint naval exercises within the ANZUS alliance (Australia, New Zealand and the United States).[20] The United States, which for security reasons does not reveal whether or not Navy vessels at sea are carrying nuclear weapons, responded by canceling the exercises altogether. Days later, Australian Prime Minister Robert Hawke told the administration U.S. aircraft could not use Australian bases to monitor a test of the MX missile scheduled for this summer.

Pressure for Arms Control in Soviet Bloc

While pursuing arms modernization, the Reagan administration has consistently maintained that it was willing to resume arms control negotiations at any time the Soviet Union wished. It was, after all, the Soviet side that abandoned both the START and the INF talks in 1983, spokesmen maintain. First, Moscow broke off the INF negotiations in November to protest the initial NATO deployment of new Pershing and cruise missiles. The following month it failed to agree to a date for the next round of START talks. Soviet leader Konstantin U. Chernenko insisted as recently as last October that Moscow would not resume INF talks until the NATO weapons were

---

[19] For background, see "West Germany's 'Missile' Election," *E.R.R.*, 1983 Vol. I, pp. 149-168.

[20] The ANZUS defense treaty was signed in September 1951. Less structured than NATO, the treaty calls primarily for strategic consultation and periodic joint military exercises.

removed from Europe. In agreeing to return to Geneva, Moscow reversed its position. It also appears to have dropped its prior insistence on a moratorium on testing anti-satellite weapons as a condition for negotiations on space weaponry.

Since the agreement to resume negotiations, the Soviet Union has focused its attention on SDI, repeatedly asserting that no progress can be made on INF and strategic weapons unless some agreement can be worked out to prevent the "militarization of space." Some Western observers have deduced from such statements that Moscow is desperately trying to head off a new and highly expensive round of the arms race that it can ill afford. The Soviet economy has for the past several years suffered from repeated crop failures as well as depressed world prices for its oil exports.[21]

Secretary of State George P. Shultz expressed this view during recent testimony before the Senate Foreign Relations Committee. In contrast to the growing military and economic might of the West, he said, "the Soviets face ... profound structural economic difficulties, a continuing succession problem and restless allies; its diplomacy and its clients are on the defensive in many parts of the world." But this picture is not shared by all administration officials. Defense Secretary Weinberger told the same hearing Jan. 31 that the Soviet Union boasts a numerically stronger nuclear arsenal and is "dramatically improving" its quality, while "expanding the geographical reach" of its conventional forces.

History of Arms Control

THE GENEVA negotiations are but the most recent chapter in the turbulent history of arms control. Ever since the nuclear genie was let out of the bottle nearly 40 years ago, negotiators have tried in vain to halt the development of nuclear weapons.

The United States was the first country to explode nuclear devices and is the only country to have used them, destroying the Japanese cities of Hiroshima and Nagasaki in August 1945. Only by bringing Japan quickly to its knees, it was reasoned, could the Pacific war be ended without the additional loss of thousands of U.S. servicemen. Ten months later, on June 14, 1946, the United States presented a plan to the newly created

---

[21] For background on economic issues within the Soviet bloc, see "Communist Economies," *E.R.R.*, 1984 Vol. II, pp. 957-976.

United Nations to ban the production of nuclear weapons and to place all peaceful applications of nuclear technology under international control. The Baruch plan — named for its co-author, financier Bernard Baruch — called for the creation of an agency to oversee nuclear development and inspect member nations' facilities. The United States, which alone possessed the technology to produce nuclear weapons at that time, pledged to destroy its bombs as soon as the agency was established. The Soviet Union, however, insisted that the American arsenal be dismantled before it would agree to the agency's creation, and the Baruch plan became the first of many arms control proposals to fall victim to disagreements between the postwar superpowers.

The next two decades witnessed a steady worsening of U.S.-Soviet relations. It was during this so-called Cold War period of frosty diplomatic exchanges that the Soviet Union developed a nuclear capability of its own and rapidly built an arsenal of atomic weaponry to counter that of the United States. Both sides began modernizing their weapons, and the arms race was on. The first breakthrough in nuclear arms technology came as a result of reducing warhead size and weight. The bombs dropped over Japan were so heavy that they had to be transported by large bombers. By making them smaller and lighter, arms designers on both sides were able to load them instead onto rockets, which were a faster, and thus less vulnerable, means of delivering the bomb to its target. In time, both the United States and the Soviet Union developed intercontinental ballistic missiles (ICBMs), large rockets that could be shot up into the atmosphere to release their payload — the nuclear bomb — which would then follow a path determined by the physical law of "ballistic trajectory" toward its ultimate target halfway around the Earth.

The unprecedented danger and expense entailed in the spiraling arms race prompted both sides to propose several arms control initiatives during the 1950s and 1960s. This period saw considerable progress in areas not directly concerned with the armaments themselves. The bilateral Hot Line Agreement (1963) set up a direct link between the White House and the Kremlin to facilitate emergency communications and reduce the risk of war. Four multilateral agreements of the same period also were aimed at reducing the risk of nuclear conflict. The Antarctic Treaty (1959) banned "any measures of a military nature" on that continent; the Limited Nuclear Test Ban Treaty (1963) banned weapons tests under water, in the atmosphere and in outer space, including "the moon and other celestial bodies"; the Peaceful Uses of Outer Space Treaty (1966) went a step further and banned all nuclear weapons from

Arms Control: A Glossary

Anti-Ballistic Missile (ABM): A defensive system to intercept and destroy strategic ballistic missiles or their elements during flight, consisting of interceptor missiles, launchers and radars.

Cruise Missile: a small (18-ft.), jet-powered guided missile that can fly at very low altitudes to minimize radar detection.

Intercontinental Ballistic Missile (ICBM): A land-based, rocket-propelled missile with an intercontinental range (defined as over 5,500 kilometers under SALT). Usually launched from an underground silo, it is vulnerable to attack but is also the most destructive strategic weapon.

Intermediate-Range Nuclear Forces (INF): Land-based missiles and aircraft with ranges of up 5,500 kilometers that are capable of striking targets beyond the general region of the battlefield but not capable of intercontinental range.

MX missile

Multiple Independently Targetable Re-entry Vehicle (MIRV): The portion of a strategic missile that carries a number of nuclear warheads, each of which can be directed to a separate target.

Mutual Assured Destruction: The ability of opposing sides to inflict an "unacceptable" degree of damage upon an aggressor after absorbing any first strike, or first offensive move of a nuclear war.

MX (Missile Experimental): A new, 10-warhead U.S. ICBM developed to replace the increasingly vulnerable Minuteman ICBM force and to counter the SS-18 and SS-19, Soviet ICBMs.

Short-Range Nuclear Forces: Land-based missiles, rockets and artillery capable of striking only targets in the general region of the battlefield.

Strategic Nuclear Forces: Ballistic missiles and bomber aircraft that have intercontinental range. U.S. strategic nuclear forces directly threaten Soviet territory and vice versa.

Submarine-Launched Ballistic Missile: Ballistic missiles carried in and launched from a submarine. These are harder to detect than land-based or air-launched missiles.

space; and signatories to the Nuclear Non-Proliferation Treaty (1968) agreed not to transfer nuclear weapons to nations that do not possess them. These agreed in turn not to embark on nuclear weapons programs of their own.[22]

Agreement to negotiate the far more difficult issue of existing weapons was longer in coming. After its humiliation in the Cuban missile crisis of 1962 — under U.S. pressure Russia withdrew its missiles from the island — the Soviet Union rapidly increased its nuclear arsenal. By the time agreement was finally reached to begin arms negotiations in 1968, each side already possessed nuclear arsenals capable of destroying the other. Deterrence was based on the mutual realization that a nuclear first strike could not destroy all the enemy's warheads and would merely provoke a retaliatory response. The concept, known as mutual assured destruction — or MAD — was to dominate the strategic thinking of both sides. President Johnson's defense secretary, Robert S. McNamara, gave top priority to the limitation of anti-ballistic missiles (ABMs). He believed they would be ineffective against an all-out attack and were destabilizing, in that each side was rushing ahead to develop newer offensive weapons to counter ABMs.

Delayed first by the Soviet invasion of Czechoslovakia in August 1968 and then by the election of a new president, Richard M. Nixon, the Strategic Arms Limitation Talks — SALT — finally began in Vienna April 16, 1970. After two years of hard bargaining, President Nixon went to Moscow and joined Soviet Communist Party Secretary Leonid I. Brezhnev on May 26, 1972, in signing the two accords that made up the first strategic arms limitation agreement — SALT I. The first accord, the ABM Treaty, reflected the shared belief that ABM systems are destabilizing and ineffective. The treaty — which is of unlimited duration but subject to review every five years — allowed each side only two ABM deployment sites — later amended to one — and strictly limited the technological development of ABM weaponry, including radar and interceptor missiles.[23]

SALT I's second component, an interim agreement on offensive strategic arms, was less sweeping in its effect. It froze the numbers of ICBMs and submarine-launched ballistic missiles (SLBMs) on each side for five years. The Soviet Union was left

---

[22] In addition to the United States and Soviet Union, the only country with acknowledged nuclear weapons are Britain, France and China. Several other countries possess the technical ability to produce nuclear weapons. See Joseph P. Yager, ed., *Nonproliferation and U.S. Foreign Policy*, The Brookings Institution, 1980. See also "Controlling Nuclear Proliferation," *E.R.R.*, 1981 Vol. I, pp. 509-532.

[23] By 1975 the United States had deactivated its ABM installation at Grand Forks, N.D., because it was considered to be of little military value by itself. The Soviet "Galosh" ABM system is deployed around Moscow.

with more missile launchers and land-based ICBMs than the United States, while the United States retained its technological superiority and numerical advantage in long-range strategic bombers.

It was this discrepancy in the nuclear balance, which allowed both sides to perceive themselves at a disadvantage, that was to spell eventual failure for the SALT process. The agreement also left unaddressed an important technological advance already under development. This was the multiple, independently targetable re-entry vehicle, or MIRV. A single missile could now be armed with several warheads, each aimed at different targets. MIRVs made simple missile counts obsolete at a single stroke and vastly complicated the already sticky problem of counting nuclear warheads. Although the Senate ratified SALT I by an 88-to-2 margin in September 1972, U.S. misgivings over the interim agreement were expressed in an amendment sponsored by Sen. Henry M. Jackson, D-Wash., that directed the president in future negotiations to accept arms levels equal or superior to those of the Soviet Union.

Technolgical improvements not restricted under SALT's numerical limits proceeded apace on both sides. Soviet advances included a new intermediate-range ballistic missile called the SS-20, the Tu-22M Backfire bomber, submarine-launched missiles and more accurate ICBMs with a higher throw-weight, or payload capacity. For its part, the United States deployed MIRVs to maintain its advantage in the number of nuclear warheads, expanded its Trident submarine-launched missile and B-1 strategic bomber forces, and began developing new weapons such as the MX missile and the long-range cruise missile, a small, guided aircraft similar to the buzz-bombs Nazi Germany used against England in World War II. Able to fly at low altitudes, the cruise missile can be launched from land, sea or air and is particularly difficult to classify under arms control agreements because it can be armed with either conventional or nuclear warheads.

Both sides continued to modernize their nuclear weapons while observing the numerical limits imposed by SALT I. On Nov. 24, 1974, Brezhnev and President Gerald R. Ford agreed to the framework for its successor, SALT II. The Vladivostok accord, named for the Soviet Pacific port city where the two leaders met, set an overall ceiling on the number of delivery vehicles, including strategic bombers, permitted each side. Of the 2,400 total, 1,320 missile launchers could be fitted with MIRVs. Both sides were allowed leeway to allocate their forces as they saw fit. The Soviet Union would continue to concentrate its nuclear warheads on ICBMs, while the United States distributed its arsenal more evenly among the strategic "triad" of land-based missiles, submarines and strategic bombers.

Once again, however, weapons designers in the military-industrial complex of both nations worked faster than the arms control negotiators. The Vladivostok agreement did not cover the American cruise missile or the Soviet Backfire bomber, presented as a medium-range bomber but considered capable of intercontinental missions as well. The impasse over these weapons was sidestepped under a compromise negotiating framework of September 1977, in which both sides agreed to observe the SALT I Interim Agreement until they could produce its successor.

The three-part SALT II accord that Brezhnev and President Jimmy Carter signed in Vienna on June 18, 1979, featured a Treaty on the Limitation of Strategic Offensive Arms. It set a limit of 2,400 on the total number of nuclear delivery vehicles and the following individual limits: 1,320 MIRV launchers (missiles and bombers carrying cruise missiles); 1,200 MIRVed ballistic missiles; 820 MIRVed land-based ICBMs; and 308 "heavy" ICBMs. No additional fixed launchers were permitted. It also banned any increase in the maximum number of warheads on existing types of ICBMs and limited the number of warheads allowed for each new type of ICBM to 10. Each SLBM was allowed to carry 14 warheads while an average of 28 long-range cruise missiles was permitted for each bomber. SALT II also banned the flight-testing and deployment of several missiles and the construction of new fixed ICBM launchers.

SALT II immediately came under fire from critics who said it enabled the Soviets to maintain nuclear superiority over the United States. For the next two years, as U.S.-Soviet relations deteriorated, the agreement was subjected to mounting criticism. In protest over the Soviet invasion of Afghanistan in December 1979, Carter himself stopped the ratification process by asking the Senate in January 1980 to "delay consideration" of SALT II. It was never ratified.

Arms Control Under Reagan Administration

Elected in the fall of 1980, Ronald Reagan came to office vowing to "rearm America." The SALT process was denounced as a failure and arms control figured hardly at all during the first 18 months of his administration. The Soviet Union, he and his officials repeatedly suggested, had deftly used the negotiations to slow U.S. weapons modernization while boldly forging ahead themselves to a position of military superiority over the United States.

While the strategic arms negotiations were placed on hold and

Other Arms Control Talks in Progress

In addition to the bilateral negotiations dealing with nuclear armaments, the United States and the Soviet Union have held negotiations to limit conventional forces and chemical weapons, as well as talks aimed at reducing tensions and averting the risk of war in times of crisis.

Mutual and Balanced Force Reductions (MBFR): Talks opened in Vienna in 1973 among 12 NATO and seven Warsaw Pact nations. Their aim is to enhance East-West security and reduce the likelihood of war in Europe by reducing each side's military manpower in Central Europe to a maximum level of 700,000 ground forces, or 900,000 air and ground force personnel combined. NATO claims the Warsaw Pact has a 170,000-man superiority over the West (960,000 compared with 790,000) in the area under consideration. Referred to as the "zone of reductions," the area includes West Germany, Belgium, the Netherlands and Luxembourg in the West, and East Germany, Poland and Czechoslovakia in the East. Issues blocking agreement involve on-site verification, a timetable for the reduction and the troop levels now deployed. Talks resumed Jan. 31.

Conference on Confidence- and Security-Building Measures and Disarmament in Europe (CDE): The goal of these 35-nation talks, which first opened Jan. 17, 1984, in Stockholm, is to reduce the possibility of an accidental nuclear confrontation resulting from miscalculation or a failure of communications. Its participants comprise the United States, Canada, the Soviet Union and all European countries except Albania. One recent product of these talks was the addition to the Washington-Moscow "hotline" of a high-speed facsimile capability that will allow the rapid transmission of photos and charts. The CDE talks are an outgrowth of the 35-nation Conference on Security and Cooperation in Europe (CSCE), which produced the Helsinki accords of 1975, under which both sides agreed to provide advance notification of large military maneuvers. Max Kampelman, who will lead the U.S. delegation in Geneva, headed the U.S. delegation to follow-up talks, held in Madrid and concluded in September 1983. NATO delegates to the Stockholm CDE talks have proposed additional measures for exchanging military information. This year's session opened Jan. 29.

Conference on Disarmament (CD): The 40-member Committee on Disarmament was established in 1979 to achieve a complete and verifiable ban on the production, stockpiling and transfer of chemical weapons. Although a prior agreement — the Geneva Protocol of 1925 — prohibits their use, it does not restrict the production or stockpiling of chemical and biological weapons and contains no provisions for verification. The United States has accused the Soviet Union of using such weapons in Southeast Asia and Afghanistan. On April 18, 1984, the United States introduced a draft treaty calling for a comprehensive and verifiable global ban on chemical weapons. The latest round opened Feb. 5.

the Pentagon was given the green light for increased military spending, the administration had to deal with the issue of intermediate-range nuclear forces in Europe. NATO in 1979 had announced its decision to pursue a "dual track" path to counter the Soviet Union's growing arsenal of intermediate-range missiles, the SS-4, SS-5 and the new SS-20, pointed toward Western Europe. NATO announced it would seek to draw the Soviet Union into negotiations and to begin deploying American-made Pershing II and cruise missiles on allied territory if agreement had not been reached by December 1983.

Secretary of State Alexander M. Haig and Soviet Foreign Minister Gromyko pledged in September 1981 "to spare no effort" to conclude an agreement before the NATO deadline. Talks opened in Geneva on Nov. 30 of that year. Only days earlier, Reagan had offered his own solution to the INF dilemma with his "zero-zero option": NATO would cancel deployment of the American missiles if the Soviet Union agreed to dismantle all its SS-4, SS-5 and SS-20 missiles.

But the Soviet position on INF proved irreconcilable with the U.S. contention that the SS-20s constituted a new and destabilizing class of weapons. Moscow rejected U.S. insistence on global limits of the SS-20 which, with a range of 5,000 kilometers, could threaten not only Western Europe but also American allies in Asia, including Japan. The Soviet Union insisted that British and French nuclear missiles be counted as part of NATO's arsenal; the United States refused, saying that these forces were purely national in scope and did not contribute to allied defense.

The two chief negotiators at Geneva attempted to resolve the impasse on their own during a private conversation in July 1982 later known as the "walk in the woods." U.S. chief negotiator Paul Nitze — founder of the Committee on the Present Danger and leader of the fight against SALT II — and his Soviet counterpart Yuli Kvitsinsky drove to a secluded mountaintop in the Jura range near the French border, ordered the driver to meet them at the bottom and started to walk down. According to one account: "Once they got down to business, Nitze and Kvitsinsky were sitting on a log. It was starting to rain. Nitze had brought along a typed outline of an agreement, from which he began to read aloud. Kvitsinsky listened for a while, then suggested some modifications. Incorporating these changes would make it a joint paper. Nitze asked Kvitsinsky if he realized that. 'Yes,' replied the Soviet. 'Let's go through with the rest of it.' " [24]

---

[24] Strobe Talbott, *Deadly Gambits* (1984), p. 127.

By the time they had reached their car, Nitze and Kvitsinsky reportedly had defined a compromise agreement that prohibited the Soviet Union from developing a long-range ground-launched cruise missile and froze SS-20s deployed in the Asian U.S.S.R. at current levels. In exchange, the United States would cancel deployment of the Pershing. Their efforts were to prove fruitless. Both governments disavowed the proposal and the stalemate persisted. On Nov. 23, 1983, Kvitsinsky announced the Soviet decision to "discontinue" the talks in protest against NATO's resolve to deploy the Pershing and cruise missiles on schedule the following month.

Meanwhile, after 16 months in office, Reagan outlined his first strategic arms control proposal. In an effort to distinguish it from the "failed" SALT process, Reagan named his proposal START, for Strategic Arms Reduction Talks. START's basic aim, as described by chief negotiator Edward L. Rowny, was "to break the mold of past negotiations which concentrated on limiting strategic offensive arms at high levels" and "to improve strategic stability through substantial reductions in the more destabilizing strategic offensive arms." [25] The initial proposal, which Reagan presented May 9, 1982, called for both sides to

Paul H. Nitze

reduce the number of land- and sea-based missile warheads by about one-third to 5,000 and to reduce the number of deployed ballistic missiles to no more than 850, a cut of one-half for the United States, somewhat more for the Soviet Union.

Reagan subsequently modified his START proposal to accommodate the recommendations of the Commission on Strategic Forces — known as the Scowcroft commission after its head, former National Security Council member Brent Scowcroft. While reaffirming the goal of reducing each side's ballistic-missile warheads to 5,000, the president in June 1983 relaxed the overall limit of 850 deployed ballistic missiles. These changes were included in a draft treaty that the United States offered July 7.

Under pressure from congressional arms control advocates, Reagan in October incorporated into the U.S. bargaining position the "build-down" concept, which called for retiring older weapons as a corollary to modernization with the aim of reducing the total number of warheads over time. The Soviet Union, which had linked INF and START talks all along, rejected the

[25] Rowny spoke June 21, 1984, before the Royal United Services Institute of London.

modified proposal and, at the end of the negotiating round on
Dec. 8, refused to agree to a resumption date for START.

Focus on 'Star Wars'

A S THE DATE for the Geneva talks approaches, the United
States and Soviet Union have not altered their basic positions on either strategic or intermediate-range missiles. Officially, these remain as irreconcilable as they were when the
two sets of talks were interrupted at the end of 1983.

Some observers speculate that the format to be followed in
Geneva, establishing an "interrelationship" among the two categories of offensive weapons as well as strategic defense, may
offer a means of breaking the stalemate. By merging the negotiations on INF and strategic forces, it is said, the two sides
might satisfy Moscow's insistence on including the British and
French INF arsenals — totaling some 140 missiles armed with
420 warheads — in NATO's overall weapons count.[25] These
would seem less significant if the entire Euromissile issue were
to be considered in the context of the 10,000 or so strategic
weapons possessed by both sides.

Soviet Foreign Minister Gromyko seemed to indicate that a
merger might be acceptable. "Earlier we conducted talks separately on strategic arms and on intermediate-range arms — and
the two sides then agreed to try to conduct them this way
because it might be easier this way to find accords — while it
has now become absolutely clear that it is impossible to hold
talks and to try to reach agreement on strategic armaments
without solving also the question of intermediate-range weapons," he said during his Jan. 13 interview on Soviet television.

Whether or not this statement reflects Soviet interest in the
merger idea, Reagan administration officials are reportedly opposed. The inclusion of INF with strategic weapons may give
the NATO allies, who are closely involved in the INF talks, too
great a say in the formulation of the U.S. position on strategic
weapons. Given the West Europeans' strong desire for an arms
control agreement between the superpowers, it is said, the
United States would come under pressure to make concessions
on strategic weapons.

The administration appears determined to continue its buildup of these weapons and to be wavering on its promise to abide

---

[25] *The New York Times,* Feb. 1, 1985.

by the terms of the unratified SALT II treaty. Reagan said in 1981 that the United States would not exceed the limits the treaty imposed on strategic weapons so long as the Soviet Union did likewise. But the administration's recent report on Soviet non-compliance charged Moscow with several treaty violations, and Reagan on Jan. 26 for the first time indicated the United States may decide to ignore SALT II when a new, 24-missile-bearing Trident submarine — the USS *Alaska* — puts to sea next October. Under the treaty's terms, the administration would have to retire an older, 16-missile Poseidon submarine or dismantle eight land-based Minuteman II ICBMs when the Trident is completed. Adelman of the Arms Control and Disarmament Agency has said recommendations will be made to the White House in October on whether to continue to abide by SALT II.

Meanwhile, weapons systems in all three areas of the American nuclear "triad" are being modernized. In addition to the Trident, which is quieter and thus more difficult to detect than older submarines, the sea leg of the triad will soon be reinforced by the long-range, highly accurate D-5 (also called the Trident II) submarine-launched missile. The Tomahawk cruise missile is also slated for deployment on board some 100 surface ships and submarines by the end of the decade. The stealth bomber, designed to evade detection by enemy radar, and air-launched cruise missiles incorporating stealth technology are also due for completion by the early 1990s. The MX, whose fate may be decided as the talks get under way, is only one of several new developments strengthening the land-based missile force.

Negotiating 'Star Wars,' the Non-Agreement

Judging from the barrage of Soviet criticism, the Soviet Union can be expected to concentrate its negotiating stance on preventing the Strategic Defense Initiative from proceeding beyond the research stage now in progress. Announcing the program on March 23, 1983, Reagan hailed the SDI concept as nothing less than visionary: "What if free people could live secure in the knowledge that their security did not rest upon the threat of instant U.S. retaliation to deter a Soviet attack, that we could intercept and destroy strategic ballistic missiles before they reached our own soil or that of our allies?" The purpose of SDI, he said, was to strengthen deterrence. The feasibility of such a non-nuclear defense system was expected to be determined by the early 1990s.

According to official descriptions, SDI would constitute a "layered defense" using different technologies to destroy attacking missiles during each phase of the ballistic trajectory. An ICBM could be destroyed during its "boost phase" shortly after launch; during the "post-boost phase" before the warheads are released; in the "mid-course phase" while the released war-heads are soaring through space; or during the "terminal phase" as they re-enter the atmosphere *(see graphic, p. 23)*. A panoply of exotic-sounding weapons utilizing lasers and mirrors and based both on the ground and in space — hence the "Star Wars" connection — are envisioned.

SDI supporters, including Kampelman, insist that it must not be used as a "bargaining chip," to be dispensed with in return for Soviet concessions. "Strategic defense would compensate for the inevitable difficulties of verification and for the absence of genuine trust by permitting some risk-taking in [arms control] agreements," Kampelman and two co-authors wrote in a controversial article published shortly after his appointment to the Geneva talks. "This is another reason why strategic defense should not be traded in the forthcoming negotiations in return for promises that can be broken at any time." [26]

Repeating the concerns expressed by some American sci-entists, Soviet officials and academics condemn SDI out of hand. ". . . [I]ts creation will certainly increase the danger of the first (pre-emptive) strike and the probability of making wrong decisions in a crisis situation," a group of Soviet scientists wrote in a study issued last year. "That is why strategic stability will be diminished, although the two sides will retain a rough parity in their strategic armaments." [27] Another Soviet commentator predicted that SDI will further escalate the arms race. "The other side cannot shut its eyes to these war preparations, of course," arms control analyst Alexei Fedorov wrote. "It will do everything to make the Pentagon realize that [Soviet] ballistic missiles have not become 'a heap of junk' while the U.S. offen-sive strategic potential hangs over it like the sword of Damocles." [28]

Some observers believe the Soviet Union plans to resume testing and deployment of its anti-satellite (ASAT) systems. Like SDI, ASAT involves space weaponry. But while SDI would use space- and ground-based weapons to destroy attacking mis-siles, ASAT would destroy only satellites, including SDI sat-ellites and existing communications and spy satellites. The So-viet Union has had an ASAT program since the early 1970s. But

---

[26] Zbigniew Brzezinski, Robert Jastrow and Max M. Kampelman, "Defense in Space Is Not 'Star Wars'," *The New York Times Magazine,* Jan. 27, 1985, p. 47. Brzezinski was national security adviser to President Carter. Jastrow, a physicist at Dartmouth College, founded the Goddard Institute for Space Studies. Following his appointment as chief U.S. negotiator, Kampelman reportedly tried to have his name removed as the article's co-author but was turned down by the newspaper.

[27] Committee of Soviet Scientists for Peace against Nuclear Threat, "A Space-Based Anti-Missile System with Directed Energy Weapons: Strategic, Legal and Political Implica-tions," Institute of Cosmic Research, All-Union Academy of Sciences, 1984.

[28] Alexei Fedorov, "Is the 'Star Wars' Program a Defense Plan?" undated, Novosti Press Agency.

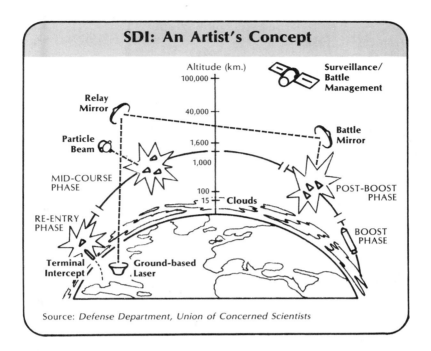

SDI: An Artist's Concept

Altitude (km.)
100,000
40,000
1,600
1,000
100
15

Surveillance/ Battle Management

Relay Mirror

Battle Mirror

Particle Beam

MID-COURSE PHASE

Clouds

POST-BOOST PHASE

RE-ENTRY PHASE

BOOST PHASE

Terminal Intercept

Ground-based Laser

Source: *Defense Department, Union of Concerned Scientists*

after the United States began developing its own ASAT system, Russia in 1983 proposed a ban on further ASAT development.[29] No mention of such a ban has been made by the Soviets since October, leading some observers to believe they want to develop their system to counter SDI.

Because the eventual testing and deployment of the space-based components of SDI are prohibited by the terms of the 1972 ABM Treaty, negotiators involved in the space weapons category of talks in Geneva will discuss this as well as the alleged Soviet violations of that treaty. Meanwhile, some administration officials are openly discussing an approach to arms control that makes it hard to see why the negotiators should bother to meet in Geneva at all. In an article published just as the agenda for next month's talks was announced, ACDA Director Adelman wrote in support of "arms control without agreements." [30] According to this approach, each side would develop a strategic defense system, such as SDI, with the expectation that the other would do the same. President Reagan envisioned such a development when he offered to share SDI technology with the Soviet Union: if both sides constructed a viable strategic defense, he said, perhaps both would then dismantle their nuclear arsenals once and for all.

[29] The U.S. ASAT missile is designed to be launched in flight from an F-15 fighter aircraft. A congressionally imposed moratorium on space testing of the ASAT expires March 1, and the first test reportedly is set for June.

[30] Kenneth L. Adelman, "Arms Control With and Without Agreements," *Foreign Affairs*, winter 1984-85.

Selected Bibliography

Books

Goldblat, Jozef, *Agreements for Arms Control: A Critical Survey*, Stockholm International Peace Research Institute, 1982.

Gray, Colin S., *American Military Space Policy*, Abt Books, 1982.

Hecht, Jeff, *Beam Weapons*, Plenum Press, 1984.

Labrie, Roger P., ed., *SALT Handbook*, American Enterprise Institute, 1979.

National Academy of Sciences, *Nuclear Arms Control: Background and Issues*, National Academy Press, 1985.

Talbott, Strobe, *Deadly Gambits*, Alfred A. Knopf, 1984.

Union of Concerned Scientists, *The Fallacy of Star Wars*, Vintage Books, 1984.

Articles

Adelman, Kenneth L., "Arms Control With and Without Agreements," *Foreign Affairs*, winter 1984-85.

Brzezinski, Zbigniew, Robert Jastrow and Max M. Kampelman, "Defense in Space Is Not 'Star Wars'," *The New York Times Magazine*, Jan. 27, 1985.

Draper, Theodore, "Pie in the Sky," *The New York Review of Books*, Feb. 14, 1985.

Greb, G. Allen, and Gerald W. Johnson, "A History of Strategic Arms Limitations," *Bulletin of the Atomic Scientists*, January 1984.

Hedlin, Myron, "Moscow's Line on Arms Control," *Problems of Communism*, May-June 1984.

Lehrman, Lewis E., "The Case for Strategic Defense," *Policy Review*, winter 1985.

Newhouse, John, "Talks about Talks," *The New Yorker*, Dec. 31, 1984.

Nitze, Paul H., "Living With the Soviets," *Foreign Affairs*, winter 1984-85.

Reports and Studies

Carter, Ashton B., "Directed Energy Missile Defense in Space," Office of Technology Assessment, April 1984.

Congressional Budget Office, "An Analysis of Administration Strategic Arms Reduction and Modernization Proposals," March 1984.

Editorial Research Reports: "Reagan's Defense Buildup," 1984 Vol. I, p. 309; "West Germany's 'Missile' Election," 1983 Vol. I, p. 149; "Controlling Nuclear Proliferation," 1981 Vol. II, p. 509; "MX Missile Decision," 1981 Vol. I, p. 409.

International Institute for Strategic Studies, "The Military Balance 1984-1985," 1984.

U.S. Arms Control and Disarmament Agency, "Arms Control," September 1984.

U.S. Government Printing Office, "The President's Strategic Defense Initiative," January 1985.

U.S. Department of State, "Security and Arms Control: The Search for a More Stable Peace," October 1984.

Graphics: Cover by Staff Artist Kathleen Ossenfort; p. 23 by Assistant Art Director Robert Redding; p. 7 by Bill Fitz-Patrick, The White House; p. 13 U.S. Air Force.

GERMAN
RECONCILIATION

WEST
GERMANY

EAST
GERMANY

by

David Fouquet

Apr. 19
1 9 8 5

GERMAN RECONCILIATION

FOR a week in May, Germany will be the focus of world attention. First, President Reagan and leaders of six other big Western industrial powers will gather in Bonn for their annual review of international economic and trade matters. Reagan will then extend his stay in Germany until May 6, just before the 40th anniversary of the collapse of Nazi Germany, ending World War II in Europe.[1]

The two events starkly illustrate the dilemma of modern Germany — a powerful participant in the community of nations, yet still haunted by an aggressive and sinister past that often impedes its ability to play its present role. While few people still seriously question Germany's place as a positive force in international affairs, recent trends and the current wave of 40th anniversary memories have raised questions about the future of Germany and the consequences for its neighbors.

In May 1945, Germany and many of those neighbors lay devastated and broken by six years of war. But within a decade the *wirtschaftwunder* ("economic miracle") was set in motion, bringing prosperity to Germany as never before and restoring its self-esteem. Four decades of peace have followed Germany's defeat, but it has been a troubled peace, leaving the country, Europe and most of the world divided politically, militarily and ideologically between East and West. Since 1949 two German nations have existed side by side: the Federal Republic (West Germany) and the Democratic Republic (East Germany), embracing the territory controlled respectively by the Allied and Russian armies at the time of Germany's surrender.

East and West Germany have both, at different times, referred in their constitutions and official pronouncements to reunification as a basic and ultimate goal. But they have made little progress toward the formation of a single Germany. The greatest obstacle has been their increased involvement in two competing alliances. Even before the Federal Republic was established, that part of Germany was being connected to the

---

[1] Reagan flies from Washington to West Germany April 30, attends the economic summit May 2-4 along with Chancellor Helmut Kohl of West Germany, President François Mitterrand of France, and Prime Ministers Margaret Thatcher of Britain, Brian Mulroney of Canada, Bettino Craxi of Italy, and Yasuhiro Nakasone of Japan. Later the president is due to visit Spain and Portugal and to address the European Parliament in Strasbourg, France, before returning home May 10.

Western system, beginning especially in 1947 with the Marshall Plan of U.S. aid for rebuilding the German industrial base. Afterward came the new republic's membership in the North Atlantic Treaty Organization (NATO), and the European Economic Community (EEC). Similarly, East Germany became a member of the Warsaw Pact military alliance and the Soviet-bloc's Committee for Mutual Economic Assistance, known as Comecon — the Russian counterparts to NATO and the EEC.

Identity Problems Among Divided People

"The division is the most tragic price Germans have had to pay for what happened from 1933 to 1945," Professor Hans-Adolf Jacobsen of Bonn University, the author of numerous works on political science and East-West relations, said in a recent interview.[2] The two German nations are not only divided politically and physically, but the people in each state seem unusually restless and beset by internal divisions. On both sides, many see an unease with the established order and an ill-defined searching for a different future.

Within the two Germanies this trend is variously described as a "new patriotism," a "German identity," or a "common responsibility for peace." In the Western alliance there is a distrust of these notions as portents of a West German drift toward neutralism and pacifism. The Soviet Union indignantly professes to see what is happening as "revanchism," a word that conveys the idea of Germans desiring to overturn the postwar political order in central Europe.

"It's an irony of history," Jacobsen remarked, "that we were in the past criticized for being good soldiers [for Hitler], and now we're criticized for being pacifists." But he noted that what is regarded with such concern is largely a continuation of a fundamental foreign policy objective of the Federal Republic, first reconciliation with its neighbors and allies in the West and then the countries to the east.

The goal of integrating West Germany into NATO and the EEC began with the Federal Republic's first chancellor, Konrad Adenauer (1949-63). The new Bonn government heartily followed the Western policy of containing communism. For many years the "Hallstein Doctrine" — named for Adenauer's foreign minister, Walter Hallstein — was the guiding tenet of the Federal Republic's foreign relations. It stated that Bonn would <u>not ha</u>ve diplomatic relations with any country that formally

---

[2] Interviewed by the author at the professor's home, March 7, 1985.

Scale of Miles
0 20 40 60 80

Baltic Sea

North Sea

Schleswig-
Holstein

Hamburg
• **Hamburg**

Bremen
• **Bremen**

NETHERLANDS

Lower Saxony

POLAND

Oder

East Berlin
☆★**Berlin**

Elbe

EAST GERMANY
Pop. 17 mil. (est.)

Oder

North Rhine-Westphalia

Neisse

• **Düsseldorf**

Leipzig \ **Dresden**

Bonn ★ *Rhine*

Hesse

Elbe

• **Frankfurt**

CZECHOSLOVAKIA

Rhineland-
Palatinate

LUX.

Saarland

• **Nuremberg**

WEST GERMANY
Pop. 61 mil. (est.)

Bavaria

Rhine

Stuttgart •

FRANCE

Baden-
Württenburg

Danube

Danube

• **Munich**

SWITZERLAND

AUSTRIA

recognized East Germany. Bonn gradually retreated from this doctrine but it wasn't until 1969, 20 years after the republic was founded, that the government turned its drive toward reconciliation in an eastward direction. That came in 1969 when Chancellor Willy Brandt pursued *Ostpolitik* (literally "East politics"), a word that has since entered many languages to describe an attempt to improve relations with the communist regimes of Europe.

Another change in West Germany's political direction came about Oct. 2, 1982. Nearly 13 years of domination by the Social

Democratic Party (SDP) came to an end that day in the Bundestag, the lower house of the national parliament. Helmut Schmidt, the once-powerful chancellor, lost a vote of confidence and promptly resigned. Schmidt was replaced immediately by Helmut Kohl, leader of the Christian Democratic Union. The CDU achieved a working majority with the aid of its traditional partner, the Bavarian Christian Social Union (CSU), and a new ally, the small Free Democratic Party (FDP), known also as the Liberal Party although it is usually right of center. Schmidt's loss resulted when the FDP deserted his coalition out of unhappiness with his own party's left wing, which opposed new missile deployment and wanted higher social-welfare spending.

This shift toward the right was confirmed in elections five months later, on March 6, 1983. The new CDU-CSU-FDP alliance won almost 60 percent of the national vote. The changeover meant the return of the once-dominant Christian Democrats — the party that had led the country's reconstruction from 1949 to 1969. The message of the victors was economic and financial austerity. The election was also noteworthy because it marked the entry of the radical upstart Green Party into the Bundestag chambers.

Troubling Leadership Question in Bonn

Kohl, a jovial, optimistic man, came to the top spot with the advantage of being the first chancellor who had no adult involvement in Germany's war years.[3] As he frequently mentioned, he was only 15 when the war ended in 1945. But he also has a reputation as a lackluster leader. This is in sharp contrast with his two predecessors, Schmidt (1974-82) who was noted for brilliance and use of power, and Willy Brandt (1969-74) for his ideas and force of personality. Almost instantly, Kohl and his new majority found themselves caught in internal squabbling, election setbacks, scandals and difficult policy choices.

First in September 1983, the Kohl forces suffered an unexpected loss to the Social Democrats in lander (state) elections in Hesse. Bavarian Prime Minister Franz Josef Strauss, the longtime right-wing leader of the Bavarian CSU, became upset when Kohl did not give him a key ministerial post and took to publicly upbraiding the chancellor. Kohl's backers were further dismayed at the Liberals' slippage in popularity after they deserted Schmidt's government, raising the prospect that in national elections scheduled for 1987 they might not win enough votes (5 percent) to be accorded representation in the Bundestag. In that event, Kohl might be unable to retain a majority in the chamber. However, the Liberals made gains in March 10

---

[3] Willy Brandt, who fled Hitler and spent the war years in Sweden, did not serve in the German armed forces. But he is identified in the public mind with wartime events.

elections in the Saarland and West Berlin. An election due May 12 in North Rhineland-Westphalia may give a clearer indication of their standing.

The Liberals' outlook also dimmed upon Foreign Minister Hans Dietrich Genscher's retirement as party leader in March. He was succeeded by the largely unknown Martin Bengemann, who became economics minister last year, replacing Count Otto von Lambsdorff. The count and several prominent politicians of all the major parties, including Kohl himself, were accused of taking secret payments from industrialist Friedrich Karl Flick. Formal charges against some of them resulted in the resignations of Lambsdorff and Rainer Brazel, president of the Bundestag, who was CDU leader before Kohl.[4]

Helmut Kohl

A considerable amount of blame attached to Chancellor Kohl and his easygoing style. The top German newsweekly magazine, *Der Spiegel,* commented that his approach consisted of "no team, no confidence, no competence." He is reputed to be bored with details, and lengthy briefings. A foreign European leader, speaking in confidence to journalists, expressed his concern at what he saw as a "leadership crisis" in Germany. A recent lengthy feature on the German political scene in *The New York Times Magazine* expressed the view: "Simply put, Chancellor Kohl is not in charge. His homey, avuncular style is strong on resounding platitudes, weak on intellectual rigor, or even content; he is best at the improvisatory stump speech and worst at mastering position papers or running a large bureaucracy."[5]

Political Shifts From Adenauer to Kohl

Kohl nevertheless is regarded as firmly in office. The opposition Social Democratic Party is going through leadership and identity crises of its own. The postwar triumvirate that guided it first to respectability and then to power is fading. Brandt,

---

[4] Two other political mishaps plagued Kohl's first year in office. One concerned allegations by the country's military intelligence services that a top officer frequented homosexual bars. The defense minister's demand for his resignation had to be withdrawn after the allegations were found to be false. The other was the government's embroilment in an awkward row over an environmental issue. Last summer, going against a parliamentary majority, the interior minister and the administration in Lower Saxony approved the start-up of a coal-fired power plant without filters to control pollution. The resulting furor led to a special session of the Bundestag to work out a compromise solution.

[5] James M. Markham, "Those Troubled Germans," *The New York Times Magazine,* Feb. 10, 1985.

Schmidt and parliamentary leader Herbert Wehner are in the twilight of their careers. Hans Jochen Vogel, who followed Schmidt as party leader, has been unable to unite the party's feuding factions and capitalize on Kohl's weaknesses.

The Social Democrats' share of the vote dropped to 40 percent in March 1983. It has become fashionable to speculate about Vogel's replacement immediately after national elections in 1987, or even earlier. Those most frequently mentioned as possible successors are Johannes Rau, prime minister of North Rhine-Westphalia, West Germany's most populous state situated in its industrial heart; and Oskar Lafontaine, the far-left mayor of Saarbrücken and prime minister of the Saarland since March. He has advocated taking the Federal Republic out of the NATO military command.

Social Democrats are divided ideologically between their party's moderate wing, led first by Schmidt and now by Vogel, and the left wing which tries to win over the young and disaffected voters who support the emerging Green Party. Schmidt is in semi-retirement, concentrating on editorial comments and his avocation as an amateur concert pianist. Brandt, over 70 and sometimes in bad health, nevertheless seeks to move the party toward an opening with the Green electorate.

It was Brandt who some 25 years earlier turned the party toward the center of the political spectrum, away from Marxist ideology. He adroitly capitalized on the weakening of Christian Democratic Chancellor Ludwig Erhard (1963-66). Disagreements over financial policies led the Liberals to drop out of the ruling alliance in 1966, forcing Erhard to resign. This led to a "grand coalition" of the two major parties, with Kurt-Georg Kiesinger of the Christian Democrats as chancellor (1966-69) and Brandt of the Social Democrats as vice chancellor and foreign minister. This arrangement lasted until 1969. Brandt's party made election gains that year and, joined by the Liberals, achieved a majority in the Bundestag, which made him chancellor.

Brandt directed West German foreign policy toward a "regulated relationship." He stopped just short of establishing diplomatic ties with East Germany but pushed for broad areas of accommodation.[6] He won a second term in 1972 but strikes and

---

[6] Brandt met with East German President Willi Stoph in March 1970 and agreed to a 20-point program of accommodation; this and subsequent discussions with East German leaders led to a treaty that was eventually ratified by Bonn in December 1972. In August 1970 Brandt signed a non-aggression treaty with Russia and in the following December concluded a treaty with Poland recognizing the postwar boundary lines in Europe by which Poland acquired nearly one-fourth of Germany's prewar territory. A preliminary agreement governing access to Berlin was concluded with East Germany in 1971, while a treaty voiding the 1938 Munich Agreement was negotiated with Czechoslovakia in 1973. At Munich in 1938, British and French leaders gave in to Hitler's demands, enabling him to invade Czechoslovakia without fear of their going to its aid.

rising inflation plagued his government. Despite his personal popularity and prestige — Brandt won the Nobel Peace Prize in 1971 — he was considered to be erratic and moody.

Schmidt, a determined pragmatist, succeeded Brandt in 1974 and guided the country to an envied economic position during a time other industrial countries were suffering from the effects of soaring oil prices. He, together with Erhard, are viewed as the personification of the "economic miracle," becoming fixed in the public's mind along with such symbols of industrial prowess as the Volkswagen automotive enterprise, the steelworks of the Ruhr, the giant chemical firms, the Hannover fair and the pace-setting practice of worker participation in management.

Although Schmidt gained a reputation as probably the most intelligent and effective of world leaders, he nevertheless alienated many in his party and country by backing U.S. efforts to deploy additional nuclear weapons in Europe. The British journalist Jonathan Carr writes in his new biography *Helmut Schmidt:* "Despite the acclaim abroad, and his widespread popularity at home, Schmidt had grave problems holding his coalition together. A restive group of Parliamentarians [members of the Bundestag] on the left wing of the SDP posed a constant danger to the slim majority the coalition parties had won in the 1976 election." At last it crumbled in 1982.

Reshaping German Opinion

ONE of the most beguiling aspects of West German political life has been the emergence of the Green Party. Frequently thought of as a radical "children's crusade," this party has achieved a significance out of proportion to its 35,000 members. Five years after its founding, the party stunned the country in the 1983 elections by winning two million votes, 6.2 percent of the total, and electing 27 members to the Bundestag.

With its roots in the mass protests Europe experienced in 1968 and the subsequent peace demonstrations and anti-nuclear-power movements, the party has vastly broadened its base. It has gathered not only restless youth but disillusioned voters of many political stripes. Greens were elected to local and regional bodies, forcing public debate on basic issues and placing the established parties on the defensive. An official of the Konrad Adenauer Foundation, the Christian Democratic research body in Bonn, commented recently on a study the organization had conducted: "The core of the Green voters comes from high middle-class backgrounds ... and includes teachers, social workers, persons in service occupations — which does not exactly conform to the Green image."

The image of an unorthodox and anti-establishment movement has accompanied the party and its founders, a young American-educated woman, Petra Kelly,[7] and a retired general, Gert Bastian. Others, such as Otto Schilly and Frank Schwalba-Oth have given the movement a more radical tint. Schilly, a Bundestag member, was legal counsel for the Baader-Meinhoff terrorists,[8] and Schwalba-Oth achieved notoriety for throwing a container of blood on a U.S. military officer during a protest. Traditional parties have acknowledged many of the issues the Greens have raised, but they also occasionally hint that the movement is dangerously extremist. Some suggest that it has been at least partly financed and infiltrated by Russians and East Germans. Still others cite its nostalgic attachment to nature and a "pan-German" identity as a link to more sober and mystical aspects of Hitler's National Socialism.[9]

By stressing their pacifism, the Greens have largely avoided being tarnished by the terrorists. They also have turned the arguments against their accusers, saying that West German authorities in the past showed more complacence toward neo-Nazi terrorism than left-wing terrorism. Some neo-Nazi groups were banned in the 1980s after a series of violent acts, including a bombing during the Munich beer festival in September 1980 that left 13 dead and 200 persons injured. This country, perhaps more than any other in Europe, has been obsessed with extremism and terrorism, from both the far right and far left.

Green leaders themselves hold contradictory views of their amorphous movement. Endless arguments take place between "fundamentalists" who maintain the Greens represent an apolitical protest movement that should have no formal links to other parties, and "pragmatists" who feel they must play the game of political democracy to change the system. Petra Kelly takes the second view, as expressed in news interviews. In contrast, Rudolf Bahro, a Marxist refugee poet from East Germany, speaks of "shameful collaboration with the power system."[10] Despite the Greens' successes, some commentators ask

---

[7] Kelly is the daughter of an American military officer and a German mother. While living in the United States, she is reported to have been influenced by the civil rights and anti-Vietnam War movements.

[8] Named for Andreas Baader and Ulrike Meinhof, leaders of a gang that operated in the late 1960s. Both were imprisoned and, according to prison authorities, committed suicide. More recently, Germany has been troubled by terrorists known as the Red Army Faction, which has been held responsible for a number of bombings and murders.The country was jolted by a series of violent incidents in December and January that were attributed to the Red Faction. Two of its leaders, Christian Klar and Brigitte Mohnhaupt, were recently convicted by a court in Stuttgart of the 1977 murders of Siegfried Buback, the chief federal prosecutor, banker Juergen Ponto and a business leader, Hanns-Martin Schleyer.

[9] For a development of this thought, see Jane Kramer's "Letter from Europe," in *The New Yorker*, Nov. 26, 1984.

[10] He was quoted in the international edition of *Newsweek*, Dec. 24, 1984, and she in the magazine's July 12, 1982, issue.

whether elections in the Saarland on March 10 may be a portent. The Greens suffered their first big setback, winning only 2 percent of the vote and no seats in the state parliament.

Disaffection Amid West German Affluence

The national debate that the Greens have inspired — some say provoked — is evident in slogans and catch phrases about the environment, pacifism, neutrality and the "German question," an all-inclusive term for the division of prewar Germany into separate countries and how the Germans deal with the situation. While some knowledgeable observers say that most of the people are apathetic about these matters, most residents whom a foreign observer meets in this well-educated and affluent society appear interested and concerned. The environment, especially, seems to claim attention. It is a rare day in the Federal Republic without some reference in newspapers or on television about acid rain and its damage to German forests, or the need for cleaner automobile emissions.

Germans, in explaining this growing awareness of environmental problems, point to the fact that despite a declining birth rate, their country is one of the most densely populated on Earth.[11] In addition, they remark, the rate of heavy industrialization has revived a basic and traditional love for natural surroundings. Although at first slow to translate the people's concern for the environment into political action, the Kohl government became embroiled in a debate with Britain, France and other members of the EEC about West Germany's intention to require that all new cars be equipped with anti-pollution devices. But imposing new standards on an already troubled automobile industry would mean some difficult choices affecting roughly a quarter of the West German work force.

In its 1984 economic survey of Germany, the international Organization for Economic Cooperation and Development[12] remarked that "after a recession lasting almost three years, the recovery in economic activity started at the beginning of 1983, and by early 1984 real GNP [gross national product — the total value of the country's goods and services] exceeded the prerecession level." Always obsessed with inflation,[13] Germany has managed to keep the rate at around 3 percent. Moreover, the

[11] According to 1983 population estimates, density in the Federal Republic averaged 642.5 per square mile, roughly 10 times greater than in the United States, but less than in Japan (811) and the Netherlands (1,002). As calculated by the Population Reference Bureau, Inc., in Washington, D.C., West Germany's "natural" population (excluding emigration and immigration) declined 0.2 percent last year.

[12] The Paris-based organization represents 24 leading non-communist industrial nations.

[13] In 1923, Germany's inflation was the worst ever recorded anywhere, soaring that November to an annual rate of 3.45 quintillion percent — a term expressed by the number 345 followed by 16 zeros.

trade-oriented economy is experiencing a boom in exports. Exports grew by 13 percent last year, according to the Kiel Institute on World Economics, and one-third of those exports went to the United States in response to the strength of the dollar in relation to the West German mark. Shipments across the Atlantic rose 48 percent above the previous year's.

But the country has been afflicted with high unemployment; early this year 2.6 million persons were jobless, a record number in the postwar years. This was partly the result of a "baby boom" that occurred in the years following World War II. Children born during those years have been entering the labor market at a time when relatively few older workers have been retiring. Generous unemployment, education and training benefits, enacted during the establishment of the postwar "welfare state" in Germany and other European democracies, helped contain the social unrest that might have resulted from massive unemployment. Even so, there is a pool of well-educated, unemployed and disaffected young people who became attracted to radical views about society, the economy and politics.[14]

The single-minded pursuit of gain which had made Germans among the most prosperous people on Earth is now seen bearing a heavy price in human terms. The drive to get ahead produced a highly competitive society that placed great value on status symbols and put pressure on the young to do well in school. Some link this pressure to West Germany's suicide rate, the world's highest among children under 15. The incidence of heart disease, as in other prosperous industrial countries, has been increasing, and West Germany has the world's highest rate of cancer deaths. German doctors attribute the diseases to industrialization, bad eating habits,[15] smoking and drinking. Participants in a medical congress in Dusseldorf in 1981 were told that liver disease was fast becoming the people's sickness, with alcohol and pollution playing a major role.

Questioning Ties With Allies, Neighbors

The youthful Green movement has increasingly called into question the division of Germany and West Germany's attachment to the Western alliance. This questioning has aroused uneasiness beyond as well as inside the country. A catalyst for much of this agitation was the NATO decision in 1979 to install new nuclear missiles in Europe and the virtual collapse of

---

[14] For background, see "European Welfare States Under Attack," *E.R.R.*, 1981 Vol. I, pp. 289-308, and "Europe's Postwar Generations," *E.R.R.*, 1981 Vol. II, pp. 933-956.

[15] *The Economist*, the London-based business magazine, reported March 23, 1985: "Statistics produced for a recent agricultural show in West Berlin show resolutely the West Germans are battling against the fashionable Western trend toward fewer calories, less cholesterol and more fruit and vegetables. West German meat consumption has risen by 15 percent in the past 10 years and by 40 percent since 1964."

Fortress Germany

Probably the world's greatest concentration of troops, missiles and military installations are on German soil, East and West. American, British and French forces have remained in West Germany since World War II, in the zones they occupied at the war's end.

They are there currently under terms of the 1954 Status of Forces Agreement, which led to West Germany's entry into NATO the next year. Belgium, Holland and Canada also supply NATO troops in West Germany. These foreign forces in 1984 numbered 392,000, of which 233,000 were Americans. Some 65,000 were British, 50,000 French, 32,000 Belgian, 6,700 Dutch and 5,400 Canadian. Additionally, all but 38,000 of West Germany's 335,000 soldiers are under NATO's command. Military installations cover one million acres of West German soil, and the country is the scene of some 5,000 military exercises yearly.

Across the border in East Germany are 380,000 Soviet troops, augmented by 115,000 East German armed forces. In both countries are thousands of nuclear weapons — missiles, artillery shells and bombs — most of them for tactical (short-range) use. Recent attention has focused on 108 intermediate-range Pershing II missiles being placed in West Germany to replace the same number of older Pershing I missiles.

Sources: West German government; U.S. Department of Defense; Institute for Strategic Studies (London); and *Nuclear Weapons Data Book* by Thomas B. Cochran and others.

détente after the Soviet invasion of Afghanistan at the end of that year. Hundreds of thousands of people, perhaps a combined total reaching into the millions, took to the steets in organized protests against placing U.S. Pershing II and cruise missiles in Europe. It was the issue, more than any other, that transformed social concerns into a national political movement.

Out of this drive grew a sense of unity with East Germans. They shared a common destiny and a common problem, for Russian missiles were installed in the Democratic Republic. Increasingly, West Germans sought out contacts with East Germans and other dissidents in the Soviet bloc to discuss peace, disarmament and the environment. Sometimes these contacts came through church functions, rock concerts and youth exchanges tolerated by the authoritarian systems. One result was an embryonic peace and protest movement in those countries.[16]

The influence of the two superpowers was being examined in a different light. This scrutiny became more intense in 1984 after the new missiles were deployed and Russian negotiators walked out of U.S.-Soviet arms control talks in Geneva.[17] One of Germany's top foreign-policy strategists, Christoph Bertram, wrote in the liberal Hamburg weekly *Die Zeit* on Oct. 14, 1983: "The controversy over the deployment is only a symptom of a deep-rooted difference of views: the views of those for whom security rests with America's nuclear shield and those for whom this shield is the root of insecurity."

Many Greens as well as other Germans strongly deny there is any anti-American prejudice in this questioning. They typically maintain that West Germany is probably the most Americanized society in the world. But even the right-of-center supporters of American policies and leadership were jarred when both President Reagan and Secretary of Defense Caspar W. Weinberger openly discussed the possibility of waging a limited nuclear war in Europe. To Germans and other Europeans, this raises the specter of their destruction while the superpowers are spared. Eberhard Schulz of the Foreign Policy Association in Bonn perceives increased American attention on the Pacific, and signs that Reagan's Strategic Defense Initiative, or "Star Wars" proposal for nuclear weaponry in space, would de-emphasize the defense of Europe.

The 'German Question'

THE existence of two Germanies represents the inability of the victors in World War II to come to terms with how to deal with their defeated enemy. Soviet military forces immediately established administrative control over the territory they occupied, an area of 41,000 square miles, about the size of Ohio. American, British and French forces each established zones in the remainder of Germany, an area of 95,000 square miles, about the size of Oregon. The four powers had agreed at the Yalta Conference before the war's end to divide Germany into four zones of occupation and Berlin into four sectors, but treated as a single economic unit.

---

[16] For background, see "Christian Peace Movement," *E.R.R.*, 1981 Vol. I, pp. 353-372, and "West Germany's 'Missile' Election," *E.R.R.*, 1983 Vol. I, pp. 149-168.

[17] Two sets of talks broke off in the late fall of 1983; in January, both sides agreed to resume, and a new round began March 12 in Geneva. See "Arms Control Negotiations," *E.R.R.*, 1985 Vol. I, pp. 145-168.

It did not work out that way. Faced with a stalemate in the supervising council, the Americans, British and later the French consolidated their zones. The Russians, in protest, withdrew from the council in March 1948 and set in motion two years of harassing tactics in Berlin, including a blockade of roads and railroads into Allied-controlled sectors of the city. The famous Berlin airlift kept West Berliners fed and supplied until, at length, Soviet authorities lifted the blockade. During the time of the blockade, attitudes hardened on both sides and the rival German republics were born.

The German Federal Republic came into being Sept. 20, 1949, followed by the German Democratic Republic, Oct. 7, 1949, a "people's republic" on the Soviet model. It is theoretically governed so that the will of the state and Communist Party are one. From the beginning the strong man was Walter Ulbricht. When Soviet forces first occupied eastern Germany, he and other past leaders of the prewar German Communist Party were brought back from exile in Moscow to carry out Soviet designs.

Erich Honecker

Upon Ulbricht's death in 1973, Willi Stoph succeeded him as chairman of the Council of State, the top post, but was replaced in a 1976 reshuffle by Erich Honecker, the party secretary, and was given the premiership instead. Honecker and Stoph continue to hold those offices. Honecker is the dominant figure. Under Ulbricht and Honecker, it is often said, East Germany became Russia's most loyal ally among the Warsaw Pact nations. However, Honecker has at times encouraged *ostpolitik* as a means of giving East Germany a greater degree of economic freedom and raising its standard of living.

Honecker has surely been puzzling to the Russians as he sometimes is to Westerners. And, according to one observer, "a lot of Christian Democrats" in West Germany are confused by "the fact that he can be a German and a nationalist and, at the same time, an ardent Communist." The observer, Jane Kramer, goes on to describe "those 19th century German Catholics who gave Bismarck so much trouble when he had put Germany together and was trying to persuade them their patriotic duty was to obey their chancellor first and the Pope second, if at all." The Catholics considered themselves as German as Bismarck, but in matters of faith they "were always looking across the Alps to the Vatican." And so in matters of communist faith, Honecker "looks across to the Kremlin." [18]

Ambiguity Over Eventual Reunification

As many Germans point out, the two countries are bound not merely by political, economic and historic ties, as important as those might be. It is truly a family affair. The 854 miles of fortified barbed wire and wall that separate the two countries in fact separate blood relatives, many of whom have not seen one another since the war years. As many as one million East Germans fled across the guarded border to the West, attracted to a booming economy and escaping a repressive regime, until communist authorities erected a massive brick wall through Berlin on Aug. 13, 1961, to stem the busiest escape route.

From that time until 1983, some 200,000 more escaped. About 150,000 others, usually older people with relatives in West Germany, have emigrated legally under an unusual arrangement. The West German government pays the East German government $15,000 to $25,000 in an unofficial ransom or bounty per person. West Germans defend this arrangement on humanitarian grounds; East Germany is eager to obtain the hard currency.

The West German constitution, known as the Basic Law, continues to maintain that all Germans form one nation. The West German government does not formally recognize the Democratic Republic as a foreign state or its residents as aliens. Nor does it charge duty on incoming East German trade, thus giving East Germany an unacknowledged backdoor entry into the European Economic Community. Partly due to billions in West German credits, the Democratic Republic has become the 12th-largest economic power in the world, with a living standard which, although about half of West Germany's, is still among the highest in the communist bloc of nations.

The question of eventual German reunification flared up occasionally but rarely as an important issue until Chancellor Kohl started speaking ambiguously about "recovering" Germany, even though he reported after a visit to Moscow in 1983 that reunification "is not on the political agenda." Surveys taken as recently as last year indicate 80 percent of the West Germans favor reunification, and the issue has been widely discussed in books and political forums. Probably a large majority of West Germans see the possibility of one German nation as a distant goal and would prefer not to jeopardize the Federal Republic's status in NATO and the European Community.

---

[18] Jane Kramer, *op. cit.*, pp. 130-131.

A senior Foreign Ministry official in Bonn denied in a recent interview that the government had any "grand design" for eventual reunification. He said: "Living in a divided Germany is a fact of life.... NATO is our vital lifeline and we will never sever it. But what really nags us is the lack of freedom and human rights on the other side.... I think we can improve everyday life without throwing up the territorial question or putting the system into doubt. Hungarians have a communist regime but don't run away."

But some others, spanning the entire political spectrum, speak openly for reunification. Among the most prominent have been Peter Brandt, the former chancellor's son; historian Peter Bender, who writes of "the Europeanization of Europe"; and author Stefan Heym, who writes that "both Germanies are being duped." Some speak for formulas for making such a prospect acceptable to worried neighbors in both the East and West. A favorite is the "Austrian solution," recalling that the occupying powers of Austria — America, Britain, France and Russia — agreed in 1955 to withdraw their forces and establish an independent, neutral Austria, free of military alliances.

Still other West Germans attach less importance to reunification. "I do accept it as a political demand if it can be achieved peacefully," said Professor Jacobsen. "But there may be higher priorities. Peacekeeping is more vital." Eberhard Schulz of the Foreign Policy Association shares this outlook. "German history was never one of a nation-state and a national feeling was never as strong as in France or Britain except for the period until 1945 [the Nazi era], and we don't want to repeat that kind of nationalism."

Lingering Fears Among Germany's Allies

West Germany is delicately walking a tightrope between maintaining an East-West political stability that is needed to draw the two Germanies closer while reassuring allies and neighbors that such a reconciliation would not create a new danger in central Europe. The United States, Russia and several other countries have reacted with considerable suspicion. Probably the mildest reaction has been America's. Washington has been reassured by Kohl's steadfastness on the missile issue.

Some of the strongest reaction has come from the Kremlin in its bitter disappointment over Schmidt's and Kohl's acceptance of missiles. "We have to remember that East Germany is the keystone to Soviet security and the Soviet position in Europe," said European-affairs military specialist Stephen Szabo.[19]

---

[19] Remark on "The MacNeil/Lehrer News Hour," PBS/TV, Sept. 4, 1985. Szabo is professor of European studies at the National War College, Washington, D.C.

Moscow undertook a hostile propaganda campaign against the Federal Republic last year, charging that it wished to overturn the results of the war, reclaim lost territory and co-opt the Democratic Republic. The culmination of this anger came last August when pressure from Moscow forced Erich Honecker to cancel his trip to West Germany, which would have been the first official visit by an East German of his stature. Many experts believed that Moscow, after failing to drive a wedge between West Germany and its allies, suddenly became sensitive to the prospect of an inter-German reconciliation.

The Federal Republic's friends in the West are not immune to the country's perceived drift toward German reunification. That concern seems pronounced in France, which was the victim of three German invasions within a century, in the Franco-Prussian War (1870-71) and two world wars (1914-18 and 1939-45). The current concern seemed especially troubling since West German reconciliation with France has been a hallmark of all postwar governments in Bonn. It was symbolic that French President Charles de Gaulle's first foreign visit after taking office was to Germany where on Nov. 26, 1958, he and Adenauer held the first of a lengthy series of meetings between French and German leaders. Franco-German friendship remains among the pillars of each country's foreign policy.

Many West Germans of the immediate postwar generation insist that they have transferred their patriotism from a German nation-state to a unified and peaceful Europe. But many of the old fears linger on. They burst into the open at the time Honecker planned to visit West Germany. Italian Foreign Minister Giulio Andreotti publicly said: "There are two German states and two German states must remain." Although the statement was later retracted at Bonn's demand, his thought was reflected in much of Europe's press commentary, recalling the celebrated remark by French author François Mauriac that "We love Germany so much we're glan there are two of them."

Mixed Feeling About Anniversary Event

It is with mixed feeling that Germany and much of the rest of the world prepares to mark the 40th anniversary of the end of World War II in Europe. To Germans, as well as others, the war's end meant the total defeat of fascism. To most it was the birth of a new Germany and a long period of peace, however troubled the peace may be. It also marked the division of their country, placing many of their people in a nation that is still not free. For a small minority of irreconciled Germans, passions still run deep. Recently a young German stood in a Bonn tavern wearing a badge proclaiming: "May 8 — Capitulation. No thanks!"

Aside from those holding such views, most Germans and others were unsure about how to commerate such an event. This was evident in President Reagan's schedule. At first he reportedly planned to be in Germany on May 8, V-E Day,[20] but later decided to address the European Parliament at Strasbourg, France, that day. He declined to visit any death camps during his visit, explaining in a news conference on March 21 that it was "unnecessary," observing that "I think they [the Germans] should be recognized for the democracy that they've created and the democratic principles they now espouse." The White House later announced he would on May 5 visit a German military cemetery at Bitburg, the burial site for 2,000 German soldiers, including 30 of Hitler's SS troops. After protests from American veterans and Jewish groups, the president said he would visit one of the death camps, after all.

British Prime Minister Margaret Thatcher initially announced there would be no official commemoration of the anniversary in Britain but had to reverse her position under an outpouring of public and press criticism. The Soviet Union has made clear to its people and others that massive celebrations marking the end of "The Great Patriotic War" will be observed as a triumph over fascist militarist enemies. East German plans for the anniversary are unclear.

In West Germany, the public and its political leaders seemed uncertain over what to do. Chancellor Kohl and his supporters originally wanted a joint commemoration service with other Western leaders. Social Democrats, however, wanted a commemoration that included representatives from Soviet bloc countries. They now plan to hold "Nuremberg talks" on May 7 in which delegates from towns and cities destroyed during the war would take part. The chancellor accepted an invitation from the small remaining West German Jewish community to visit the Bergen-Belsen death camp site on April 21.

Beate Lindeman of the Foreign Policy Association and president of the German-American friendship organization Atlantic Bridge had this to say: "The roots of our confusion lie with our history. The Weimar Republic. Hitler. No other country can understand. We completely lost our identity." Much of the German effort now seems to be directed toward rediscovering an identity.

---

[20] The German armies surrendered in the West on May 7, 1945, and separately to Russian forces May 9. Meanwhile, Gen. Dwight D. Eisenhower, commander of Allied forces in western Europe, declared May 8, Victory in Europe (V-E) Day.

Selected Bibliography

Books

Bahro, Rudolf, *From Red to Green: Interviews With New Left Review,* Verso/NLB (London), 1984.

Burdick, Charles, and Hans-Adolf Jacobsen (eds.), *Contemporary Germany, Politics and Culture,* Westview Press, 1984.

Kelly, Petra (Mariane Howarth, trans.), *Fighting for Hope,* South End Press, 1984.

Laqueur, Walter, *Germany Today,* Weidenfeld and Nicholson (London), 1985.

McCauley, Kartin, *The German Democratic Republic Since 1945,* St. Martin's, 1983.

Steike, Rudolf and Michel Vale (eds.), *Germany Debates Defense: The Nato Alliance at the Crossroads,* Sharpe, 1983.

Articles

Dean, Jonathan, "How to Lose Germany," *Foreign Policy,* summer 1984.

Garton Ash, Timothy, "Which Way Will Germany Go?" *The New York Times Review of Books,* Jan. 31, 1985.

Kramer, Jane, "Letter From Europe," *The New Yorker,* Nov. 26, 1984.

Leisler Kiep, Walther, "The New Deutschlandpolitik," *Foreign Affairs,* winter 1984-85.

Lowenthal, Richard, "The German Question Transformed," *Foreign Affairs,* winter 1984.

Markham, James M., "Those Troubled Germans," *The New York Times Magazine,* Feb. 10, 1985.

Reports and Studies

Editorial Research Reports: "Germany and the Balance of Power," 1955 Vol. I, p. 397; "West German Prosperity," 1969 Vol. I, p. 63; "Europe's Postwar Generations," 1981 Vol. II, p. 933; "Germany's 'Missile' Election," 1983 Vol. I, p. 149.

German Information Center, New York, "Germany's Contributions to Western Defense," 1984.

Organization for Economic Cooperation and Development, "Economic Surveys, Germany," 1984.

Graphics: Maps by Staff Artist Kathleen Ossenfort; photos p. 31 from German Information Center, New York, and p. 39 East German government.

SOUTHERN EUROPEAN SOCIALISM

by

David Fouquet

**Sept. 21
1 9 8 4**

Editor's Note: Since this report was originally issued, Spain and Portugal have been granted membership in the European Economic Community, effective Jan. 1, 1986. In Greece, national elections were scheduled to be held on June 2. Political tensions rose there this spring when Prime Minister Andreas Papandreou's socialist government blocked the re-election of President Constantine Karamanlis and contrived to have its handpicked candidate selected in a disputed vote by the National Assembly. Though a leader of the chief opposition party, the centrist New Democracy, Karamanlis is a father figure in Greece. He led the country back to democracy in 1974 after seven years of military rule.

SOUTHERN EUROPEAN SOCIALISM

DURING a short span of little more than two years, from mid-1981 to the late summer of 1983, all five of the big democracies in Southern Europe and their nearly 170 million people came under the sway of Socialist-led governments. This leftward shift of power in France, Greece, Spain, Portugal and Italy provoked a wave of anxiety in those countries and among their northern neighbors in the North Atlantic Treaty Organization (NATO) and the European Economic Community (EEC). For the political left throughout Europe, it sent expectations soaring.

Both the fears and high expectations have all but vanished today. The Socialist leadership, though varying in ideological ambition from country to country, has generally turned to middle-of-the-road devices in trying to meet pressing economic problems and to conduct foreign policy. The question now being asked in Europe, "What has the socialist 'revolution' wrought?" brings forth no single all-encompassing answer. It has meant different — often dissimilar things — in each of the five countries.

France was the first to go Socialist, ending decades of right-of-center rule. This came with the election of François Mitterrand as president in May 1981. That fall Andreas Papandreou engineered a Socialist victory in Greece's national elections. The next year, Felipe González, at age 40, led the way to a similar electoral triumph in Spain. And 1983 witnessed the return of Socialist Mário Soares as prime minister of Portugal and the unprecedented selection of a Socialist, Bettino Craxi, to lead a coalition government in Italy. Three of these countries — Greece, Spain and Portugal — had been in the iron hand of military dictatorships until a few short years earlier.

The outcome of this sharp break with tradition has not led to radical upheavals in the established social, political or economic patterns of those countries, nor in the international balance of power. To many domestic observers, the policies followed by these Socialist-led governments have produced remarkably little internal change. And in some cases, the Socialist leadership has seemed even more pro-Western in foreign policy than previous governments.

André Fountaine, the French author and columnist, wrote in the Paris daily *Le Monde*[1] that it was a far cry from the line established at the meeting of the Second Socialist International in Basel, Switzerland, in 1912. Working-class political movements were then urged to exploit economic crises to "provoke the downfall of capitalist domination." Instead, the new Socialist governments have become the victims of the current European economic recession and have been forced to preside over a period of austerity and the partial dismantling of the welfare states they so ardently promoted throughout most of the century.

In a *New York Times* survey of these regimes published late last year,[2] the acknowledged architect of Socialist Spain's economic policy, Miguel Boyer, was quoted as saying "the economic crisis imposes tight limits on what we can do." Greece's Finance Minister Gerassimos Arsenis noted that "the road to socialism no longer passes through the welfare-statism of the 1950s and 1960s." And in Portugal, Prime Minister Soares conceded that the new brand of socialism was marked by "realism above everything else." He even contradicted Greek Prime Minister Papandreou, who had told a meeting of European Socialist leaders in Athens late in 1983 that "we can now safely speak of a real, modern Mediterranean socialism." "There is no Mediterranean socialism," Soares said.

This lack of a clear break with the conservative administrations of their predecessors, and with governments in Northern Europe and the United States, has led to identity crises and strains within the various Socialist parties. Commenting on this problem at a meeting of European Socialists in Paris in November 1982, the leader of the Belgian Socialist Party, Guy Spitaels, noted: "We're too indistinct on socioeconomic issues ... and people wonder what's the difference with a center-right approach elsewhere."

Nowhere is the gap between ideology and actual policy more evident than in France. While the austere course of action has led to disillusionment and dissatisfaction among partisan ideologues and some rank and file, it is nevertheless also perceived generally as the only valid policy choice in an economic crisis. When Mitterrand was elected president, it marked a remarkable and largely unexpected break with the past. "Europe's most conservative people," as the French have been described,[3] had been governed by right-of-center governments for the 22 years of the Fifth Republic inaugurated by Charles de Gaulle.

---

[1] *Le Monde*, April 20, 1984.
[2] Written by Paul Lewis; published Nov. 29, Dec. 1-2, 1983.
[3] In *The Economist* of London; in a special survey of France the magazine published Feb. 27, 1982.

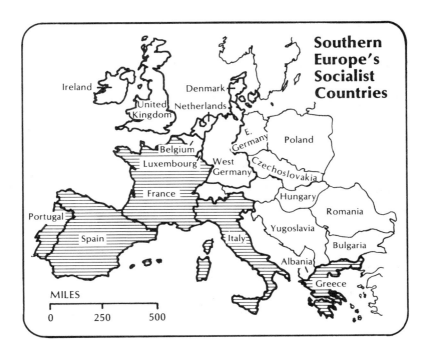

Southern Europe's Socialist Countries

Ireland
Denmark
United Kingdom
Netherlands
E. Germany
Poland
Belgium
Luxembourg
West Germany
Czechoslovakia
France
Hungary
Portugal
Romania
Spain
Yugoslavia
Italy
Bulgaria
Albania
Greece

MILES

| 0 | 250 | 500 |

And France had not been ruled by a left-wing government since Léon Blum's short-lived Popular Front in 1936. For many of those years, the French electorate had accepted the conservative leadership's arguments that it was too risky to allow the left, especially the mistrusted Communists, to govern the country. These arguments had been convincing despite considerable disillusionment, numerous scandals and social and political disturbances that rocked France in 1968.

If Mitterrand's victory over incumbent Valéry Giscard d'Estaing in the presidential election was stunning, the extent of his landslide was to be fully revealed a few weeks later when the new leader dissolved the National Assembly and called for parliamentary elections. The gamble was an immense success. His Socialist allies almost trebled their membership in the National Assembly, obtaining 284 of the 491 seats. The right-wing Gaullist Rassemblement Pour la République (RPR), led by Paris Mayor Jacques Chirac, wound up with a meager 90 seats and its more centrist partners in the previous coalition, the Union Démocratique Française (UDF), led by Giscard and Prime Minister Raymond Barre, obtained only 63 seats. The Communist Party, led by Georges Marchais, which had formed an alliance with the Socialists during the campaign, won only 44 seats.

Giscard later likened the left-wing sweep to "a Ghengis Khanlike invasion." Mitterrand, a lawyer generally regarded as a centrist, had taken over the leadership of the Socialists in 1971 following elections the year before which accorded the party only 6 percent of the vote. *The Economist* magazine, in a cover story on Mitterrand last March, referred to him as a "Socialist chameleon" and a "political Janus." This refers largely to the fact that he had been staunchly anti-Communist early in his career but later welcomed Communist support to rebuild the sagging fortunes of his Socialists.

Temporary Cooperation With Communists

He succeeded in convincing both Socialists and Communists that the only effective means of winning national elections was by joining forces. The alliance was an awkward love-hate relationship recognized, accepted and sometimes rejected by both parties which, nevertheless, became truly operational at the time of elections. Instead of fragmenting left-wing voter support, both parties agreed that the candidate with the best chance of winning a parliamentary or presidential contest would not be opposed by the other party and would get the complete support of both parties.

This strategy worked so well for the Socialists that from time to time the Communists have been fearful of being virtually absorbed by the Socialists. Seeing so many Communist voters deserting to join the Socialists, Marchais withdrew from this alliance in 1978, but rejoined a little over a year later when Communist popularity dipped even further to 18 percent of the electorate. This had led to a situation of virtual entrapment and neutralization of the Communists. Opponents on the right, however, contend that it is Mitterrand who is trapped — in a dependency on Communist votes and support.

Many French people shuddered at the prospect of Communists participating in a Western government for the first time since the 1940s, when de Gaulle himself organized a broad-based government that included Communists. But Mitterrand stuck to the alliance which had brought him to power. He gave four Cabinet-level ministries to Communists in reward for the party's support in the 1981 elections, although he had a sufficient parliamentary majority to rule without Communist backing.

It was generally reasoned that he wanted to assure Communist acquiescence and not alienate a potentially dangerous source of opposition. Communists received the relatively minor posts of transportation, health, civil service and vocational training, three of which were later downgraded to non-Cabinet status in a subsequent general reshuffling of the government —

and finally all four Communists resigned in a break with Mitterrand's government early in September 1984 *(see p. 55)*.

Mitterrand Vision: Society Transformed

In the first few heady weeks and months following its triumph, the French Socialist Party embarked on an ambitious 110-point program to improve and transform French society. Enlarging social programs and benefits, narrowing the income gaps between the rich and poor, and reducing unemployment became the new priorities in a country gripped by a world economic slump. The National Assembly promptly voted a series of sweeping measures bringing about:

● A hefty pay increase for the country's lowest wage-earners.

● Nationalization of 36 private banks, two major holding companies and nine large industrial groups and three foreign-owned operations, all with full indemnification of private owners.

● A reduction in the legal 40-hour work week and an increase in paid vacation time to five weeks a year.

● Heavier taxes on wealthy individuals and lighter taxes on others.

● Greater participation by workers in the management of their companies.

● Reduced authority by the central government and the establishment of regional assemblies.

● Abolition of state security courts which could hold closed trials and whose verdicts could not be appealed.

● Abolition of the death penalty, outlawing the use of the guillotine which had been the means of execution since the French Revolution in 1789.

● A halt to the forced departures of foreign migrant workers.

● An overhaul of state-run broadcasting and news policies to improve objectivity in information.

As popular as these measures were with Mitterrand and his supporters, they were anathema to the country's traditional and conservative elite. The earliest problem encountered by the new administration was a plunge in the value of the national currency, the franc, brought about by the massive flight of capital into Swiss bank accounts or American property and stocks. The new economic planners visualized the stimulation of the economy and a subsequent reduction of already high unemployment levels by the application of traditional socialist or Keynesian pump-priming methods.

They also arrived with an ideological distrust of free-market forces, favoring instead more state planning and intervention. They saw the wage increases for low-income workers not only

51

helping correct an economic and social injustice but a means of boosting consumer demand. The nationalization of key financial and industrial organisms was aimed at channeling direct state investment more effectively than through an independent private structure. Another goal was the conversion of France into "the European Japan" through ambitious state investment into several key high-technology sectors. Some $15 billion was to be funneled into research and development, a figure higher than the level of civilian research in the United States and close to that of Japan. There were rhetorical promises to "reconquer the domestic market" from Japanese, European and American competitors.

Economic Tailspin and Forced Austerity

The result of such a significant change in French planning and strategy by a largely inexperienced government in an already depressed economy was the massive exodus of capital, mounting inflation, rising budget and trade deficits, and continuing unemployment, fueled as elsewhere in Europe by demographic conditions involving the postwar baby boom and sluggish economies. The increased wages and government spending succeeded in stimulating imports and inflation.

The new planners also had the misfortune of starting their economic stimulation measures at a time when virtually all other industrial countries were placing their priority on curtailing inflation. France's inflation remained higher than its neighbors and undercut the country's competitiveness in international markets. The result was increased trade deficits and indebtedness that generated even less confidence in the weakening franc and the government planners.

It quickly became apparent that the government would have to devalue the set parity of the franc. It was also expected that the devaluation would have to be accompanied by austerity measures aimed at slowing down economic growth and inflation. To do so would undermine the government's plan and thus was rejected — until June 1982. By then, France's European partners, especially West Germany, made devaluation and restrictive measures a precondition to granting France a rescue loan. When it came, devaluation was accompanied by a four-month temporary wage-and-price freeze to dampen the expected inflationary impact.

In March 1983, Prime Minister Pierre Mauroy told a television audience he "completely" rejected another devaluation of the franc and boldly stated that "our biggest problems are behind us now." A few days later, on March 6, the first round of the country's municipal elections resulted in a resounding rebuff for the political left after only 22 months in office. Although the elections had no direct bearing on power at the national level, they served as a weathervane of public opinion. Opposition parties captured 50.9 percent of the vote and wrested 15 major cities away from left-wing mayors. A key victor was Jacques Chirac, who won a second six-year term as mayor of Paris and strengthened his claim as leader of the right-wing opposition. Although seemingly unrelated, another indirect blow came that same weekend from across the Rhine River, where Chancellor Helmut Kohl and his conservative coalition won a victory in West German parliamentary elections and set in motion a surge of confidence in that country's economy and currency, to the detriment of the faltering franc.

Almost immediately the French government underwent a political reorganization. Out of it, Finance Minister Jacques Delors, who had long argued for "a pause" in reform experiments and for more economic restraint, emerged as the uncontested manager of future economic strategy. Ousted from the government was the main advocate of the socialist interventionist school, Industry and Research Minister Jean-Pierre Chevènement.

Delors rejected some calls for an avowedly isolationist approach to resolving the growing crisis, which would have involved the withdrawal of the franc from the European Monetary System[4] and the erection of import barriers. On March 21, following intense negotiations with other countries in the Monetary System, the franc was devalued again. On March 25, a "healing" program for the economy was revealed. Its hallmark was "rigor." A new French emphasis on austerity was the price France had to pay to its European neighbors for their willingness to go along with yet another devaluation of the franc — a devaluation that made France's exports cheaper and imports more expensive, thus giving the country a trade advantage.

While basic sympathy for the Socialist government had kept most labor union unrest in check during the previous two years, there had been a steadily rising chorus of protest from other quarters. Justice Minister Charles Badinter became the target of right-wing ire about alleged laxity toward law enforcement, criminality and punishment following the abolition of the death penalty and the special courts. Among the first to demonstrate their displeasure were policemen, some of whom were also mem-

---

[4] The European Monetary System, established in March 1979, is a joint cooperative system under which most EEC member countries agreed to maintain the exchange rates of their national currencies stable, though not fixed, in relation to one another. This is done to shelter their monies and trade from upheavals in the international money markets. Changes in a country's currency rates, therefore, can only be made by a government following consultation and accord with the other countries.

bers of right-wing organizations. Then came an assortment of disgruntled students, doctors, farmers, shopkeepers, civil servants and supporters of the vast Catholic-school system, all protesting government action against their interests.

About-Face on Policy; Coalition's Rupture

Just as the government's policies took a decisive turn in March 1983, so did the political attitudes of the labor unions and Communists. From that time on, these former allies of the Socialists began to campaign openly against the austerity programs. Georges Marchais, the Communist Party leader, said however that his criticism did not reflect an outright split with the government. For the rightist foes of the government, its about-face was hailed as a vindication of their position. Former Prime Minister Giscard, emerging from his humiliating loss to Mitterrand in 1981, decried "the harm done to the reputation of the country" by an "incompetent" government.

The crumbling facade of left-wing unity deteriorated even further throughout 1983 and by the following January the French public was shocked to watch televised scenes of workers inside a Peugeot-Talbot plant near Paris hurling lead bolts and rivets at their colleagues. These riotous scenes were the result of a split among the workers and unions over the nationalized plant's plans to lay off nearly 2,000 workers. The working-class backlash against the austerity policies was also expressed in organized demonstrations by truck drivers, farmers and steelworkers. The truck drivers blocked roads and virtually paralyzed the country last March.

Protests arose from others besides the workers. On June 24 nearly a million people marched in Paris against a government plan to place more control over the Roman Catholic education system, which receives state support — a measure generally regarded as the opening of a campaign by the political left to create a single, lay school system.

Only a week earlier, another kind of judgment was rendered by the French public. In France, as in other EEC countries, delegates were elected to the European Parliament, a consultative body functioning since 1979 without real authority.[5] These elections had no direct bearing on the national political scene but were regarded as a test of public opinion. They resulted in only a slight improvement of the popular vote for the right-of-center parties in the traditional opposition and a small loss for the Socialist Party. But they were also characterized by

---

[5] For background on the Parliament, see "Electing Europe's Parliament," *E.R.R.*, 1979 Vol. I, pp. 345-360.

an overwhelming rejection of Communist Party candidates. The party obtained a meager 11.2 percent of the total vote, virtually the same as the heretofore unknown National Front on the extreme right. This was in marked contrast to the 20 percent share for Communists in the previous elections to the European Parliament, in 1979, and even below the 16.1 percent received in the 1981 national election that brought the left-wing coalition to power in France.

In the wake of this rebuff, Mitterrand made what observers regarded as an appeal to the political center in an attempt to stop the erosion of support for his government before national elections in 1986. On July 17 he accepted the resignation of Prime Minister Mauroy and immediately replaced him with Laurent Fabius, the 37-year-old industry minister who was widely regarded as a technocrat rather than a political figure. The Communist Party promptly said its views were incompatible with those of Fabius and refused to participate further in the government.

Fabius is committed to the modernization of French industry even at the cost of thousands of jobs, if necessary. He said on Sept 5, in his first nationally televised appearance since taking office, "Either we modernize . . . [or] France in 20 years will no longer exist as a great power." A week later he submitted a national budget, for 1985, that for the first time in 10 years calls for the increase in government spending to fall below the expected increase (3 percent) in the country's production of goods and services — the gross national product (GNP).

Surprise of Pro-Western Foreign Policy

Despite its domestic problems, the Mitterrand government has enjoyed consensus support in its foreign policy. Although the heir to a postwar tradition of French arrogance toward the United States, the Western Alliance and the European Common Market, President Mitterrand has given unreserved support to all three. Unlike many Socialist or Social Democratic regimes in Europe, the Mitterrand government has reassured many tremulous allies abroad by being much more critical of the Soviet Union than its right-of-center predecessors, which were eager to proclaim their independence from Washington and NATO.

He supported the controversial deployment of a new generation of American nuclear missiles in some NATO countries, and in general showed none of the usual French self-conscious hesitation about establishing better relations with the United States and NATO. An element of this policy has been to seek closer European defense cooperation and the strengthening of the French military and nuclear capability. Surprisingly, the opposition has not strenuously objected to the new forign policy orientation, nor to the deployment of French military forces in the troubled African state of Chad or as part of the Western multinational force in Beirut.

"Mitterrand is hard for the French to love," Jane Kramer of *The New Yorker* wrote from Paris last spring, recalling his "chilly pride" and economic bungling. "But most people here agree with him about the world outside France.... Mitterrand surprised people who thought that a Socialist president would be a 'socialist' abroad and perfectly innocuous at home, where it counted. They did not expect the old politician ... [to start] talking like Napoléon ... and they certainly didn't expect François Mitterrand to rule France instead of govern it." [6]

Other Experiences

TAKEN in isolation, the French experience might be a mere historical curiosity. Whether by coincidence or swayed by the breakthrough in France, voters in Greece, Spain and Portugal cast their ballots overwhelmingly for similar left-wing leadership. In Italy, it was the case of a Socialist being called on to form a coalition government and break a political stalemate.

Greece emerged in 1974 from a seven-year military dictatorship and Spain in 1975 from four decades of fascist authoritarianism upon the death of its "Caudillo," Francisco Franco. After a few years of centrist rule, marked by the hesitant consolidations of democratic forms, both countries turned overwhelmingly to Socialist leaders. The Greek Socialist Party (Pasok) and its leader, Andreas Papandreou, obtained 48 percent of the votes cast and a large parliamentary majority in October 1981, six months after Mitterrand's Socialists took power in France. In December 1982, Felipe González led a Socialist triumph in Spanish elections.

Both Papandreou and González had fashioned political machines out of once listless Socialist parties, just as Mitterrand had done in France. Pasok's share of the Greek vote went from 14 percent in 1974 to 25 percent in 1977 and then the triumphant 48 percent in 1981. In Spain, the Socialists increased their popular vote from 5.5 million in 1979 to 10 million in 1982, overshadowing by far their right-wing, centrist and Communist rivals, and virtually eliminating the last two as significant political forces.

---

[6] Jane Kramer, "Letter From Europe," *The New Yorker,* March 26, 1984, p. 113.

Countries at a Glance

	Area Sq. miles	Popu- lation† (millions)	GNP (US$ millions)	Unem- ploy- ment*	Inflation*
France	342,808	54.2	657,560	9.6%	7.5%
Italy	187,176	57.0	391,440	12.8	11.3
Greece	82,403	10.0	42,890	1.3	19.1
Spain	313,838	38.4	214,300	17.8	11.4
Portugal	58,583	10.1	24,750	9.0	30.4

† Mid-1984 estimates by Population Reference Bureau, Inc.
* As of July 1984 in France, Italy and Greece; March 1984 in Spain and Portugal.

Sources: EEC, International Monetary Fund, Population Reference Bureau, Inc.

Despite campaign rhetoric hinting at Greek withdrawal from NATO and the EEC and a rapid start on far-reaching social and economic measures after taking office, the leadership of Prime Minister Papandreou has been marked by what has become known as the "gradual" approach. The new government quickly adopted a popular plan of indexing wages to the cost of living and relaxing past restrictions on labor union activity. But wages shot up by 40 percent in the first year, as did the country's budget and trade deficits. Many other domestic electoral proposals have since been shelved or delayed in the quest for a more balanced budget and economic confidence.

Of all the Southern European socialist regimes, Greece has struck out on the most neutralist foreign policy, to the general discomfort of its allies. Yet it has not withdrawn from the major Western economic and defense groupings and has continued to permit American bases on its territory. Papandreou's freedom in foreign policy is obviously limited by his country's need for Western capital and trade to overcome its economic difficulties.

The domestic situation has generally been similar in the new Socialist Spain. There, however, the incoming administration of Felipe González profited from the experience of France and Greece. Instead of delaying the unavoidable currency devaluation which seems inescapably linked to the panicky flight of capital following the arrival of a new Socialist government, the González team devalued the peseta by 8 percent just a week after taking office. And although he promised during the election campaign to create 800,000 new jobs in four years, his new economic policies have been clearly committed to moderation and austerity, although officials carefully avoid those labels. As in the other countries, the priorities were to reduce double-digit inflation, and budget and trade deficits, and to modernize industry even if it required massive layoffs.

"What's a socialist industrial policy?" Felipe González asked rhetorically during a radio interview in Brussels in March 1984. "If it means the suicide of steel, shipbuilding and other industries, then I don't want any part of it." Miguel Boyer, the architect of this socialist economic policy, also remarked during a recent interview, "the economic crisis puts tight limits on what we can do." Initially committed to the withdrawal of Spain from its new NATO membership, the government announced but then indefinitely put off a referendum on the subject.[7] González sought refuge in a policy he himself calls "calculated ambiguity."

In general, the Spanish government has staked out a moderate course in foreign policy which has left some of its more radical supporters dismayed. Many think that the ultimate pattern of Spain's international policy may hinge on how long the European Economic Community makes the country wait for membership, with impatience and bitterness increasing at each delay. The previous government applied for membership to the EEC in July 1977, shortly after Portugal's bid in March of that year, and negotiations on the terms of entry for both have been proceeding since and are expected to end this year. Spain's hopes were boosted when Mitterrand told Spaniards on a visit to Madrid last June 29 he wanted the country's entry into the EEC to be "rapid and successful." French objections to the competition from French agricultural exports had put pressure on Mitterrand's government to try to delay or block Spain's membership.

Portugal: Maturity of Moderate Socialism

The other Iberian Peninsula state, Portugal, was also in the midst of a deep and troubled transition period when, in 1983, its electorate decided to put its trust in a veteran and respected Socialist leader, Mário Soares. Soares, then 59, formed his government in coalition with the smaller Social Democratic Party in June 1983 following an election victory that nevertheless fell short of giving the Socialists a majority in the 250-seat National Assembly. It marked the 15th government since the "peaceful revolution" of April 1974 which ended 48 years of dictatorship under Presidents Antônio Salazar and his associate, Marcello Caetano. That record of political instability for the country's Second Republic appears dangerously similar to the mark set by its First Republic. The First Republic had 45 governments in the years between 1910, when it was formed, and 1926, when it was overthrown by a military uprising.

---

[7] Spain entered NATO in May 1982 and the Socialist government pledged a review and consultation with the public on the subject, which is expected to lead to a referendum.

Soares, unlike many of his Southern European Socialist colleagues who came to power during the recent period, had the distinction of having had high-level political experience. It was obtained during two brief terms as prime minister in 1976-78. During that first period in office, Soares had sought to chart a course of economic moderation, although it was cut short by political infighting. His return to office left no doubt as to his recipe for the country's economic ills. Such a course was also dictated by the International Monetary Fund (IMF), in return for opening lines of credit to help Portugal overcome chronic budget, trade and debt problems.

According to a statement by the Bank of Portugal late in 1983, the government decided on a three-stage economic recovery plan. The first stage would be an 18-month program aimed at reducing external and public-sector deficits. Two longer phases would be directed at the financial sector and modernization of the country's underdeveloped industrial potential. Predictably, some of the measures to dampen domestic demand and reduce government subsidies proved to be unpopular with the public and labor unions. But some reports from Portugal also indicated that Soares' personal support remained strong. "We are beginning, just beginning, to get a sense of ourselves; unlike those in power before us, we have taken on all the risks along with the challenges," he remarked last fall.[8]

If the domestic segment of the Soares economic doctrine betrayed hardly any of the usual signs of traditional socialism, the external side of his policy was also decidedly moderate. Much of his and the country's hopes for modernization lie with a "Europeanization" process resulting from eventual membership in the EEC, which could possibly occur shortly before Spain's more difficult assimilation. The other main element has been membership in NATO and friendship with the United States, which has been an important creditor to the country since the post-revolution purge of Communist influence. Soares was instrumental in purging that influence during his previous terms of office.

Craxi's Role in Italy's Splintered Politics

The ascendancy of Socialist Bettino Craxi as the head of Italy's 43rd government[9] since the end of World War II marked the first time a Socialist had become prime minister and only the second time that anyone outside the dominant Christian Democratic Party had held the post during that postwar period.

---

[8] Quoted in the Paris-based *International Herald Tribune*, Oct. 3, 1983, from an interview.

[9] It is sometimes counted as the 44th postwar Italian government if former Prime Minister Mariano Rumor is considered to have formed new governments upon resuming office twice after he submitted resignations in 1974.

The Craxi-led government was formed Aug. 4, 1983, following elections on June 26 and 27. His selection was logical, but it also reflected the arcane reasoning of Italian politicians. Craxi's Socialists and their three smaller allied parties had increased their share of the vote from 17.4 percent in 1979 to 23.5 percent in 1983 while the Christian Democrats dropped from 38 to 33 percent. The offer by the Christian Democrats to Craxi to lead a new coalition government was therefore not just a reward for his years of tenacity in seeking the office or the improved showing of his party at the polls. It was also a means of keeping him out of the opposition, and farther away from the Communist Party, with which the Socialist Party is allied in a number of local administrations. It also saddled him with the unpleasant task of carrying out programs of economic austerity and acquiescing in American nuclear missile deployment in Sicily.

Both austerity and missile deployment were supported by the Christian Democrats. However, they were difficult for Socialists to swallow and caused Craxi to hesitate before accepting the prime minister's job. He knew the difficulty of gaining acceptance from the work force and political opponents for changes in the country's wage-price index system, the *scala mobile,* which assured employees that their wages would keep pace with the economy's double-digit inflation. Nonetheless his government proposed the measure, adding to public and union displeasure which was voiced by a million protesters in the streets of Rome on March 24.

The next month Communist opposition in Parliament forced the measure to be amended and delayed. Senator Napoleone Colajanni, the Communist leader in Parliament, summed up the political dilemma facing a Socialist-led government that applies restrictive economic programs: "We want to force the Socialists to the crossroads. Either they are truly a reformist party, in which case they must logically ally with us, or else they are just another bourgeois party like the Christian Democrats or Republicans, in which case they serve no purpose." The test in Italy as elsewhere is whether Socialist leadership can survive the clash of its traditional ideological orientation with the pressures imposed by national and international economic and political realities. The uncertain result of such choices bear on their continued existence as a political force.

The test has probably been made all the more difficult by the death June 11 of Enrico Berlinguer, who for 12 years had led Italy's Communist Party, the largest (1.3 million) in Western Europe, and one that was virtually independent of Moscow. Belinguer, who in the mid-1970s had almost persuaded the other parties to bring Communists into the ruling coalition, had

Southern Europe's Socialist Leaders

Andreas Papandreou, prime minister of Greece

(b. Feb. 5, 1919), the son of a prime minister (George Papandreou), he studied at Harvard and later (1950-63) taught economics at the Universities of Minnesota, Northwestern and California. Returning to Greece from exile in 1963, he served in economic posts but in 1967 was imprisoned, then exiled (to Sweden and Canada) by a military dictatorship. At its downfall, in 1974, he returned to Greece and founded the Panhellenic Socialist Movement (Pasek), which carried him to electoral victory in 1981.

Bettino Craxi, prime minister of Italy

(b. Feb. 24, 1934), a journalist and author who became secretary general of the minority Socialist Party of Italy in 1976 and prime minister in August 1984 at the head of a five-party coalition.

Greece

Italy

France

Spain

Portugal

François Mitterrand, president of France

(b. Oct. 26, 1916), noted for his intellect but also a man of action. A soldier in World War II captured by the Germans, he escaped and was active in the French resistance. He is the holder of several of France's highest awards. He served in several official posts in the post-war years, and became the chief architect of the Socialist Party's winning electoral strategy in 1981.

Felipe González, prime minister of Spain

(b. Mar. 5, 1942), educated at the Catholic University of Louvain in Belgium, he was a labor lawyer who pushed for workers' causes. After the return of democracy to Spain, he moved to the leadership of the country's dispirited Socialist Party, which he revitalized.

Mário Soares, prime minister of Portugal

(b. Dec. 7, 1924), a lawyer and historian who under the Salazar dictatorship was imprisoned 12 times. Upon Portugal's return to democratic rule in 1974, he returned from exile in Paris to become foreign minister and head the negotiations that led to independence for Portugal's African colonies. He was prime minister twice in 1976-78 and returned to the post in June 1983.

earned the respect of millions of non-Communists. His funeral
drew a million mourners in Rome, and it was thought that the
emotional outpouring might give the party new strength. It was
reported in late July that other leaders in the current ruling
coalition had closed ranks behind Craxi despite many differences with him. His partners, apparently fearful of a Communist political upsurge, specified that the Socialists should
abandon local and regional alliances with the Communists
"wherever possible."

European Comparisons

THE problems facing the Socialist governments of Southern
Europe are not at all unlike those confronting other governments on the continent that have entirely different ideologies.
In Northern Europe during recent years, the political pendulum
has swung in the other direction, toward the center and right.
There, the region that was often described as the cradle of
European socialism and the welfare state, has witnessed a rejection of Socialist and related parties in favor of more conservative governments. These governments, for the most part, have
been busy trying to scale down the size and cost of the welfare
state.[10]

This has been the case in most Scandinavian countries, and in
Holland, Britain and West Germany. The main exceptions have
been the return to power of the Swedish Socialist Party, under
its longtime leader Olaf Palme, in 1982, and the retention of the
Social Democratic leadership in Austria since 1970. In virtually
all European democracies, the leadership of whatever stripe has
had to cope with economic difficulties and the need for imposing unpopular measures. In case after case, the elaborate social
and welfare measures adopted by all types of governments
under better economic conditions have been reluctantly sac-
rificed by new governments trying to balance their budgets and
reduce inflation and labor costs. For instance, last April the
Palme government in Sweden imposed sweeping financial restraints to block the threat of high wage costs and inflation in
1985 from an emerging economic recovery.

As both right- and left-wing governments have experienced
the same policy constraints in recent years, a sort of solidarity in
adversity has developed among European leaders who see and
commiserate with one another regularly. Most of the leaders
seem to have rejected extreme views of how to deal with their
economic and social ills. They have accepted the wisdom of

[10] See "European Welfare States Under Attack," *E.R.R.*, 1981 Vol. I, pp. 289-308.

cutting back on welfare programs and other public spending patterns which were established in more prosperous times and which may have contributed to unattainable public expectations. All have abandoned the concept of full employment as an immediate goal in the quest for greater economic competitiveness with their neighbors.

And many have avowedly aligned themselves with the severe type of supply-side economic theory originated by the Reagan administration and introduced in Europe by the Conservative government of British Prime Minister Margaret Thatcher. The pressures and tribulations of the Thatcher government have underlined the fact that right-wing efforts at promulgating such doctrines fare no better than those of left-wing policy makers elsewhere. In fact, they sometimes seem to face stronger opposition since they do not have natural allies in organized labor.

The Thatcher experience has been nearly a mirror image of the French government's problems. Mrs. Thatcher, in pressing for her stern and unwavering efforts to reduce inflation and government spending as well as the return of many of the country's previously nationalized firms to private ownership, has had to cope with public and union opposition, of course, but also with so-called "wets," or moderates, in her own Conservative Party. But even as she persevered in her reduction of welfare programs and nationalization of state companies, she has also been forced to seek compromise with opponents.

Socialist Search for the Middle Ground

Barring any sudden parliamentary collapses, which are not unexpected or uncommon in countries like Italy, the political complexion of Western Europe seems set at least until next fall when the next round of national elections are scheduled to begin.[11] The fate of Socialists and their more conservative counterparts in the longer term seems to be intimately linked to the economic results and the effectiveness of the initially unpopular austerity programs. Only in Greece and Spain was there a strong inclination to follow more standard left-wing policy, and there only in foreign policy. Prime Minister Papandreou has staked out a position more in step with non-aligned states than with other members of the Western Alliance.

But in weathervane France there were signs that Mitterrand's policies of economic restraint were gaining grudging approval from moderates and conservatives. And the most important elements of his foreign policy, such as his smoother relations with the United States, have been accepted by his political foes.

[11] If the current governments are permitted to complete their normal terms — that is, if they are not rejected by parliamentary action — the following schedule of elections will prevail: Greece, October 1985; France, June or July 1986; Spain, 1986; West Germany, March 1987; Italy, mid-1987; Britain, 1988.

Socialists are in search of a role that will not forever doom them as permanent opposition parties, ideologically pure but politically ineffective. European Socialist parties appear no longer able to adopt the role of the champion of the working class. There are, in fact, signs that such a role is inappropriate. At a recent strategy session of Socialist leaders in Brussels, many were heard to comment about the change in their rank-and-file membership away from the traditional blue-collar industrial unionists toward a majority of teachers, public servants and others in the middle class. Most still saw themselves as advocates of greater economic and political democracy, as opposed to the conservatives' more intimate relationship with the propertied, managerial and upper classes. But Socialist governments and strategists have been drifting toward German-style social democracy or American-style liberalism.

Selected Bibliography

Books

Albert, Michel, *Un Pari pour l'Europe,* Seuil, Paris, 1984.

Brown, Bernard E., *Socialism of a Different Kind: Reshaping the Left in France,* Greenwood Press, 1982.

Lacourte, Jean, *Léon Blum,* Holmes & Meier, 1982.

McShane, Denis, *François Mitterrand: A Political Odyssey,* Universe Books, 1982.

Williams, Stuart (ed.), *Socialism in France: From Juares to Mitterrand,* St. Martin's, 1983.

Articles

"Can Mitterrand Remake France's Economy," *Business Week,* Jan. 10, 1983.

DePorte, A. W., "France's New Realism," *Foreign Affairs,* fall 1984.

Europe (magazine of the European Economic Community), selected issues.

Kramer, Jane, "Letter From Europe," *The New Yorker,* March 26, 1984.

LaPalombra, Joseph, "Specialist Alternatives: The Italian Variant," *Foreign Affairs,* spring 1983.

Lewis, Paul, *The New York Times,* series on Southern European Socialism, Nov. 29, Dec. 1-2, 1983.

OECD Observer (magazine of the Paris-based Organization for Economic Cooperation and Development), selected issues.

"Survey on France," *Financial Times* of London, July 7, 1982.

Reports and Studies

"OECD Economic Surveys," March 1983.

Editorial Research Reports: "French Parliamentary Elections (1978 Vol. I, p. 161); "European Welfare States Under Attack" (1981 Vol. I, p. 289); "Common Market in Disarray" (1984 Vol. I, p. 409).

Graphics: Maps by Staff Artist Kathleen Ossenfort;
photos from European government agencies.

SOUTH AFRICA'S 'TOTAL STRATEGY'

by

Robert Benenson

**Sept. 9
1 9 8 3**

Editor's Note: The controversy over the Republic of South Africa and its policy of apartheid, or racial separation, has had greater than usual visibility in the United States over the past year. Since November 1984, there have been daily non-violent protests at the South African embassy in Washington, D.C., with dozens of prominent persons, including several members of Congress, getting themselves purposely arrested on misdemeanor trespassing charges. Anti-apartheid sentiment has also been evident on a number of college campuses.

The step-up in American protests against apartheid came at a time when racial violence was on an upswing in South Africa. Perhaps the most explosive incident occurred on March 21 when at least 19 blacks marching in a funeral procession in Uitenhage were killed by security forces who claimed self-defense. The shootings occurred on the 25th anniversary of the Sharpeville incident, in which 69 black demonstrators were killed. Blacks in several townships have taken out their hostility on other blacks whom they believe are collaborating with the white regime, particularly members of the government-sponsored community councils. A number of officials have been brutally murdered.

The violence in South Africa intensified demands by American anti-apartheid groups for U.S. sanctions against that nation. The groups continue to call for disinvestment in South Africa by American corporations and government entities, and a ban on the sale of South African Krugerrands (gold coins). Several bills mandating such sanctions have been introduced in the 99th Congress. President Reagan condemned apartheid as immoral, but continues to conduct a policy of "constructive engagement" with South Africa.

The government of Executive President Pieter W. Botha has made several moves it sees as vindicating the Reagan administration's faith in gradual, but progressive change. Last September, the first tricameral legislature, which gives representation to the Indian and colored minorities, though not blacks, was seated. In January, Botha acknowledged the permanence of black settlements in urban areas, seemingly reversing the longstanding policy of eventual repatriation of all blacks to tribal "homelands," and suggested the set-up of an informal forum for black representation. In February, a moratorium on forced relocations to the black homelands was declared, and in April the Parliament repealed laws banning interracial marriage and sex.

Most black South African leaders, including Anglican Bishop Desmond Tutu, winner of the 1984 Nobel Peace Prize, described Botha's moves as cosmetic. On the other end of the political spectrum, South Africa's right wing denounced even these limited moves toward black-white accommodation as a sellout of white rule and the ethic of racial purity.

SOUTH AFRICA'S 'TOTAL STRATEGY'

A LMOST as inevitable as the coming of fall, another session of the United Nations General Assembly means another round of condemnations of the white supremacist government of South Africa. Up for the U.N.'s consideration during the 38th annual session, beginning Sept. 20 in New York, is a report from its World Conference on Racism calling for new efforts to coerce South Africa to end its policy of apartheid, or racial separation.[1] The conference specifically asks the Security Council to declare economic sanctions against South Africa. And it asks member nations to end all sporting, cultural and scientific contacts with that country.

The push for sanctions against South Africa hardly broke new ground. The world community, especially the Third World nations of Africa and elsewhere, have long denounced South Africa's apartheid government. Over the past 20 years, the United Nations has passed many resolutions against apartheid, created a Special Committee Against Apartheid, adopted the International Convention on the Suppression and Punishment of the Crime of Apartheid, passed in 1977 a mandatory arms embargo against South Africa, and declared 1982 to be the International Year for Mobilization of Sanctions Against South Africa. The U.N. also, in 1965, declared South Africa's occupation of South West Africa, also known as Namibia, to be illegal *(see p. 77)*.

These actions and other forms of international criticism, along with the nation's geographic isolation on the tip of the black-dominated African continent, have created the image of South Africa as a "pariah state." South Africa is hardly alone in the world though. Despite occasional and intermittently vigorous criticism from Western nations, including the United States, South Africa has normal diplomatic, economic and commercial trade relationships with most of the West. Vast mineral resources and the willingness of multinational manufacturers from the United States and Europe to locate there helped turn South Africa into a modern, industrial nation, so dominant regionally that it controls not only its own economic destiny but the destinies of the black African states around it.

---

[1] The report was approved in Geneva Aug. 13 by a vote of 104-0, with 10 abstentions. The United States and Israel boycotted the conference because of its position, as expressed in earlier U.N. resolutions, that Israel's nationalistic philosophy of Zionism is racist.

The isolation, always exaggerated, has lessened even more since the coming of the Reagan administration. Unlike the Carter administration, whose emphasis on human rights led to an antagonistic relationship with South Africa, the Reagan administration has implemented a policy of "constructive engagement" with South Africa. State Department officials say this more conciliatory policy makes the South African government more willing to discuss areas of disagreement and gives the United States more influence in pressing for reform of apartheid. But the administration is also moved by its view of South Africa as a bulwark, even an ally, in the fight against Communist expansionism. The Reagan position runs counter to the movement, supported by many churches, civil and human rights groups, universities, and even some state and city legislatures, to place economic pressure on South Africa through sanctions and disinvestment.

Colonial Background of Today's Policies

Life in South Africa and its relations with other countries are dominated by a single fact: 4.5 million whites, comprising only 16 percent of South Africa's 28 million people, have absolute control over the nation's government, economy and military forces. The 20 million blacks who make up 72 percent of the population have no political rights or representation, have been relegated to an inferior economic position, are strictly limited in their freedom of speech, movement and association, and are undergoing gradual denationalization as the South African government proceeds with the creation of "independent" black homelands.

The Colored, or mixed blood, people who make up 9 percent of the population, and the people of Indian ancestry, who make up 3 percent, though slightly more prosperous than blacks, also have no political rights or representation. However, they will gain a weak political voice under a constitutional amendment proposed last year by Prime Minister Pieter W. Botha. It is expected to be approved soon by the South African Parliament and ratified by the voters. The referendum date has already been set for Nov. 2. The amendment's main thrust is to consolidate political power in the executive branch of government, especially in Botha's hands, carrying forward South Africa's "total national strategy" — in response to the country's perception of "total onslaught" directed against it by its outside foes.

The policy of white supremacy and racial separation, or apartheid, has evolved over more than 300 years of South African history. The first Dutch settlers landed at the Cape of Good Hope in 1652. Unlike the economically motivated traders who colonized most of what came to be known as the Third

World, the Cape settlers were "boers" (farmers) who believed they had a God-given mandate to cultivate and dominate this new promised land. Along with a small group of Germans and French Huguenots, the Dutch overwhelmed the local Khoikhoi (Hottentot) tribe, developed the "Afrikaans" dialect and began calling themselves "Afrikaners." The Afrikaners meant to stay and began to regard themselves as the "White Tribe of Africa."

Afrikaner dominance was temporarily stayed by British colonialists, who took control of the Cape Colony in 1806. Several thousand British were provided land grants in the Cape Colony and in Natal in eastern South Africa. Although the British were primarily interested in developing and exploiting the resources of their colonies, they also developed a philosophy that it was the "white man's burden" to "civilize" primitive peoples. Viewing Great Britain as too sympathetic to blacks, especially after it ended slavery in its colonies, including South Africa, in 1838, thousands of angered Afrikaners set off on the "Great Trek" into the nation's interior. After weathering attacks and massacres by various African tribes, the Afrikaners circled their ox-drawn wagons in a formation known as a "laager," [2] and, armed with guns, defeated the spear-bearing Zulus at Blood River in December 1838. They set up the independent republics of Orange Free State and Transvaal, but these too came under British domination after the discovery of diamonds and gold there.

Although the philosophy of apartheid is generally associated with Afrikaners, the groundwork was laid by the British, including mining and industrial entrepreneur Cecil John Rhodes. He devised the hut tax in 1894, payable only in South African currency, which forced the African natives into wage labor. Consolidation of the white position in South Africa was delayed, however, by the Anglo-Boer War (1899-1902). Refusing to submit to total British domination, the Afrikaners of Transvaal and the Orange Free State *(see map, p. 71)* fought the British. The conflict was bloody. More than 5,000 British soldiers died in the fighting, and the Afrikaner people suffered great privations.

More radical Boers felt betrayed by the surrender negotiated by their leaders; but conciliatory Boer leaders such as Louis Botha and Jan Christaan Smuts convinced the British government to give South Africa independent Commonwealth status. In 1910, the Union of South Africa was created, with a whites-only government. "This is where the problem started," said David Ndaba, an official with the U.N. Mission of the African National Congress, an exiled South African dissident group. "If

---

[2] The defensive posture taken by many present-day white South Africans who view themselves as beset by unfair world opinion came to be known as the "laager mentality."

the British didn't do that, I think South Africa would have been treated as one of the colonial cases ... [and we would have received] independence maybe like Kenya, Nigeria, Zimbabwe, Zambia, Lesotho."

The South African government, led by Afrikaners seeking accommodation with the British, passed a number of laws aimed at controlling the African majority and creating a pool of African labor. The Native Lands Act of 1913 created tribal reserves or "homelands," scattered areas comprising 13 percent of South Africa's land. Blacks were forbidden to purchase property outside the reserves, and were permitted to live in urban areas only when their labor was needed by white employers. To control the "influx" of blacks into urban areas, the government enacted "pass laws" requiring blacks to carry identification cards. These would show whether they were legal residents of the townships that had been erected outside the big cities to confine the black urban workers and their families. Workers were barred from striking, and black union activity was suppressed. Legislation reserved skilled, better-paying jobs in business, industry and mining for whites.

Ongoing Removal to Black Homelands

The system of racial separation lacked a master plan until the Nationalist Party came to power in 1948. Many Nationalist leaders belonged to the Broederbond, a semi-secret society whose goals included preservation of Afrikaner culture and Afrikaner dominance of South Africa's government. Among younger party members were those, like future Prime Minister John Vorster, who had tried to sabotage the South African war effort on the British side in World War II. The Nationalist leaders hewed to the philosophy described by Afrikaner theorist G. A. Cronje in 1945: "The more consistently the policy of apartheid could be applied, the greater would be the security for the purity of our blood and the surer our unadulterated European racial survival." Cronje wrote that Afrikaners should promote apartheid because "it is according to the Will of God."

The Nationalists set about in earnest to create a legal structure of racial separation. In 1950, the Group Areas Act created separate zones in towns and cities for whites, Africans, and each Colored group (mixed-blood Coloreds, Indians, Chinese and Malays). Since pass laws and other influx-control measures had been unable to stop job-seeking migrants from ballooning the size of Johannesburg townships such as Soweto and shantytowns outside Cape Town, Parliament in 1952 made it a punishable offense for blacks to be in "white" areas unless they could prove residency since birth, 10 years' continuous employment or 15 years' legal residency, direct family relationship with a

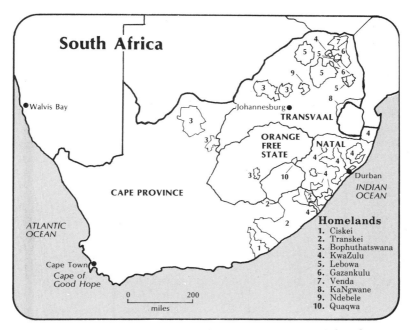

Map: South Africa

Walvis Bay

Johannesburg

TRANSVAAL

ORANGE FREE STATE

NATAL

CAPE PROVINCE

Durban

INDIAN OCEAN

ATLANTIC OCEAN

Cape Town
Cape of Good Hope

0   200
miles

Homelands
1. Ciskei
2. Transkei
3. Bophuthatswana
4. KwaZulu
5. Lebowa
6. Gazankulu
7. Venda
8. KaNgwane
9. Ndebele
10. Quaqwa

qualifying male, or permission from a government labor bureau to remain. Violators were jailed, fined and/or deported to the homelands.

The government worked to establish its social blueprint. The 1949 Prohibition of Mixed Marriages Act banned marriages between Europeans and non-Europeans. The 1950 Immorality Act, which banned sexual relations between persons of different races, was amended in 1957 to include "any immoral or indecent act" between black and white. The Population Registration Act of 1950 required the categorization of each South African into a racial grouping: white, African, and Colored. The classifications are often made on the basis of appearance, and dozens of people are reclassified on appeal every year. The Reservation of Separate Amenities Act of 1953 provided the legal basis for segregation in public facilities, including transportation, restaurants, and parks; the act also created the separate-but-unequal doctrine, which permitted authorities to provide certain services for whites, while providing inferior or no service for blacks.

Segregation in public facilities came to be known as "petty apartheid." But whites sought to ensure their dominance, and even to make themselves a majority of South Africa's citizenry, through the policy of "separate development," or "grand apartheid." Beginning with the Bantu Authorities Act of 1951, the government has moved to create "independent" states out of the tribal reserves. Ten "homelands," each assigned to a different African tribe, were created; all black South Africans were assigned to a homeland according to their tribal ethnicity, and since 1951, about three million blacks have been involuntarily removed from "white" areas to the homelands. When South Africa grants independence to a homeland, all blacks who have tribal or ethnic associations with it are declared citizens of the homeland, even if they have never lived there, and lose their South African citizenship. If the homelands policy is carried out to its fullest extent, all South African blacks would be de-nationalized, and whites would thus be in the majority among remaining South African citizens.

Four homelands have been given their "independence" by South Africa: Transkei (1976), Bophuthatswana (1977), Venda (1979) and Ciskei (1981). None is recognized by any other country. South African officials say world opinion is tainted by a misimpression that the homelands policy indicates some kind of oppression against blacks. They say that South Africa, as part of its grand design, is granting blacks the political rights they desire, in their own independent states, and that only international prejudice against South Africa prevents their recognition as sovereign states. "You have, for example, Botswana, Lesotho and Swaziland [former British colonies], which could equally have been parts of South Africa, and if their independence had been given them by South Africa, then presumably that also would not have been recognized," said Brand Fourie, South African ambassador to the United States.[3]

But most international observers are skeptical. South African officials admit that the black states have no control over their foreign policy or defense; critics claim that the leaders of the states — such as Lucas Mangope of Bophuthatswana, Kaiser Mantanzima of Transkei and Lennox Sebe of Ciskei — are puppets of Pretoria. Only Bophuthatswana, with its booming gambling casinos, has approached any kind of economic stability. South Africa's Bureau of Economic Research reported last November that only about one million of the 4.6 million blacks in the "independent" homelands were economically active in 1980 at the time of its survey. In the six other homelands, more than 5.2 million of the 6.2 million blacks were reported to have no measurable income at all. The leader of one of those homelands, Chief Gatsha Buthelezi of KwaZulu, has refused South Africa's offers of independence.

International skepticism of the government's intentions was intensified by Pretoria's[4] attempt to rid itself of some of the homeland territory last year. South Africa's government offered

---

[3] All quotations in this report were, unless otherwise noted, obtained in interviews conducted by the author between Aug. 4 and 9, 1983.

[4] Pretoria is the administrative capital of South Africa and the name is synonomous with the government; however, Parliament sits in Cape Town.

to settle a long-standing border dispute with Swaziland by turning over parts of KaNgwane and KwaZulu to the Swazis. The transfer would have made about 850,000 blacks, still regarded as South Africans, into citizens of Swaziland. However, the plan was voided by the South African Court of Appeals last September.

Results of Apartheid: Inequality, Revolt

According to statistics compiled by The Africa Fund in New York, black welfare has been handicapped by the apartheid system. The average monthly wage for black manufacturing workers in 1980 was $308, less than a quarter of the white average of $1,273.[5] The relative disparity was even worse in mining: 1979 figures showed blacks earning a monthly average of $175, compared to $1,056 for whites. Infant mortality figures per 1,000 in 1980 were 12 for whites, 69 for urban blacks and 282 for rural blacks. The Study Commission on U.S. Policy Toward Southern Africa, funded by the Rockefeller Commission, reported in 1981 that only 15 percent of the black children who entered primary school in 1967 had reached the final year of high school. The commission also found that the South African government was spending over 10 times more for the education of white than black students.[6]

Another result of the apartheid system is a festering anger among black South Africans that occasionally erupts into open protest and violence. Black opposition to white domination is nothing new. Among the heroes of black South Africans are the Zulu chiefs Dingane, who led Africans against the Afrikaners at Blood River, and Bambata, whose unsuccessful revolt against British rule led to the total disarming of blacks in 1906.[7]

Blacks turned to nonviolent protest, through the African National Congress (ANC), founded in 1912. Claiming an inability to get a hearing from the South African government, a group of ANC members, including Nelson Mandela, Oliver Tambo and Walter Sisulu, created the Youth League of the ANC in 1944 with a program of nonviolent resistance patterned after the actions of Mohatma Gandhi in India. In 1952, it staged a campaign of defiance against segregation and pass laws, and boycotted farm products produced by convict labor. In 1955, a convention of blacks and sympathetic whites, Coloreds and Indians drew up the Freedom Charter, which called for a South Africa where "Every man and woman shall have the right to vote for and stand as candidates for all bodies which make

---

[5] Other non-white South Africans were slightly better off. Coloreds averaged $355 a month in manufacturing, $461 in mining. Indians earned $399 in manufacturing; the few Indians involved in mining earned $518.

[6] *South Africa: Time Running Out*, University of California Press, 1981.

[7] Bambata was killed, and photographs of his severed head were turned into postcards by British soldiers, an event that remains a symbol of white rule to many black South Africans.

laws." It further stated that "our country will never be prosperous and free until all our people live in brotherhood, enjoying equal rights and opportunities."

The government, meanwhile imposed more restrictions on critics of its policies. The Suppression of Communism Act was passed in 1950 and during the next 25 years, according to South African legal expert John Dugard, "was invoked against ardent non-Communists as well as professed Communists, as the definition of communism is wide enough to encompass most radical opponents of the status quo." [8] The government charged 156 signers of the Freedom Charter with treason, claiming that the document urged the overthrow of the government; all were later acquitted. The government also used force; on March 21, 1960, police in Sharpeville opened fire on a black mob organized by the Pan-Africanist Congress (PAC) to protest pass laws, killing 70. The protest and its aftermath resulted in the banning of both the PAC and the ANC.

In 1961, Mandela and others created a military wing of the ANC, known as Umkhonto We Sizwe, Zulu for "Spear of the Nation." Inexperience with underground organizing led to the group's easy infiltration; Mandela, Sisulu and several others were convicted and sentenced to life imprisonment, while many other ANC supporters, including current leader Oliver Tambo, fled into exile in neighboring countries. [9] At his trial, Mandela declared his innocence, saying "the criminals that should have been brought before this court are the members of the Verwoerd government." [10]

With the 1960s and 1970s came other measures to control dissent. The Terrorism Act of 1967 made punishable not only acts of violence but also (1) advocacy of any political aim to be brought about by violent or forceful means, and (2) acts that cause substantial financial loss to a person or the state, create "feelings of hostility" between races, or "embarrass the administration of the affairs of the state." The use of detention without charge or trial and the practice of banning became common. Persons who were banned were severely restricted in their speech, movement and association; their words could not be quoted or published; and sometimes they were exiled to remote parts of the country or placed under house arrest.

The student-led "black consciousness" movement in the mid-1970s culminated in protests, sparked by a government decision to make Afrikaans the official language in black schools. Protest

---

[8] *South Africa: Time Running Out*, p. 68.

[9] Mandela, now 65 and still in prison, remains the titular head of the ANC.

[10] Hendrik Verwoerd served as prime minister from 1958 until his assassination by a deranged white man in 1966.

riots erupted in Soweto in June 1976 and spread to other black urban enclaves during the following months, resulting in police confrontations and a black death toll of about 1,000. The government, operating under the Riotous Assemblies Act of 1956, afterward required a permit for all outdoor meetings and gatherings except sporting events.

Several black leaders were banned, including Steven Biko, the black consciousness organizer and theorist. Biko was subsequently arrested for violating a banning order and in September 1977 died of brain damage while in police custody. Despite accusations by his supporters that Biko was beaten to death by police and an international outcry over the incident, an inquest found the officials innocent of wrongdoing. Several other government opponents have died in detention, including Dr. Neil Aggett, a white union leader who was found hanged in his Johannesburg jail cell in February 1982.[11]

In recent years, the exiled ANC has stepped up its campaign of armed attacks — terrorism according to Pretoria — from neighboring countries. The ANC bombed a state-run synthetic fuel plant in June 1980 and a nuclear power station in December 1982. That same month, in an escalation from its stated policy of avoiding loss of human life, the ANC exploded a bomb in a car outside the Pretoria headquarters of the South African Air Force, killing 19 persons. South Africa responded promptly with force; its warplanes attacked an area suspected of ANC activity near Maputo, Mozambique, killing at least six persons.

Government Claims of Reforming System

South African officials insist that suppressive laws and violence are exceptions to the norm in a relatively peaceful and prosperous country, and complain that a biased Western press is in part responsible for South Africa's tarnished image. There have been some reforms that have loosened restrictions on the everyday activities of blacks. Prime Minister Botha has used the phrase "Change or die!" many times over the years and has said that he is not willing to die to defend petty apartheid. Local authorities have exercised their option or have applied for government exemptions in order to end segregation of such public facilities as museums, parks and libraries. South Africans are sports-conscious, and the government has made a point of publicizing its integrated athletic teams in the hope of breaking down an international sports boycott.[12]

---

[11] An official inquiry ruled Aggett's death a suicide. His family argued that he killed himself after being tortured in interrogation, but a court found no wrongdoing by authorities.

[12] The government in 1962 lifted a ban on participation by black South Africans in Olympic Games — although the International Olympic Committee (IOC) has placed the Games off-limits to all South African athletes since 1970. Since 1976 the country has permitted multiracial teams to represent it in other international sports events. However, few such events are open to them because of the boycott, which was initiated in the 1970s.

The government also contends that blacks are making economic advances. Blacks were prohibited from striking until a series of wildcat walkouts in the Durban-Port Elizabeth area in 1973 forced a change in that policy. A commission headed by Dr. Nic E. Wiehahn suggested in 1979 that job reservations be eliminated and black labor unions be permitted. Reservations are no longer required by law except in the mining industry where a powerful white union holds sway, and black unions have proliferated, albeit under the watchful eye of the government which quickly cracks down on political activities. Although great wage disparities remain, the gap between white and black wages narrowed between 1970 and 1980 in manufacturing and mining.

The most controversial "reform" plan put forth by the Nationalist government is Botha's constitutional proposal to give limited political representation to the Colored and Indian populations. A tricameral legislature would be created, with separate houses for the three ethnic groupings. The Colored and Indian houses would deal with matters specific to their communities, while issues cutting across ethnic lines — and therefore, most national policy — would be decided by a white-dominated President's Council, which already exists, and by a white "executive president," an office yet to be created combining the offices of prime minister and president  — which now is mostly ceremonial. Blacks would not be included, a policy which the government defends by referring to the "independent" homelands and black municipal councils as evidence of black self-government.

Pieter W. Botha

Government officials say the "power-sharing" proposal is a dramatic leap forward for South Africa. But blacks and their supporters see the policy as nothing but a means of government co-optation of other disadvantaged groups. According to the 1982 report of the U.N. Special Committee Against Apartheid, "A growing coalition of civil organizations, action committees, youth groups and trade unions firmly rejected the new constitutional proposals which they viewed as nothing but a device to divide the population and perpetuate apartheid." The Colored Labor Party was deeply split when its leadership announced its support for the proposals last January. Many black leaders say that the proposals have galvanized black opposition to the government and reawakened the black consciousness movement.

Regional Domination

I T IS not only South Africa's domestic policy that provokes controversy. South Africa has been at odds with the world community over its continued control of Namibia, also known as South West Africa. South Africa captured the territory from German colonists in 1916, during World War I, and in 1919 received a mandate from the League of Nations to administer it. Despite United Nations' demands that South West Africa be turned over to U.N. control, the Nationalist government in 1948 gave South West Africa representation in Parliament and exported the apartheid system to the territory. Although sparsely populated (just over a million people) and mostly desert, it is rich in diamonds and other minerals, and has a deep-water port at Walvis Bay which, despite its geographical location in the middle of Namibia's coast, has been annexed by South Africa as part of Cape Province.

South Africa remains in control of Namibia despite a U.N. resolution in 1965 that declared the South African occupation illegal and another in 1971 that declared the South West Africa People's Organization (SWAPO), which is fighting a guerrilla war against South African occupation, as the "authentic representative of the Namibian people." South Africa has about 100,000 troops in Namibia or, as critics point out, nearly one soldier for every 10 Namibian residents. The South Africans have frequently used Namibia as a base for its successful incursions against SWAPO bases in Angola to the north.

The United States has played a central role in the negotiations for a Namibian settlement since the early days of the Carter administration. At that time, the role of SWAPO in a Namibian government was the main issue. In 1978, the U.N. Security Council approved a plan, agreed to in principle by South Africa and SWAPO, for a cease-fire, withdrawal of troops from Namibia and a process for U.N.-supervised elections.

But since early 1981, South Africa has linked its withdrawal from Namibia to the departure of 25,000 Cuban troops from Angola. It is a policy encouraged — some say dictated — by the Reagan administration. Those troops have been in Angola at the invitation of President Jose Eduardo dos Santos to help fend off the South African-backed insurgency of the National Union for Independence (UNITA) since shortly after the nation obtained independence in 1975. The Cuban issue has created a vicious circle: the South Africans refuse to leave Namibia (and southern Angola) until the Cubans are out, but the Angolans refuse to send the Cubans home until the South Africans depart.

Ambassador Fourie, who was a chief South Africa negotiator on Namibia for five years, insisted that the Cuban departure is "the last remaining issue to be resolved." However, many diplomatic observers see recent successes by UNITA, which dominates almost all of southern Angola, as stiffening South Africa's resolve. If the Marxist government of dos Santos is forced to come to terms and possibly even share power with UNITA leader Jonas Savimbi, then the Namibian settlement is likely to be more beneficial to South Africa. South Africa also notes that dos Santos will never be able to send the Cubans home unless he ends the civil war by reconciling with Savimbi.

U.N. Secretary-General Javier Peŕez de Cuellar visited South Africa, Namibia and Angola Aug. 22-24 in an attempt to break the stalemate. The secretary-general was able to obtain South African agreement on most of the issues, including the U.N.'s qualifications as an impartial observer to conduct Namibian elections. However, de Cuellar said the Cuban troop issue, the main obstacle, was outside the mandate given him by the U.N. Security Council, and statements by South African and Angolan officials indicated that the problem is no closer to resolution.

Economic Hold on Neighboring Nations

The five "front line" states which South Africa borders or surrounds are unanimous in their opposition to its Namibian policy and apartheid government. These states — Lesotho, Swaziland, Mozambique, Zimbabwe, Botswana — are all ruled by their black majorities. Mozambique has a Marxist government. Although Zimbabwe (formerly Rhodesia) has a mixed economy, its president, Robert Mugabe, rose to power as a Marxist and persistently assails South African "racism." But these nations dare not cut off relations with South Africa, for it dominates the region's economy.

Much of South Africa's wealth is based on the vast mineral reserves discovered in the 19th century. Among its main exports are gold, diamonds and coal. Iron ore reserves have allowed South Africa to build a thriving steel industry. More than half of the world's reserves of several so-called "strategic minerals," such as platinum group metals, manganese and chromium, are in South Africa. The mineral wealth provided the base for industrial growth dominated by Western multinational corporations, including over 300 based in the United States. ARMSCOR, the government's armament manufacturer whose growth was spurred by the international arms embargo, turns out more than $1 billion in sophisticated weaponry each year. And South Africa is a net exporter of agricultural products, including sugar, fruit, fish, and the staple of many African nations, corn.

As a result, South Africa towers above its developing neighbor states. South Africa's 1982 gross national product of $80 billion was nearly nine times that of the five front-line states combined, although its population is only one-third larger than theirs. Put another way, South Africa produces more than three-quarters of the total GNP of all nations south of Zaire and Tanzania (including Angola, Namibia, Zambia, and Malawi). Its per capita GNP of $2,200, according to the British magazine *The Economist*, was three times the regional average. South Africa's per capita income in 1980 was $2,250; for the top ranking front-line state, Botswana, it was under $1,000.[13]

Comparisons do not provide the whole picture of South Africa's dominance. Only agriculturally rich Zimbabwe has been able to avoid importing corn from South Africa, and even its situation is threatened by drought and unrest in some rural provinces. While the front-line states are heavily dependent on South Africa for trade, most of South Africa's commerce is with industrialized nations such as the United States, Britain, Japan, West Germany, Switzerland and France. The underdeveloped nations are reliant on revenues derived from remittances of

---

[13] "Destabilisation in Southern Africa," *The Economist*, July 16, 1983.

79

migrant workers employed in South Africa's mines and factories.

Botswana, Lesotho and Swaziland (known as the BLS states) have joined in the South African Customs Union, with a nation they avow to despise politically. The most vulnerable of these nations is Lesotho. Carved out of a former British enclave and independent only since 1966, it is surrounded by South Africa and depends on South Africa's transport network for its imports and exports. South Africa is Lesotho's main trading partner. The small chiefdom gets half of its food and all of its oil and electricity from South Africa. More than half of its labor force works in South Africa; many of the workers commute daily between the two countries.

The dominance South Africa holds over Lesotho is illustrated by a recent incident. Angered by the presence of ANC sympathizers in Lesotho, South Africa demanded the expulsion of 3,000 South African refugees from Lesotho and, beginning in May, slowed commerce and instituted border "security checks" which stymied the flow of workers to and from their jobs in South Africa. In late July, Lesotho informed the U.N. high commissioner for refugees and the secretary-general that the refugees would be removed, and asked for international assistance. Stating that his country was being "suffocated," Lesotho Foreign Minister Evaristus R. Sekhonyana said, "We will have to comply with the demands. Lesotho has no options." [14]

South Africa's Use of Its Military Power

Lesotho has also felt the wrath of South Africa's military machine. Last December, South African commandos armed with rockets and machine guns attacked what was called an ANC stronghold in Maseru, Lesotho's capital, killing more than 40 persons. Lesotho government spokesmen said that many of the dead were South African refugees and Lesotho nationals, including some women and children. The Lesotho raid, the Mozambique bombing in May and the raids against SWAPO positions in Angola have shown that South Africa is ready, willing and able to use its military muscle against what it sees as security threats throughout southern Africa.

Such actions are based on the South African government's expressed belief that it is the subject of a "total onslaught" by leftist forces backed by the Soviet Union. As portrayed in 1980 by Defense Minister Magnus Malan, the "total onslaught is an ideologically motivated struggle" aimed at "the overthrow of the present constitutional order and its replacement by a sub-

---

[14] Quoted in *The Washington Post*, Aug. 12, 1983.

ject communist-oriented government." [15] Yet other South African officials deny that it is their neighbors' political philosophy that results in South African military response. "If they would have their form of government [and] wouldn't export it, well, it's their business," said Ambassador Fourie. "But our real argument is, we say, 'You cannot house terrorists in your country to operate against South Africa.' "

Some observers say that South Africa has gone beyond defensive and counter-terrorist measures. In an article entitled "Destabilisation in Southern Africa," journalist Simon Jenkins wrote this summer in *The Economist* that South Africa is attempting to ensure its internal stability and regional dominance by destabilizing the governments of neighboring countries. Jenkins cited extensive evidence that South Africa is supporting and training anti-government guerrillas in Mozambique, Lesotho and Zimbabwe. According to Jenkins and others who concur in this view of South African policy, the idea is not to overthrow the neighboring governments but to keep them economically dependent and militarily preoccupied with civil strife and insurrection. [16]

Fourie denies that South Africa is trying to destabilize its neighbors. "If we wanted to ... it is the easiest thing in the world to do," he said "All you need do is stop the railway lines, close your port facilities ... then you can really destabilize these countries overnight almost."

The American Role

A N EPISODE that occurred in 1975 typified the touchy relationship between the United States and South Africa. Throughout that year, under a policy formulated by Secretary of State Henry Kissinger, the Ford administration had been providing aid to South African-backed forces in a civil war in newly independent Angola. Congress learned of the activities in December 1975, and with the memories of the Vietnam conflict still fresh, passed an amendment to a defense appropriations bill prohibiting the use of funds "for any activities involving Angola directly or indirectly." The anti-communist forces soon collapsed and South African troops assisting them were forced to retreat to Namibia. South African officials still harbor hard feelings over the incident. "You know your country failed in this

---

[15] Quoted by Kenneth W. Grundy in "South Africa's Domestic Strategy," *Current History,* March 1983.
[16] *The Economist,* July 16, 1983, pp. 19-28.

miserably," Gen. Constand Viljoén, the South African defense chief, told *The New York Times* recently. "The collapse in 1975 was a disaster." [17]

South Africa suffered other setbacks in its relations with the United States. The Carter administration's interest in human rights and the cultivation of closer ties with Black Africa often were manifested in verbal attacks on South Africa. In his Senate confirmation hearing as Carter's nominee as U.S. representative to the United Nations, Andrew Young said that "a rather hard-line policy might be necessary to make South Africa move internally." Young maintained this critical posture throughout his tenure in the U.N. post. In September 1977 during the Carter presidency, the deputy U.S. ambassador to the United Nations, Donald McHenry, canceled a negotiating session with South African officials on Namibia to attend the funeral of Steven Biko.[18]

The Reagan administration has not been entirely uncritical either. The under secretary of state for political affairs, Lawrence S. Eagleburger, said in a speech in June: "The political system in South Africa is morally wrong. We stand against injustice, and, therefore, we must reject the legal and political premises and consequences of apartheid." [19] Yet the Reagan administration has adopted a conciliatory policy of "constructive engagement" with South Africa, and even President Carter, whose criticism offended Pretoria, once called South Africa a "stablilizing force" in southern Africa.

This ambivalent attitude is caused by the opinion of many American diplomatic, political, business and military leaders that South Africa is important in the East-West balance of power. "In this rich and diverse land of talented and diverse peoples, important Western economic, strategic, moral and political interests are at stake," said Chester Crocker, assistant secretary of state for African affairs, in August 1981. Crocker later added that "South Africa is an integral and important element of the global economic system, and it plays a significant economic role in its own region." [20]

Mineral wealth is invariably cited in assessments of South Africa's strategic importance to the United States. South Africa produces about half of the world's platinum and has almost three-quarters of the world's reserves. The only other important platinum producer is the Soviet Union. A similar situation exists for other strategic minerals, such as chromium, vanadium and manganese.

---

[17] Quoted in *The New York Times*, June 4, 1983.
[18] For background, see "African Policy Reversal," *E.R.R.*, 1978 Vol. II, pp. 501-520.
[19] Speech to the National Conference of Editorial Writers in San Francisco, June 23, 1983.
[20] Speech before the American Legion in Honolulu, Aug. 29, 1981.

South Africa's 'Total Strategy'

The sea lanes off South Africa, known as the Cape Route, serve as a highway for the ships that carry much of the West's oil supply from the Persian Gulf and other forms of Asian trade as well. "The importance to the West of the Cape Route is beyond question," wrote the Study Commission on U.S. Policy Toward Southern Africa in 1981. "Some 2,300 ships travel it each month. They deliver 57 percent of Western Europe's imported oil and 20 percent of U.S. imported oil. Some 70 percent of the strategic raw materials used by NATO is also transported via the Cape Route." Thus, South Africa is seen as a strategic ally simply because of its location on the tip of the continent.

Because of its military power, South Africa is also seen by many Westerners as a strategic force against Soviet expansionism in southern Africa. Although Soviet influence is limited to the Marxist countries of Angola and Mozambique and to the SWAPO and ANC insurgency movements, U.S. military advisers have long professed concern that a weakening of South Africa would lead to Soviet domination of Namibia and possibly all of southern Africa, including South Africa. The South African concept of "total onslaught" fits with the Reagan view of virtually unlimited Soviet expansionism.

The United States has economic interests in South Africa as well. According to the Investor Responsibility Research Center in Washington,[21] 400 U.S. companies have affiliates in South Africa. These include some of the nation's biggest corporations: General Motors, Ford, Mobil and Caltex Oil hold over half of the $2 billion of direct U.S. investment in South Africa. U.S. companies also employ about 100,000 South Africans, 70 percent of whom are black. Over 6,000 companies, according to IRRC, do business with South Africa through sales agents or licensing agreements. Many banks lend money to South African corporations; some, including Citibank and Bank of America, lend money to the South African government.

New Policy of Constructive Engagement

The Reagan administration's policy that smoothing relations with South Africa is in the best interests of the United States was spelled out in Crocker's speech. "The United States also seeks to build a more constructive relationship with South Africa, one based on shared interests, persuasion and improved communication," Crocker said. According to the authors of this policy of "constructive engagement," the United States seeks to bring about reform of apartheid not through scolding and at-

---

[21] The IRRC, founded in 1972, describes itself as a non-profit corporation "to conduct research and publish impartial reports on contemporary social and public policy issues and the impact of those issues on major corporations and institutional investors." In a directory of U.S. corporations in South Africa, published in May 1982, IRRC said it was financed by subscription fees paid by more than 170 investing institutions.

tempted intimidation, but through open, diplomatic discussion that will increase the South Africans' willingness to listen while insuring American strategic interests.

A change in official attitude toward South Africa soon became clear after Ronald Reagan assumed office. In March 1981, Jeane Kirkpatrick, the U.S. representative to the U.N., vetoed a Security Council condemnation of South Africa for its invasion of southern Angola in search of SWAPO bases. In November 1982, the administration put its stamp of approval on a $1.1 billion loan by the International Monetary Fund to South Africa. Although the president and his aides have expressed general opposition to South Africa's social system, their protests against instances of alleged human rights violations have been muted.

Administration officials say restraint on U.S. intervention in South African internal affairs has led to reforms, including Botha's constitutional proposal. "I do not see it as our business to enter into this debate or to endorse the constitutional proposals now under consideration for South Africa," Eagleburger said in his speech. "Yet the indisputable fact which we must recognize is that the South African government has taken the first step toward extending national political rights beyond the white minority."

Some observers say that the Reagan policy is being credited for some other ameliorative actions in South Africa. Pretoria lifted a ban on 50 dissidents in June, dropping the number of persons still banned to 11. *Washington Post* correspondent Allister Sparks reported from South Africa on Aug. 14, "Local political and diplomatic observers have attributed this to pressure from the United States, and it is being cited as the first significant achievement of the Reagan administration's policy of 'constructive engagement' with South Africa."

However, the Reagan policy is not seen as constructive by opponents of the South African government. Zimbabwe President Robert Mugabe, who had previously taken a soft line toward Reagan's African policy, said in an interview with *The Washington Post* on Aug. 18 that U.S. support "had the effect of encouraging South Africa to continue along the same old path of resistance to the wishes of the majority of the people in Namibia and South Africa, and, in fact, to become more aggressive against the front-line states." David Ndaba of the ANC went further, accusing the United States of giving the South African government a freer hand to crush dissent.

Anti-apartheid groups in the United States have been hardly less vehement in their criticism of constructive engagement. According to Timothy Smith, executive director of the Interfaith Center on Corporate Responsibility (ICCR) in New York, constructive engagement has been a "complete failure" as a total philosophy. "The churches we work with would say the Reagan administration had gone totally overboard to naively assume ... that a constructive engagement, business-as-usual policy was going to be a force for change in South Africa," Smith said. "[The South African leaders] know how to co-opt constructive engagement and to make some minuscule changes that can please the Reagan administration while not at all changing the central force of keeping the white minority in power."

Pressures on Corporations to Disinvest

The ICCR is a coalition of churches that work together to channel their $7.5 billion in investments in a socially conscious direction. It is one of the largest of the many church, student, civil rights and political groups that favor economic pressure as a means of forcing change in South Africa. These groups, active for nearly two decades but particularly in the past 10 years, try to put pressure on banks and businesses to reduce or break their economic ties with South Africa. Tactics include withdrawing funds from banks lending money to the South African government, selling stock in companies that trade with or operate subsidiaries in South Africa (a practice known as "divestment"), and lobbying state legislatures and city councils to end investments of pension funds and other assets in companies and banks doing business with South Africa.

The movement to put the financial squeeze on South Africa has had some success. A number of banks have adopted stated policies of not doing business with South Africa, or not lending money to the South African government and its agencies. Several U.S. corporations, including Polaroid and Chrysler, have closed their South African operations. Several others, including General Electric, were dissuaded from expanding their operations in South Africa. State and city governments have also acted to drop South African links. Because of laws passed in 1982, state colleges and universities in Michigan are required to drop their investments in South Africa, and the state employees and teachers' pension funds in Massachusetts must divest. The Philadelphia City Council also banned city investments in South Africa last year. "These are places where the South Africa agenda has not been debated before and suddenly it's in scores of new places with substantial capital," said Smith. "I don't think they can like that at all."

Many corporations have resisted pressure to disinvest or reduce their South African commitments by stating that they can accomplish more to change the apartheid system by raising wages, ending workplace segregation, encouraging collective bargaining and otherwise improving the economic lot of black workers, than they could by withdrawing. About half of the U.S. companies in South Africa have subscribed to the Sullivan Principles, drawn up in 1977 by Rev. Leon Sullivan, chairman of Opportunities Industrialization Centers of America, a minority job-training organization, and board member of General Motors. The Sullivan Principles include: nonsegregation in all eating, comfort and work facilities; equal and fair employment practices; equal pay for comparable work; initiation of programs to train black and other non-white workers for supervisory, administrative, clerical and technical jobs; and increasing their number in management and supervisory positions.

Many anti-apartheid groups see the Sullivan Principles as lip service, and say that even those companies that have instituted programs to improve conditions for black workers have done nothing to remedy the basic inequities in the apartheid system. Smith disagrees, stating, "I think companies have made significant steps over the last decade, because of the encouragement of Sullivan, of good people in the companies who are pushing for changes, and the pressure groups like ourselves." But Smith added, "I don't think that's a formula for social change in South Africa."

Uncertain Outlook for Peaceful Changes

There are widely varying views on the efficacy of economic pressures in changing South Africa's racial policies. Reagan administration officials take a position similar to that of the U.S. corporations based in South Africa. "Disinvestment by U.S. firms would undo an avenue of positive effort," said Lawrence Eagleburger. "This apparent quest for symbolic dissociation is, in reality, a formula guaranteed to assure America's irrelevance to South Africa's future."

South African officials scoff at efforts by foreign pressure groups as no more than a lot of sound and fury. Ambassador Fourie said that attempts at economic pressure had not hurt South Africa "thus far," and added that the U.S. pressure groups did not "vitally want to improve things in South Africa" but were using the situation in "an internal political kind of argument." But opponents of the apartheid government insist that pressure is worthwhile. "The only hope for a relatively peaceful change is when international pressure is exerted on the apartheid regime, because frankly it is not possible for 4 million whites to dominate and rule over 23 million black people," said David Ndaba. "It has only been possible because of the economic and military power they have at their disposal."

There are some who hold out hope that the push for peaceful change may come from within South Africa's ruling white minority. For the white population, South Africa functions as a democracy. The minority Progressive Federal Party, dominated by English-speaking British descendants, has campaigned consistently for reform and has come out strongly against the tricameral parliament proposed by Botha. White dissent, though watched carefully and occasionally restrained by the government, is generally tolerated. The South African Council of Churches has described apartheid as a "heresy," and many of the English-language churches are split over the apartheid issue. A small group of white women have gone to the black townships to aid hunger victims during the current drought plaguing southern Africa. The traditional white dissident groups continue their anti-apartheid protests.

"Certainly the white community is not totally monolithic in supporting apartheid forever," said Timothy Smith of ICCR. Smith said that there are South African whites who are motivated for reform out of fear, "enlightened self-interest," or "Christian compassion and commitment to sharing of power and wealth." However, Smith noted that the whites who are willing to talk about power-sharing with blacks have "no significant political power at this point."

The limited potential for reform was illustrated by the split in the Nationalist Party following Botha's announcement of his parliamentary reform plan. Right-wingers claimed that the reform was the first step toward a multiracial government that would soon include blacks, and a group led by Dr. Andries Treurnicht bolted to form the Conservative Party. In by-elections last May, one Nationalist candidate won handily, but Treurnicht, running as a Conservative, won easily, and a veteran Nationalist leader barely retained his seat against a Conservative. "The government was looking over its right shoulder, not its left shoulder" in the elections, said Smith.

South African government officials say that, if left alone, they will evolve a system over time in which all races will have economic and social opportunity, along with full political rights within their racial communities. But black activists, especially those dedicated to the overthrow of apartheid, say that Pretoria's idea of reform is an institutionalization of an unequal and oppressive system, and they urge South African blacks to oppose such efforts. While some black leaders, such as Zulu chief Buthelezi, retain hope that apartheid can be broken through patient negotiation, others believe that only massive protest and escalated violence can change the system. "In the words of Nelson Mandela, we believe that between the anvil of mass political action and the hammer of armed struggle, we will crush the white racist rule of South Africa," said David Ndaba.

Even foreign anti-apartheid activists who reject the use of violence echo the warning of the Study Commission that time is running out on South Africa. "Yes, real change might happen in 15 years," said Smith. "Does South Africa have 15 years?"

Selected Bibliography

Books

Harrison, David, *The White Tribe of Africa*, University of California Press, 1981.

Hauck, David et al., *Two Decades of Debate: The Controversy Over U.S. Companies in South Africa*, Investor Responsibility Research Center, 1983.

South Africa: Time Running Out, Study Commission on U.S. Policy Toward Southern Africa, 1981.

Articles

" 'Cruel, Inhuman, Degrading' Situation in South Africa," *U.N. Chronicle*, March 1983.

Jenkins, Simon, "Destablisation in Southern Africa," *The Economist*, July 16, 1983.

Knight, Robin, "South Africa: A Country Up Against the Wall," *U.S. News & World Report*, May 23, 1983.

Liebenow, J. Gus, "American Policy in Africa: The Reagan Years," *Current History*, March 1983.

North, James, "Blacks and Whites Together," *The New Republic*, Nov. 1, 1982.

Treen, Joseph and Holger Jensen, "Apartheid's Harsh Grip," *Newsweek*, March 28, 1983.

Ungar, Sanford J., "Namibia: The Last Buffer," *The Atlantic Monthly*, June 1983.

Reports and Studies

Editorial Research Reports: "Southern Africa in Transition," 1975 Vol. I, p. 245; "Africa and the Big Powers," 1976 Vol. II, p. 641; "African Policy Reversal," 1978 Vol. II, p. 501.

Goldberg, Glenn S., "IRRC Directory of U.S. Corporations in South Africa," Investor Responsibility Research Center, May 1982.

"Report of the Special Committee Against Apartheid," United Nations, 1982.

"Tricameral Legislature Proposed," South African Embassy, Washington, April 1983.

Graphics: Cover map by Staff Artist Robert Redding; inside maps by Staff Artist Belle Burkhart; photo from South African Embassy, Washington.

FEEDING A
GROWING WORLD

by

Mary H. Cooper

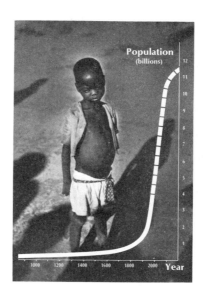

Oct. 26
1 9 8 4

FEEDING A GROWING WORLD

H UNDREDS of thousands of people in Africa are dying from starvation or diseases related to malnutrition, victims of the worst drought in a decade. The toll could surpass the drought of the early 1970s when an estimated half million Africans died. In the intervening 10 years, the population in many African countries has increased more rapidly than food production, forcing them to rely on foreign sources for food.

Even when food is available in sufficient quantities, much of it never reaches the people in need. In Chad, where millions of people need immediate food relief, there is no rail or paved road system to transport food. There, as in Ethiopia, political unrest and civil war make distribution even more difficult.

The drought may also spell catastrophe for some of the few African nations that have viable economies. Kenya, one of the few drought-stricken nations to have accumulated sizable currency reserves from its exports to the developed world, is facing widespread hardship. The East African country's food needs far outstrip its production capacity, largely because of its 4 percent annual population increase.

Across the world, another food emergency threatens the lives of thousands of Indonesians left stranded when a recent typhoon destroyed roads and housing. Relief workers complain that promised food aid has not materialized. Supplies that have been delivered are not reaching the people for whom it was intended. Again, lack of adequate distribution channels, as well as inadequate government interest, are blamed. Again, local food production comes nowhere near meeting the emergency.

These emergency situations reveal the precarious state of food supplies in a growing world. Although the overall rate of population growth has slowed from about 2 percent to about 1.7 percent in the last 10 years, the total number of people is increasing steadily. The United Nations, which estimates global population to be 4.6 billion today, predicts it will reach 6 billion by the end of the century and 11 billion by 2025 if present trends continue. The Population Reference Bureau projections are somewhat lower; it estimates that population will be 8.1 billion by 2020 *(see box, p. 93)*. And while there is an aggregate food surplus in the world, the demand for food is already outstripping agricultural production in many countries, particularly in Africa *(see map, p. 95).*

The greatest increases in population are occurring in areas of the world that are least capable of supporting them. Indeed, some of the wealthier developed countries are witnessing a trend in the opposite direction. Some, such as France, are attempting to reverse their declining populations and the potential decline in their own economic and political power.

By contrast, the World Bank estimates that the populations of the developing nations are increasing by more than 2 percent a year. The average couple in these countries has at least four or five children. Ironically, it is in the very countries where industrial development and agricultural "carrying capacity" are lowest that population increase is highest. Of the 80 million children born each year, the United Nations estimates, 73 million are born to poverty-stricken parents in Africa, South Asia and Latin America.

New U.S. Approach to Population Growth

The first concerted effort to address world population growth was made a decade ago, when the United Nations sponsored the World Population Conference in Bucharest, Romania. The 136 government delegations attending the conference in 1974 approved unanimously a "World Population Plan of Action," which stressed the importance of including family planning projects in each nation's economic development plans. The statement set no targets for family size and declared that "all couples and individuals have the basic right to decide freely and responsibly the number and spacing of their children and to have the information, education and means to do so." [1]

The Bucharest meeting reflected the growing sense of urgency over the "population explosion." Typical of the period was a widely cited study prepared for the Club of Rome entitled *The Limits to Growth,* which concluded: "If the present growth trends in world population, industrialization, pollution, food production, and resource depletion continue unchanged, the limits to growth on this planet will be reached sometime within the next one hundred years." [2] This concern was quickly channeled into family-planning programs in developing countries. During the last 10 years, 39 developing countries — accounting for three-quarters of the world's population — have adopted

---

[1] "World Population Plan of Action," adopted by the World Population Conference, Bucharest, 1974. For background, see "World Population Year, *E.R.R.,* 1974 Vol. II, pp. 581-600.
[2] Donella H. Meadows *et al., The Limits to Growth: A Report for the Club of Rome's Project on the Predicament of Mankind* (1974), p. 24. The Club of Rome is an international association of scientists, economists and other professionals who study issues related to global resources.

Population Growth Projections
(in millions)

	Mid-1984* (Est.)	Natural Increase**	2000	2020
World	4,762	1.7%	6,250	8,086
More developed	1,166	0.6	1,270	1,350
Less developed	3,596	2.1	4,980	6,736
Excluding China	2,561	2.4	3,676	5,191
Africa	531	2.9	855	1,405
Asia	2,782	1.8	3,680	4,646
Asia (excluding China)	1,748	2.1	2,377	3,101
North America	262	0.7	297	328
Latin America	397	2.4	562	798
Europe	491	0.3	510	510
U.S.S.R.	274	1.0	316	364
Oceania	24	1.3	29	36

** *The effects of migration are not included in the current annual rate of natural increase.*

Source: Population Reference Bureau

policies of some kind to slow population growth. Although foreign assistance is crucial to carrying out these policies, the 39 governments are assuming an increasing portion of the costs.[3]

The principles expressed in the World Plan of Action were endorsed again this summer in Mexico City, where 148 government delegations attended the second U.N.-sponsored population conference, held Aug. 6-14. The United States was a signatory to the resolution despite a controversial change in its approach to population growth. The United States has been the largest contributor to family planning projects in developing nations.[4] But at the Mexico conference, U.S. delegation head James L. Buckley presented a statement that departed significantly from prior U.S. policy.

While reaffirming the Reagan administration's support for "population strategies based on voluntary family planning," Buckley, a former Republican senator from New York, challenged the view that slowing population growth is essential to economic development. Citing Hong Kong and South Korea as

---

[3] See J. Joseph Speidel and Sharon L. Camp, "Looking Ahead," *Draper Fund Report*, June 1984.

[4] In fiscal 1984, which ended Sept. 30, the United States contributed $240 million to family planning programs overseas, or 44 percent of all such contributions by the industrialized nations.

examples of rapid economic growth amid teeming populations, he stated that "population growth is, of itself, neither good nor bad. . . . People, after all, are producers as well as consumers." Taking up Reagan's oft-stated theme of the benefits of capitalistic economic systems, Buckley added: "We believe it no coincidence that each of these societies placed its reliance on the creativity of private individuals working within a free economy."

The new U.S. position also allowed American contributions to be used only for programs that are "not engaged in" and do not "provide funding for abortion or coercive family planning programs." While the U.S. contribution to the U.N. Fund for Population Activities (UNFPA) — $46 million in fiscal 1985 — was assured after the organization stated it would comply with the new conditions, the prospects for continued U.S. support of private family-planning agencies are less certain *(box, p. 97)*.

The United States is nearly alone in its assessment of population control. Ironically, its new position resembles the stance championed by some Third World nations a decade ago, when the industrialized world appeared to be more enthusiastic about controlling population growth than the countries experiencing the highest growth rates. "Development is the best contraceptive" was the slogan adopted by China and other developing countries where officials believed the Western nations wanted to halt Third World population growth to protect their own political dominance. Now, in the opinion of Arthur Haupt of the Population Reference Bureau, "the vast majority [of Third World countries] show at least a wariness of rapid population growth. The American view isn't held in its entirety by hardly any of the less developed countries." [5]

Sub-Saharan Africa's Declining Food Output

Many demographers say the overall decline in population growth over the last decade is illusory. If China — where a draconian birth-control program has produced a 10 percent fall in the birth rate — is excluded from the assessment of Third World population trends, the picture is far less rosy. Sub-Saharan Africa alone appears to be in a position to eradicate all progress toward reducing population growth and increasing development made in other parts of the world. "Of all the major regions of the developing world, sub-Saharan Africa has had the slowest growth in food production and the fastest growth of population during the past twenty years," a recent World Bank

[5] The Population Reference Bureau is a Washington-based non-profit research and educational organization concerned with population and demographic issues.

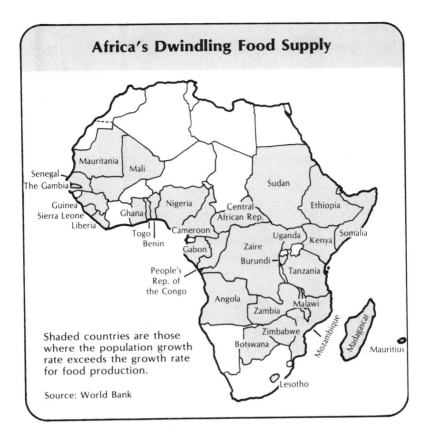

Africa's Dwindling Food Supply

Shaded countries are those where the population growth rate exceeds the growth rate for food production.

Source: World Bank

report pointed out. "It is the only region where food production is losing the race with population growth."[6]

Drought has undoubtedly exacerbated the continent's problems. The U.N.'s Food and Agriculture Organization (FAO) has identified 24 countries in need of emergency food aid — including several whose agricultural production normally meets food demand. The crisis seems certain to worsen. Of the 3.3 million tons of cereals the FAO estimates are needed in the area, only 2.3 million tons had been pledged by September. Inadequate storage facilities and the lack of means to transport and distribute the food once it arrives also hamper relief efforts.

But Africa's woes have longer-term roots as well. None, in the view of the World Bank, is more pervasive than the accelerating growth of population and inappropriate development programs that do not directly address the problems of improving food self-sufficiency. The population of sub-Saharan Africa is growing faster, at 3.1 percent a year, than that of any other continent. According to the World Bank report, the total population,

[6] World Bank, "Toward Sustained Development in Sub-Saharan Africa: A Joint Program of Action," September 1984, p. 14.

95

"which rose from 270 million in 1970 to 359 million in 1980, seems set to double by the turn of the century and significantly more than triple by the year 2020." [7] In addition, it continues, research has failed to improve the output and resistance to drought and pests of such local crops as millet and sorghum.

Population Growth Trends

O PINIONS VARY widely over which policies are best suited to slow world population growth, but most demographers agree on its principal causes and probable consequences. Rising birth rates occur both as a result of parental choice and a lack of contraceptive methods.

In most industrialized countries, the cost of raising each child is high, both in terms of additional family expenses and reduced family income for the parent who leaves the work force to care for the child. In most developing nations, however, each additional child represents a net family asset. Because mothers are paid little or nothing for their work, the time taken for child-rearing is far less costly than in the industrialized West. In rural areas, where women are better able to combine work with child care, more children mean more hands for agricultural work as well. In areas where schooling is not readily available for older children and teenagers, the incentive to have many children to contribute to family income remains high.

In areas of high infant and child mortality rates, young parents tend to have many children with the expectation that not all will survive. According to a World Bank report, one child in five dies in his first year in some areas of Africa, one in seven in parts of Bangladesh, India and Pakistan.[8] The close spacing of children often weakens mothers and children alike, worsening each baby's chances for survival. Parents also often see children as their sole source of support in old age, especially in poor countries lacking any type of state pension system or tradition of local support for the community's elderly. World Bank interviewers found that up to 90 percent of parents in Indonesia, Korea, the Philippines, Thailand and Turkey expected to turn to their children for support in old age.

Local customs can play an important role in determining a country's birth rate. Especially where women have little access to education and jobs outside the family, birth rates tend to

---

[7] "Toward Sustained Development in Sub-Saharan Africa," *op. cit.*, p. 26.
[8] World Bank, *World Development Report 1984*, May 25, 1984.

U.S. Policy on Population Control

Congress first began appropriating funds for family planning assistance to Third World nations in the early 1970s. Since then the United States has been the largest contributor to family planning programs administered by private agencies, multilateral organizations and the national governments themselves.

However, the new U.S. policy, which holds that economic development is the most efficient means of controlling population growth, has raised questions about the U.S. government's continued commitment to helping control the world's population growth.

One of the more controversial aspects of the new U.S. policy is its language on abortions, which are legal in most countries of the world. U.S. law already stipulates that all family programs receiving U.S. contributions must be voluntary and that U.S. contributions cannot be used for "forced or coerced" abortions or sterilizations. The new policy would ban aid to any private agency that "actively promotes" abortion, even if no U.S. funds are used directly for that purpose.

The main agency that could be affected by this language is the International Planned Parenthood Federation, which is active in 119 countries. Federation officials have said that eight of its affiliates have provided counseling to women seeking abortions. But at least one anti-abortion group in the United States has charged that the international organization has "aggresively promoted" abortions in developing countries. The private family planning agency is expected to discuss its response to the U.S. policy at a November meeting in London.

remain high. In many societies, particularly in Bangladesh and parts of Latin America and Africa, large families are regarded as an asset, and women are expected to marry early and have many children. Furthermore, the numerous family-planning programs introduced during the last decade have had differing results. In some countries they did not reach enough women to have an appreciable effect on rising birth rates.

Poverty is the biggest common denominator among countries experiencing high population growth. The World Bank, in fact, observes that "the higher a country's average income, the lower its fertility and the higher its life expectancy." [9] Accordingly, the regions with the lowest incomes — sub-Saharan Africa and India — also have the highest fertility and mortality levels — five to eight children per woman and life expectancies as low as 50 years. In the slightly more prosperous countries of East Asia and Latin America, life expectancy is some 10 years higher and women have an average of three to five children.

---

[9] *Ibid.*, p. 69.

There are some notable exceptions to this rule. China and Indonesia, for example, are relatively poor countries where fertility rates have fallen considerably in recent years. In contrast, some wealthier developing countries, including oil-exporting Mexico and Venezuela, have been less successful in reducing their birth rates than might have been expected. In these predominantly Catholic countries, Vatican opposition to all "artificial" means of birth control has undoubtedly hindered efforts to reduce population growth.

Consequences of Rapid Population Growth

Views on the consequences of rapid population growth have evolved considerably since 1798 when Thomas Malthus theorized that population increases geometrically and is slowed only by rising death rates caused by the resultant food shortages.[10] His observations were based on trends before the Industrial Revolution, when increases in population and therefore in the labor supply led to falling wages and thus reduced incomes. Over time population growth tended to contract. But this natural check on growth was largely removed with the dawn of the industrial age in the mid-1700s and improved living conditions. Mortality rates fell and overall fertility rates rose throughout most of Europe.

But birth rates in what is now the developed world soon leveled off and never approached the levels registered in the Third World during this century. In many countries today, the marked decline in infant mortality brought on by improved medical care has not been consistently offset by reduced birth rates. Since World War II, population growth has averaged 2 to 4 percent in the developing countries, far above the 1.5 percent level registered in Europe during the Industrial Revolution.

Furthermore, countries no longer have emigration outlets for their rising populations. Europe's growing numbers of the 1800s were largely absorbed by North and South America and Australia. And for those who did not emigrate, there were in most cases established national economic and political systems better equipped to cope with the pressures brought on by increasing populations than are offered in today's developing countries.

Although demographic trends have not conformed to Malthus' hypothesis, many observers agree with his central premise that population growth may eventually outstrip the Earth's ability to sustain its people. The Club of Rome study, for example, gave humanity at most a century to curb population growth.

---

[10] Malthus offered this theory in his *First Essay on Population.*

Feeding a Growing World

This view has been challenged not only by the Reagan administration in its Mexico City statement, but by some economists who see population growth as a positive contribution to world development. Julian Simon, a University of Maryland professor who is perhaps the best known advocate of this position, has emphasized the innovative force inherent in rising populations. While recognizing that famine and poverty may be among the short-term effects, he states that market forces and human ingenuity will in the long run correct any imbalances due to population increases. "The main fuel to speed our progress is our stock of knowledge, and the brake is our lack of imagination," Simon writes. "The ultimate resource is people — skilled, spirited, and hopeful people who will exert their will and imaginations for their own benefit, and so, inevitably, for the benefit of us all." [11]

Other demographic experts take a middle ground. In its 1984 *World Development Report*, the World Bank agrees that rising populations will not necessarily exhaust the world's finite resources but challenges Simon's assertion that more people automatically translate into technological advance. It paints a picture of poverty, illiteracy and population growth forming a vicious circle that requires a more complex solution than birth control alone. ". . .[R]apid population growth," it concludes, "is, above all, a development problem." [12]

In this way, the report distinguishes between the crowded but growing economies of Hong Kong and Singapore and the stagnating economies of Bangladesh and Kenya. The former have higher education levels and established economies, thanks to heavy investment by developed countries. Their population growth levels are also stabilizing. The latter have attracted comparatively little foreign investment, and their education levels are low and declining. At the same time, their populations are growing rapidly, ensuring that whatever resources are now used for education must increase significantly just to maintain existing educational services, let alone expand them. In addition to growing numbers of school-age children, high-fertility regions can expect large increases in the labor force. Lack of economic growth, however, means many people will not be able to find work, worsening poverty within these countries and further widening the gap between the world's rich and poor nations.

One troubling aspect of rapid population growth is urbanization. Big cities — once the result of industrialization — are increasingly found in the developing world *(see table, p. 101)*.

---

[11] Julian L. Simon, *The Ultimate Resource* (1981), p. 348.
[12] *World Development Report 1984, op. cit.*, p. 80.

Hungry peasants are flocking to urban centers ill-equipped to accommodate them. Jobs, food, sanitation and housing are at a premium in Bombay, Mexico City, São Paulo and dozens of other Third World cities. But urbanization is only half the problem, according to the World Bank, which predicts that the rural population of all Third World countries, if unchecked, will grow by another one billion people by 2050. Instead of focusing on costly projects to redistribute the population away from the large cities, as the Mexican government has done in recent years, the bank suggests that rapidly urbanizing countries concentrate their meager resources on developing rural areas to stem the flow of people into the cities.

Results of Recent Family Planning Programs

By all accounts, the most effective program to curb population growth to date is China's "birth planning policy." First introduced in 1956, the program initially promoted late marriage and birth control. This effort was short-lived, however. Under the Great Leap Forward, begun in 1958, birth control was condemned as a ploy by the capitalistic nations to maintain their hegemony over the Third World. With the death in 1976 of Mao Tse-tung and the rise to power of China's "pragmatic" leadership, birth control again became a national priority.

Contraceptives, abortion and sterilization are available free of charge throughout China. Birth quotas are set at the commune, factory or neighborhood level by committees. Couples must apply to these committees for permission to have a child; permission is granted or denied according to a priority system. Since 1979 China has promoted an even stricter "one-child family" policy. Incentives in the form of bonuses, better jobs or housing, or access to further training or education are offered to couples that promise to have only one child. Those who fail to comply may be penalized.

The aggressive policy has been effective: China's birth rate has fallen by more than one half since 1965. But the price appears to be high. Press reports abound of forced abortions and a rising incidence of female infanticide, the result, critics say, of the one-child policy.

Other Third World nations have also reduced their birth rates, albeit to a lesser extent than China. When a city-based family planning program failed to have an appreciable effect on the birth rate in rural areas of Indonesia, the government decentralized the program to the village level and delegated responsibility for local family planning services and distribution of contraceptives to the traditionally powerful local leaders. Recent statistics suggest that peer pressure to conform at the

Projected Urbanization
(Cities with more than 10 million residents)

1950	(millions)		(millions)
New York, northeast New Jersey	12.2	London	10.4
2000			
Mexico City	31.0	Cairo, Giza, Imbaba	13.1
São Paulo	25.8	Madras	12.9
Tokyo, Yokohama	24.2	Manila	12.3
New York, northeast New Jersey	22.8	Greater Buenos Aires	12.1
Shanghai	22.7	Bangkok, Thonburi	11.9
Peking	19.9	Karachi	11.8
Rio de Janeiro	19.0	Bogota	11.7
Greater Bombay	17.1	Delhi	11.7
Calcutta	16.7	Paris	11.3
Jakarta	16.6	Tehran	11.3
Los Angeles, Long Beach	14.2	Istanbul	11.2
Seoul	14.2	Baghdad	11.1
		Osaka, Kobi	11.1

Sources: United Nations; World Bank

village level has reduced the birth rate in Java and Bali faster than in any other developing country except China.[13] The percentage of married women, aged 15 to 49, who use contraceptives ranges from 6 percent in sub-Saharan Africa to 25 percent in South Asia, 40 percent in Latin America and 65 percent in East Asia.[14]

Birth control efforts in Latin America have had varied results. Throughout the region, population growth remains high and is projected to increase by at least 2 percent a year, closer to 3 percent in Central America. This relatively poor performance is attributed to the persistence of the gap between rich and poor throughout the region. Mexico's family planning program has succeeded in reducing the average annual population growth from 3.2 percent between 1970 and 1980 to 2.4 percent in 1984. But, conceded Mexican President Miguel de la Madrid, "... [i]nternal financing was insufficient to meet the demographic pressures as they were translated into growing social demands for public expenditure and investment."[15] The coun-

---

[13] See Bruce Stokes, *Helping Ourselves* (1981). See also Martha Ainsworth, "Population Policy: Country Experience," *Finance and Development*, September 1984.

[14] "World Development Report 1984," *op. cit.*, p. 127.

[15] Miguel de la Madrid H., "Mexico: The New Challenges," *Foreign Affairs*, fall 1984, p. 66.

try's current fertility rate is still about twice that necessary to maintain its population level. Of particular concern to the Mexican government is the rapid internal migration of peasants to Mexico City, already a teeming metropolis unable to provide minimal services to its inhabitants, most of whom are relegated to the slums encircling the city.

As in Mexico, fertility fell by about one-third in Colombia during the 1970s. There, as in some other Latin American countries, doctors played an important role. "Doctors got it all started in the mid-1960s," Jean van der Tak of the Population Reference Bureau explained. "They got family planning going out of their concern over the number of women dying from illegal abortion." On the other hand, van der Tak blames doctors for obstructing effective programs in India. "Doctors *are* the problem in India," she said. "They are nominally responsible for family planning services, but they don't have the time. Most of them are men and there are not enough of them to do the job anyway. They want to keep their control over the services but they don't want to leave the cities and go to the countryside where family planning services are most needed."

Site of the world's first national family planning program, India saw its fertility rate fall rapidly, from 6.5 children per woman at the time the program was set up in 1952 to 4.8 in 1982, despite the country's low average income. Results vary markedly among India's states. By 1978, the state of Kerala, with its low infant mortality and high level of literacy among women, had seen its fertility rate sink to 2.7, while the rate in poorer Uttar Pradesh remained at twice that level. Despite India's successes, its population as a whole is rising by 16 million people a year, the fastest growth rate in the world.

Policy Implications of Country Experiences

Demographers and family planning experts see reason for both hope and despair from these experiences. Some, including Kingsley Davis of Stanford University's Hoover Institution, decry the lack of attention given to birth control in earlier years when there was a greater chance of averting the population explosion of the post-World War II period. Davis says recent efforts fail to address the root of the problem. "About all that a program of contraception, abortion, and sterilization can do is satisfy the demand [for birth control] quickly once that demand gets under way," Davis wrote. "But the purpose of population policy is to create the demand, not wait until something else creates it. As yet, except in China and Singapore, there is no anti-natalist policy worthy of the name." [16]

---

[16] Kingsley Davis, "Declining Birth Rates and Growing Populations," *Population Research and Policy Review*, no. 3, 1984, p. 73.

Others urge governments to act more aggressively to stem population growth. Speaking earlier this year in Nairobi, Kenya — a country whose birth rate has actually risen since 1965 — World Bank President A. W. Clausen emphasized the link between poverty and rapid population growth. "Economic and social progress helps slow population growth; but, at the same time, rapid population growth hampers economic development. It is therefore imperative that governments act simultaneously on both fronts. The international community has no alternative but to cooperate, with a sense of urgency, in an effort to slow population growth if development is to be achieved. But it must be slowed through policies and programs that are humane, non-coercive, and sensitive to the rights and dignity of individuals."

Clausen's predecessor, Robert S. McNamara, repeated this urgent call for action by both the countries involved and the international community. Citing the lack of political will by some governments to introduce and enact effective family planning programs, he predicted that "failure to act quickly to reduce fertility voluntarily is almost certain to lead to widespread coercive measures before the end of the century." For their part, he wrote, the developed countries should continue to provide technical and material assistance to birth control programs, conduct research in the effort to find safe and effective means of contraception and provide the results of their demographic research to high-fertility countries enabling them to institute programs best suited to their own goals.[17]

Implications for Food Policy

I N CONSIDERING the relationship between the rising world population and the availability of adequate food supplies, one must also consider whether a country is agriculturally self-sufficient. The fact that drought-stricken countries of sub-Saharan Africa are experiencing large-scale famine illustrates the difficulty of effectively channeling the world's food surpluses to areas of immediate need.

The United States is expected to produce bumper crops of corn and soybeans this year. Large wheat surpluses have already been harvested in the Common Market countries of Europe. At the same time, millions of people are dying of starvation or

---

[17] Robert S. McNamara, "Time Bomb or Myth: The Population Problem," *Foreign Affairs,* summer 1984, p. 1129. McNamara, defense secretary from 1961 to 1968, served as president of the World Bank from 1968 to mid-1981.

suffering from malnutrition. International response to appeals for emergency food relief has been far from adequate; only about one half of the requested food has reached the stricken countries.

The United States is the largest contributor of international food aid.[18] Through the Food for Peace program (PL 480, Title II), the U.S. government either provides food directly on a government-to-government basis or donates food to voluntary relief agencies, such as CARE or the Catholic Relief Service, which then transport it to targeted countries and may or may not help distribute it among the population. Under Food for Peace the U.S. government also contributes a quarter of the total food aid allocated through the World Food Program, administered by the U.N.'s FAO. The Food for Peace program has been faulted for indiscriminately dumping surplus grain and providing a disincentive for local food production in the destination countries.[19] But its supporters say the program should be more heavily funded.[20]

Unfortunately, Food for Peace and other food relief programs initiated in the grain-surplus nations can do little to improve distribution within the country of destination, one of the main obstacles to relief efforts. Many countries in need of immediate aid, such as Chad, lack seaports to receive food shipments. Once it arrives in city distribution centers, there is frequently no way to transport the food to the rural areas where it is needed. Food often spoils because of inadequate storage facilities. Internal strife often makes these distribution problems insurmountable. In both Ethiopia and Chad, civil war has made large parts of the country inaccessible to food relief.

Local Solutions to Chronic Food Shortage

Emergency relief efforts are no long-term substitute for agricultural self-sufficiency or, at the very least, the financial capacity to import food independently through foreign trade. "If the people of the Sahel had dollars to spend," said Haupt, editor of the monthly publication *Population Today*, "they would have international Safeways."

Many Third World nations have never recovered from the oil price shocks of the 1970s. Just as they were beginning to accumulate foreign reserves from the sale of agricultural products and minerals abroad, the oil crisis plunged the industrial nations into recession and demand for these commodities in the

---

[18] For background on U.S. agricultural policy, see "Farm Policy's New Course," *E.R.R.*, 1983 Vol. I, p. 233.

[19] See, for example, comment by James Bovard in *The Wall Street Journal*, July 2, 1984.

[20] The Reagan administration requested and Congress approved $1.4 billion for fiscal 1985 for Food for Peace. An additional $150 million in emergency food aid to the countries of sub-Saharan Africa was approved last summer.

Growth in Food Production

(Average Annual Percentage Change)

	Total		Per Capita	
	1960-70	1970-80	1960-70	1970-80
Developing countries	2.9%	2.8%	0.4%	0.4%
Africa	2.6	1.6	0.1	−1.1
Middle East	2.6	2.9	0.1	0.2
Latin America	3.6	3.3	0.1	0.6
Southeast Asia*	2.8	3.8	0.3	1.4
South Asia	2.6	2.2	0.1	0.0
Southern Europe	3.2	3.5	1.8	1.9
Industrial market economies	2.3	2.0	1.3	1.1
Non-market industrial economies	3.2	1.7	2.2	0.9
World	2.7	2.3	0.8	0.5

Does not include China.

Sources: Food and Agriculture Organization; World Bank

industrial nations dried up. Despite subsequent recoveries in the developed nations, demand for Third World products has not reached its former level. The fall in exports, together with rising external debt among many nations now experiencing food shortages, has reduced their capacity to meet food needs through foreign trade.[21]

Past efforts to improve the agricultural self-sufficiency of developing nations have yielded impressive results. The "Green Revolution" of the 1960s and 1970s successfully applied the research capabilities of the industrialized world to produce genetically modified plants — such as fast-maturing, dwarf varieties of rice, corn and wheat — that significantly increased agricultural output in areas of Latin America, India and South Asia.[22] As a result, most of the developing countries are today producing as much food per capita as they have in the past despite rapidly increasing population growth.

But many — including China and India — are barely keeping up, while others — including the majority of sub-Saharan African countries — are falling behind in per capita food production, making them ever more vulnerable to natural disasters. These countries present special geological and climatic problems that the Green Revolution did not address. Although sub-

---

[21] For background on the debt burden and trade problems among the developing nations, see E.R.R., "World Debt Crisis," 1983 Vol. I, pp. 45-64, and "Global Recession and U.S. Trade," 1983 Vol. I, pp. 169-188.
[22] For background, see E.R.R., "Green Revolution," 1970 Vol. I, pp. 219-238.

Saharan Africa abounds in uncultivated land, almost half of it is closed to livestock or cultivation because it is infested with tsetse flies, the carriers of sleeping sickness (trypanosomiasis). In addition, some countries in the region — 14, according to a World Bank estimate — lack sufficient land to sustain their growing populations if cultivated according to traditional, subsistence farming methods. In many the rough terrain and remoteness of tillable lands make it very expensive to introduce modern agricultural techniques. Much arid land can be cultivated only if costly irrigation networks are constructed.

Various international technical aid and training programs are focused on helping the African countries improve their agricultural productivity. The U.S. Department of Agriculture, in conjunction with the Agency for International Development (AID), conducts some 150 such projects worldwide, 30 of them in Africa. In most of these projects, Dr. Peter Koffsky of USDA's Africa program explained, surveys are conducted to assess the local agricultural conditions; it is then up to the national governments to act on the basis of these surveys. Other projects are more direct: Koffsky cited the example of the USDA's Dry Land Cropping Systems Research project undertaken in Kenya in conjunction with the FAO. "In the Kenya project," he said, "we work with farmers to assess which crops are best, such as drought-resistant maize. But long-term policy is hard to assess. The effectiveness of the projects varies considerably."

Many technical innovations have yet to be applied in much of Africa. Multiple cropping — harvesting more than one crop each year on the same plot — is one method used in some Asian countries to feed their growing populations. New plants better adapted to arid conditions and poor soil offer some promise to sub-Saharan Africa. The use of fertilizers, which has greatly increased agricultural productivity in the developed nations, could also improve self-sufficiency in this region, but they are expensive. The FAO estimates that seven sub-Saharan nations — Burundi, Kenya, Lesotho, Mauritania, Niger, Rwanda and Somalia — will be unable to feed their populations by the end of the century even if all these improvements are fully adopted.

Some observers say the main obstacle to agricultural self-sufficiency is political rather than technical. By holding down prices to make food affordable, it is said, the governments of many developing nations have discouraged local production, driving farmers off the land, encouraging migration to cities and pushing their countries into ever heavier dependence on external food assistance.

Urbanization is presenting its own food problems in many developing countries. When people migrate to urban centers, they become totally dependent on commercial sources of food and thus vulnerable to any breakdown in the distribution system. Slum dwellers, who may have migrated to the cities to escape starvation in the countryside, often become victims of severe malnutrition and disease related to poor sanitation.[23]

Prospects for Sustaining Future Growth

If conditions today are grim in many parts of the world, will future generations be able to feed themselves? Optimists like Julian Simon find little cause for concern. "...[T]here is little reason to believe that, in the foreseeable long run, additional people will make food more scarce and more expensive, even with increasing consumption per person," he wrote. "It may even be true that in the long run additional people actually *cause* food to be less scarce and less expensive, and cause consumption to increase."[24]

Stunted corn, Mozambique

If World Bank projections are correct, the Earth will have the capacity to feed its growing numbers. Because world grain production is projected to grow by 3.5 percent a year until the end of the century, while annual demand is expected to increase by only 2.6 percent, the World Bank expects food output to be adequate to meet the global demand over this period. Even in the 21st century, when the world's population is expected to level off at about 11.4 billion people, the World Bank predicts that the Earth will still be able to continue providing today's average per capita intake of food.

But quite a different picture emerges when individual regions, countries or population groups within countries are considered. Even barring further drought and technical or political obstacles to increased food production, two Third World regions — sub-Saharan Africa and Latin America — are identified as potential disaster areas because of their rapid population growth and slow income growth. Unless corrected, this combination promises eventually to produce widespread starvation.

---

[23] See James E. Austin, *Confronting Urban Malnutrition* (1980).
[24] Simon, *op. cit.*, p. 69.

Selected Bibliography

Books

Cuca, Roberto, and Catherine S. Pierce, *Experiments in Family Planning: Lessons from the Developing World,* Johns Hopkins University Press, 1977.

Eckholm, Erik P., *Losing Ground: Environmental Stress and World Food Prospects,* W. W. Norton & Co., 1976.

Gupte, Pranay, *The Crowded Earth: People and the Politics of Population,* W. W. Norton & Co., 1984.

Meadows, Donella H., *et al., The Limits to Growth: A Report for the Club of Rome's Project on the Predicament of Mankind,* Universe Books, 1972.

Simon, Julian L., and Herman Kahn, eds., *The Resourceful Earth, A Response to 'Global 2000',* Basil Blackwell, 1984.

Articles

Ainsworth, Martha, "Population Policy: Country Experience," *Finance & Development,* September 1984.

Davis, Kingsley, "Declining Birth Rates and Growing Populations," *Population Research and Policy Review,* no. 3, 1984.

Gilland, Bernard, "Considerations on World Population and Food Supply," *Population and Development Review,* June 1983.

McNamara, Robert S., "Time Bomb or Myth: The Population Problem," *Foreign Affairs,* summer 1984.

Mellor, John W., and Bruce F. Johnston, "The World Food Equation: Interrelations among Development, Employment, and Food Consumption," *Journal of Economic Literature,* June 1984.

Population Today, selected issues.

Shepherd, Jack, "Africa: Drought of the Century," *The Atlantic,* April 1984.

Reports and Studies

Berg, Alan, "Malnourished People: A Policy View," World Bank Poverty and Basic Needs Series, June 1981.

Brown, Lester R., "Population Policies for a New Economic Era," Worldwatch Paper 53, March 1983.

Brown, Lester R., and Edward C. Wolf, "Soil Erosion: Quiet Crisis in the World Economy," Worldwatch Paper 60, September 1984.

Editorial Research Reports: "Soil Erosion: Threat to Food Supply," 1984 Vol. I, p. 229; "World Food Needs," 1974 Vol. II, p. 825; "World Population Year," 1974 Vol. II, p. 581.

Winrock International, "World Agriculture: Review and Prospects into the 1980s," December 1983.

World Bank, "Toward Sustained Development in Sub-Saharan Africa: A Joint Program of Action," August 1984.

—— "World Development Report 1984," May 25, 1984.

Graphics: Cover illustration by Art Director Richard Pottern, cover photo and p. 107 photo by Sen. John C. Danforth, R-Mo. (Both photos were taken in Mozambique, Africa). Map, p. 95, by Assistant Art Director Robert Redding.

CHINA Quest for Stability and Development

by

Mary H. Cooper

**Apr. 13
1 9 8 4**

Editor's Note: The Chinese government's program to relax state control over the economy was expanded in October 1984 with the announcement that the country's 400,000 economic enterprises were authorized to set their own wages and prices and to decide how to invest their earnings. Such sweeping liberalization of economic management was without precedent in China, and appeared to demonstrate the determination of Prime Minister Zhao Ziyang and Communist Party Secretary Hu Yaobang to fully implement the radical economic reforms first defined by aging leader Deng Xiaoping.

But Peking recently admitted it may have relaxed central economic control too swiftly. Zhao announced in March that some of the state controls removed last fall were being reimposed to halt inflation and to crack down on widespread abuses of the new program.

China has also continued to open its doors to foreign investment as another means of modernizing its predominantly agricultural economy. After first allowing foreign oil companies to explore for oil within its coastal waters in 1980, China this spring extended the oil exploration agreements to onshore sites as well. In March the largest co-production agreement between China and a foreign company was signed. Under the $800 million contract, U.S. aerospace giant McDonnell Douglas will sell China 26 etliners and assemble 25 of them in Shanghai.

CHINA:
QUEST FOR STABILITY
AND DEVELOPMENT

R ONALD REAGAN'S coming trip to China will be the third by an American president since 1972, pointing up the importance this country places on achieving a good working relationship with its erstwhile enemy.[1] In this election year, Reagan will use the highly publicized event to underscore his most widely acclaimed foreign policy success to date, improved diplomatic and trade relations with the world's most populous nation. In the view of this most ideologically anti-communist administration in recent memory, communist China offers a unique opportunity both to counter Soviet expansionism and open up a vast export market for U.S. goods.

Reagan's trip follows Chinese Premier Zhao Ziyang's 10-day visit to the United States in January. Zhao's was the first such trip by a high-level official from China since that country's top leader Deng Xiaoping visited in 1979. The flamboyant Deng toured the country like a politician, donning a cowboy hat in Texas and taking the controls of a NASA spacecraft on a simulated flight, to reassure Americans that China's turn to the West was sincere. In contrast, the businesslike atmosphere surrounding the Zhao-Reagan exchange reflects the difficulties encountered in bilateral relations over the past five years.

Differences over trade issues and U.S. support for Taiwan have lent a more sober tone to U.S.-China relations. Like Zhao's Washington visit, Reagan's trip to China is not expected to produce any breakthroughs in bilateral relations, but should serve to underline U.S. support of China's ambitious modernization program. "In this sense," said Scott Seligman of the National Council for U.S.-China Trade, "the trip's symbolic importance cannot be underestimated."[2]

Considerable symbolic significance also is attached to the signing of various bilateral agreements on these occasions. Two

---

[1] Reagan's trip to Peking, Xian and Shanghai is scheduled for April 26-May 1. In addition to talks with Chinese leaders, the president will participate in several events including visits to the Great Wall and the Shanghai Foxboro Co. Ltd., a U.S.-Chinese joint venture. He also is scheduled to address the Chinese people on television April 28. The other incumbent presidents to visit China were Richard Nixon (1972) and Gerald R. Ford (1975).
[2] The Washington-based private, non-profit organization represents over 400 U.S. companies engaged in trade with China. Established in 1973 with the encouragement of both governments, the council advises its members on doing business in China and, through its Peking office, serves as a link between U.S. firms and Chinese enterprises. Its Chinese counterpart is the China Council for the Promotion of International Trade (CCPIT).

agreements signed by Zhao and Reagan during the premier's visit encouraged greater exchange of scientific information and provided a framework for expanding trade and developing China's coal and offshore oil reserves. Two additional agreements to be signed during Reagan's trip or soon thereafter — a treaty barring double taxation of companies and another protecting U.S. investments in China — are expected to encourage further U.S. business participation in China's economic modernization program. Agreement on nuclear power development may also be reached. In January Zhao indicated China's opposition to the spread of nuclear weapons to other countries; his statement may have created an opening for China and the United States to resolve their differences on this issue.[3]

The greatest improvement in U.S.-China relations has been in trade. In 1971, the year before the two countries signed an agreement to move toward normalizing relations, trade totaled $4.9 million. Ten years later in 1981 it reached a high point of $5.5 billion. Last year's figure of $4.4 billion would have been far higher if a midyear dispute over textile trade and a consequent Chinese boycott of U.S. grain had not resulted in the first U.S. trade deficit with China since 1977 *(see table, p. 119).*[4]

Bilateral trade is expected to increase substantially; the administration eased restrictions on high-technology exports to China late last year. In testimony before the House Energy and Commerce Committee's special subcommittee on trade with China, Commerce Secretary Malcolm Baldrige predicted Feb. 22 — the 200th anniversary of U.S.-China trade — that the new export rules would bring U.S. exports of these products to $2 billion this year alone.

Twelve-Year Process of Normalization

In contrast to the burgeoning commercial links between the two countries, U.S.-China diplomatic relations are tenuous at best, resting precariously on a series of joint communiqués whose ambiguous wording permits the two countries to sidestep fundamental differences on key issues. Of these, none is more serious than the Taiwan issue, defined by Chinese leaders as the main obstacle to better bilateral relations. When the communists took over the mainland in 1949, the Nationalist govern-

---

[3] China joined the International Atomic Energy Agency Jan. 1, but continues to oppose the 1970 Nuclear Nonproliferation Treaty, which allows inspectors of the 112-nation agency to check for possible military use of fissionable material. The United States, Soviet Union and Britain have signed the treaty, while the other two known nuclear arms states — China and France — have not. The administration has conditioned U.S. assistance in China's nuclear power development on China's adoption of safeguards to prevent nuclear proliferation.

[4] Despite a new textile agreement reached last August, China protested American quotas on Chinese textiles — even after they were lifted — by refusing to honor its commitment to purchase at least six million tons of U.S. grain annually through 1984.

ment (Kuomintang) fled to the island of Taiwan (Formosa), which it has ruled ever since. American interest in Taiwan solidified during the Korean War (1950-53), which pitted U.S. forces allied with South Korea against the Chinese who supported North Korea. Zhang Wenjin, China's current ambassador to Washington, said that during the Korean War "the United States turned Taiwan into an unsinkable U.S. aircraft carrier," obstructing reunification with the mainland and making U.S.-China diplomatic relations "unthinkable." [5]

This state of affairs continued until the chill in relations between China and the Soviet Union of the late 1960s created an opening for the successful American diplomatic initiatives of the early 1970s. These resulted in President Nixon's trip to the People's Republic of China in February 1972 when the two countries pledged to work toward "normalization" of relations. On that trip Nixon signed the Shanghai Communiqué

Zhao and Reagan at White House

in which the United States acknowledged that "all Chinese on either side of the Taiwan Strait maintain there is but one China and that Taiwan is a part of China" and affirmed "its interest in a peaceful settlement of the Taiwan question by the Chinese themselves."

Negotiations on normalization continued until Dec. 15, 1978, when — catching the public by surprise — President Jimmy Carter announced he had just signed a joint communiqué establishing full diplomatic relations between the two countries as of Jan. 1, 1979. The United States recognized the People's Republic as the sole legitimate government of China, acknowledged that Taiwan was a part of China, promised to remove U.S. troops from the island within four months and agreed to terminate official governmental relations with Taiwan Jan. 1, 1979. Refusing to abandon Taiwan altogether, the United States said it would continue to supply the island with "defensive" weapons. America's new relationship with Taiwan was formalized April 10, 1979, when Carter signed the Taiwan Relations Act (PL 96-8). Despite Peking's objections, the law maintained

---

[5] Ambassador Zhang spoke at the Johns Hopkins School of Advanced International Studies Nov. 16, 1983.

all treaties with the island and provided for continuing bilateral relations through a private corporation — the American Institute in Taiwan — staffed largely with former State Department personnel.

A third U.S.-China joint communiqué, signed Aug. 17, 1982, further defined both countries' relations with Taiwan. In return for Peking's promise to seek reunification only by peaceful means, the Reagan administration promised a gradual reduction of arms sales to the island. U.S. concessions on Taiwan still are not satisfactory to Peking. "Only when arms are no longer provided to Taiwan," said Ambassador Zhang, "can U.S.-China relations be normal."

Reagan's Policy Shift on China, Taiwan

The signing of the 1982 communiqué represents an about-face in Reagan's views on China. During his 1980 election campaign he talked of reversing the Carter-initiated normalization process and restoring diplomatic relations with Taiwan. Continued arms sales to Taiwan during Reagan's first months in the White House led to a visible worsening of relations with Peking. Reagan's change of heart apparently was dictated by a growing recognition of China's value as a potential counterweight to the Soviet Union, considered the main threat to world peace by both China and the United States. After the signing of the August 1982 joint communiqué on Taiwan, bilateral relations began to improve. Trade picked up markedly under the terms of a new trade agreement signed the same year, and the stage was set for the Zhao-Reagan exchange of visits.

In addition to stimulating the U.S. economy and satisfying Reagan's big-business constituency, Washington sees other benefits in improved commercial relations with China. The administration's decision to liberalize export restrictions last year was based in part on the conclusion that "U.S. security interests include the benefits to the United States which will come from a more stable and secure China" whose participation in the world economy could be hastened with a greater infusion of U.S. technology. Improved trade relations were also seen as a means of making China "less vulnerable to Soviet coercion or intimidation," thus protecting U.S. security interests in Asia.[6]

In a clear departure from his earlier pronouncements, Reagan also has proposed closer military relations with Peking. Wary of upsetting the China-U.S.-Soviet balance and becoming overly dependent on U.S. finished products, China has rebuffed the administration's overtures for a military alliance or "strategic

---

[6] Donald M. Anderson, acting deputy assistant secretary of state for East Asian and Pacific affairs, testifying before the House Foreign Affairs Committee's Subcommittee on International Economic Policy and Trade Nov. 17, 1983.

partnership" and steered clear of large weapons purchases from the United States. But later this year the two countries plan to undertake military exchanges focusing on training and logistics. Purchase of a limited quantity of anti-tank and anti-aircraft missiles, early warning radar devices and other defensive weapons is said to top the agenda of Chinese Defense Minister Zhang Aiping, scheduled to visit Washington this summer.

China in Transition

C HINA'S TURN toward the West began in the last years of Mao Tse-tung's leadership, when the threat of Soviet expansionism and the excesses of the Cultural Revolution prompted Premier Chou En-lai to seek improved relations with the United States. But internal politics have made for a rocky road to modernization. Deng Xiaoping, vilified by the Cultural Revolution as a "capitalist roader," re-emerged in the mid-1970s and appeared to be in line to succeed the ailing Chou. But when Chou died in April 1976, Mao's wife, Jiang Qing, launched a campaign against Deng and the premiership was handed to Mao's chosen successor, Hua Guofeng. Deng's fortunes seemed to be permanently eclipsed in April 1976 when Jiang and her allies, known as the "Gang of Four," succeeded in having him stripped of all leadership positions.

The long-ailing Mao died at age 82 on Sept. 9 of the same year, setting off a power struggle between Jiang and other radicals acting in Mao's name and the more moderate party veterans. Barely a month later, on Oct. 6, a coalition led by Hua arrested 30 high-ranking party and government officials including the Gang of Four.[7] Already premier, Hua now also was named party chairman and chairman of the military commission. Deng returned to the political scene, becoming China's second-ranking leader in July 1977.

Over the next four years Deng consolidated his leadership by whittling away at Hua's official positions. Deng's close associate, Zhao Ziyang, replaced Hua as premier in 1980, and another Deng supporter, Hu Yaobang, was named party chairman in 1981. Once these power shifts were made, the party Central Committee officially proclaimed the Cultural Revolution a disaster, the result of "leftist errors." The stage thus was set for

---

[7] Jiang and her collaborators were brought to trial in 1980 and sentenced to life imprisonment. For an account of Jiang's role in Chinese politics, see Ross Terrill, *The White-Boned Demon* (1984). For background on the Cultural Revolution and the period after Mao's death, see "China After Mao," *E.R.R.*, 1974 Vol. I, pp. 101-120; "China's Opening Door," *E.R.R.*, 1978 Vol. I, pp. 641-660.

the ideological justification both of Deng's rise to power and the economic reforms he espoused. While avoiding the denigration of China's chief mentor of the past half century, the new leadership began to limit its praise of Mao's accomplishments to the pre-Cultural Revolution era *(see box, p. 125)*.

Moderating China's Communist Economy

The December 1978 Third Plenum of the 11th Central Committee formalized China's commitment to the "Four Modernizations" program first outlined the previous February. That program called for decentralizing industrial planning and decollectivizing the countryside. No longer was China compelled to heed Mao's call to preserve egalitarianism and eliminate the residues of capitalism in Chinese society. Deng himself — in a statement reminiscent of the "trickle-down" reasoning dear to supply-side economists in this country — wrote that it was acceptable "to make some people rich first, so as to lead all the people to wealth."

Subsequently the leadership introduced a new "responsibility system" permitting small-scale private enterprise. As an incentive to greater productivity, farmers were required to furnish only a certain quota of grain to the state and allowed to plant and market privately additional cash crops of their choosing. The land still was owned by the state, but the farmers could build their own houses on it and manage their family holdings. Central planning of industry was reduced, with factory managers freer to diversify production, market their products and allocate part of the profits at their discretion — or bear any losses without recourse to bailout by the state. Foreign investment was encouraged with the creation of the China International Trust & Investment Corporation, and single enterprises were allowed to export their goods. [8] It later was announced that China's legal system would be overhauled to accommodate the far-reaching economic reforms.

Incentives and the Four Modernizations

China's ambitious goal of quadrupling its gross national product by the year 2000 was adopted in September 1982 at the 12th party congress, followed by publication of the sixth five-year plan (1981-85), which detailed the progress expected in all sectors of the economy. The plan emphasized modernization of plant and equipment during the 1980s, which would permit the more rapid growth envisioned for the 1990s.

Of the economic sectors targeted for development under this "Four Modernizations" program — industry, agriculture,

---

[8] For a detailed review of Deng's political reforms, see H. Lyman Miller, "China's Administrative Revolution," *Current History*, September 1983.

science and technology, and defense — industry has received the greatest infusion of investment to date. China has turned increasingly to private banks and international lending agencies to meet its growing borrowing needs; the World Bank recently announced it would lend $1 billion in 1984 to China, a member since 1980. China also has gained access to outside investment capital by encouraging joint ventures between foreign and Chinese companies. Of 188 joint ventures, 105 were set up in 1983 alone, for a total investment of $515 million, according to the Ministry of Foreign Economic Relations and Trade.[9] Typical of such joint ventures is the Beijing Jeep Corp., established in 1983 by the Beijing Automobile Plant and American Motors Corp. AMC will provide the technology for the production of modified Jeeps assembled with Chinese labor. In exchange for its $16 million investment, AMC has the right to acquire a 49 percent interest in the company. Another American corporation, Minnesota Mining and Manufacturing, in 1983 became the first foreign concern to wholly own a small factory in China. European and Japanese companies also have extensive joint venture arrangements in China in a wide range of industries.[10]

---

[9] Figures cited by the Chinese news agency Xinhua, Feb. 23, 1984, translated and published by *Foreign Broadcast Information Service* (*FBIS*), a U.S. government publication.

[10] The People's Republic initially restricted joint-venture activity largely to four "special economic zones" located in Guangdong (Shenzhen, Zhuhai and Shantou) and Fujian (Xiamen) Provinces. Joint ventures now are being encouraged in many regions of the country.

Apart from much-needed investment capital, what China wants most from the West is modern science and technology. According to Chinese statistics, more than 130 contracts for technology transfer were concluded between 1973 and 1981, primarily for energy and power-generating equipment, electrical machinery and precision instruments. China's main suppliers of this material were West Germany, followed by the United States, France, Britain and Japan.

As a result of its aggressive reform policies, China's economy has outpaced expected growth rates. The State Statistical Bureau reported that industrial production rose by 10.2 percent last year, twice as fast as predicted.[11] Output targets for 31 key industrial and agricultural products already have been met, two years ahead of schedule. Thanks in large part to the responsibility system, Chinese per capita income rose by 6 percent in 1983, to $250, boosting consumer demand for such products as color televisions, bicycles, refrigerators and electric fans, considered luxury items only a few years ago.

But below the surface of these impressive gains, many problems remain. State Economic Commission Minister Zhang Jinfu explained: "The technological level and the level of operation and management are on the whole comparatively backward in the 400,000 or so industrial enterprises existing in our country, the quality of products is low, the variety small in number, the consumption of energy resources and raw materials high, and the economic results poor." [12]

Of primary interest to Chinese planners is the development of offshore oil reserves, estimated to be potentially among the largest in the world. Although China already produces 2.2 million barrels of oil per day from its onshore fields, 10 percent of which is exported, yet-untapped offshore reserves may allow the country to double its oil output by the year 2000. Twenty-seven oil companies from nine countries are now engaged in exploration of the continental shelf in the South China Sea and adjoining areas off the coast of China. If the proven reserves meet official expectations, oil production may account for much of future U.S. investment in the country.[13]

In the countryside, where the responsibility system has had its most visible impact, agricultural production has increased

[11] *FBIS*, Feb. 16, 1984, reprinted from Xinhua, Feb. 11, 1984.
[12] Interview published in *Jinji Ribao*, Oct. 10, 1983, reprinted in *FBIS* Nov. 2, 1983, pp. K 12-16.
[13] Coal is China's primary energy source, and negotiations on a $500 million joint project with the Los Angeles-based Occidental Petroleum Corporation for development of an open-pit mine in northern China — the largest joint venture in China to date — appear to be moving toward a successful conclusion. But inadequate railway facilities and the danger of pollution may prevent the full exploitation of this abundant fuel.

U.S.-China Trade, 1971-1983
(in $ millions)

	U.S. Exports	U.S. Imports	Total Trade	U.S. Balance
1983	2,173	2,244	4,417	-71
1982	2,912	2,284	5,196	628
1981	3,603	1,895	5,498	1,708
1980	3,749	1,058	4,807	2,691
1979	1,717	592	2,309	1,125
1978	818	324	1,142	494
1977	171	203	374	-32
1976	135	202	337	-67
1975	304	158	462	146
1974	819	115	934	704
1973	740	65	805	675
1972	64	32	96	32
1971	0	5	5	-5

Source: Department of Commerce

dramatically. While grain production — dictated by government quotas — has risen only slightly, the production of cash crops has boomed and the standard of living of most farmers has improved apace. But here, too, economic reform is not without risk. There are reports that basic facilities, such as large-scale irrigation systems, have not been properly maintained since decollectivization, as farmers concentrate their energies on producing cash crops. Small-scale cultivation is labor-intensive and poorly suited to the mechanization of agriculture envisioned under the "Four Modernizations."

Over-cultivation spurred by the profit incentive is exposing large areas of China's limited arable land — just over 10 percent of the country — to erosion. The condition of the rural elderly and disabled also has been jeopardized because no general welfare system has replaced the communal care these people once received. Any significant breakdown of the rural economy, sustained by 80 percent of China's one billion inhabitants, could have disastrous effects on the entire society.[14]

The last of the "Four Modernizations," defense, receives the lowest priority by China's economic reformers. The 4.2 million-member People's Liberation Army (PLA) — the world's largest armed force — is considered by military analysts to be in dire need of technology and training. The army's weapons are 20 years out of date when compared with the two superpowers that sit with China in the so-called "strategic triangle." Despite U.S. offers, China has eschewed large arms purchases, evidently

---

[14] For a more detailed discussion of Chinese agriculture, see Kuan-I Chen, "China's Changing Agricultural System," *Current History*, September 1983.

preferring to obtain instead the technology with which to rearm itself independently.

Peking's Foreign Policy

C HINA'S OPENING to the West for technological aid and trade opportunities has not been matched by a similar pro-Western tilt in foreign policy. During his trip to Washington in January, Premier Zhao reiterated China's intention to follow an "independent foreign policy," focusing on enhanced relations with other Third World nations. International peace and stability is a frequently stated aim of China's diplomacy.

To further international stability China carefully avoids giving the impression of favoring either the United States or the Soviet Union. While striving to reach agreement with Washington on a number of trade and technological issues, China has criticized U.S. policy in Central America and Lebanon as examples of "superpower hegemonism," rebuffed U.S. offers of a strategic alliance and continued to strongly condemn U.S. arms sales to Taiwan.

At the same time, China is working with the Soviet Union toward resolving the differences that led to the Sino-Soviet split of the 1960s.[15] China has defined three main conditions for normalization with Moscow: a reduction of Soviet forces along the 4,000-mile border separating the two nations as well as complete Soviet withdrawal from Mongolia; withdrawal of Soviet forces from Afghanistan, considered a threat both to neighboring China and to its ally, Pakistan; and — perhaps most important — withdrawal of Soviet-supported Vietnam from Kampuchea (Cambodia).

These preconditions are the subject of bilateral negotiations begun in October 1982. But the fourth round of Sino-Soviet talks — concluded in Moscow March 26 — did not produce significant results. Although Sino-Soviet trade is expected to increase by 50 percent this year alone, to $1.2 billion, Moscow has rejected Peking's sweeping conditions for full normalization, and party-to-party relations have not been renewed. The recent Kremlin succession also holds little promise for a breakthrough. In his first foreign-policy address Soviet leader Konstantin U. Chernenko indicated March 2 the Soviets have no intention of withdrawing their support of the Vietnamese occupation of Kampuchea.

---

[15] For background, see "Sino-Soviet Relations," *E.R.R.*, 1977 Vol. I, pp. 81-100.

China's concern over Soviet intentions in East Asia finds a sympathetic audience in the Reagan administration, which has criticized Soviet policy in the region for its "heavy emphasis on military intimidation, the easy resort to force, the absence of any sense of trust, the inability to communicate, and the paranoia that exists just below the surface of an unconvincing rhetoric of peace and good will." [16] Such concern has been heightened by reports of an intensified Soviet military presence not only along the Chinese border, where about 720,000 troops and 125 SS-20 mobile missiles are deployed, but also in Vietnam, where Soviet air and naval forces are stationed at the bases of Cam Ranh Bay and Da Nang, built by the United States during the Vietnam War.

Premier Zhao reassured the administration in January that any improvement in Sino-Soviet relations would not jeopardize Sino-American ties, saying China did not consider its position in the strategic triangle "equidistant" between the Soviet Union and the United States. In the view of Soviet-affairs expert Seweryn Bialer, "China's position in the triangle will remain skewed in favor of the [United States]. Sino-American relations will remain closer than either Sino-Soviet or Soviet-American relations. The U.S. remains the pivotal country in the triangle and derives the most advantage from it." [17]

China watchers advise against attributing too much significance to either American or Soviet actions in China's recent initiatives toward Russia and the United States. "Powerful forces inside China are moving Peking to discuss seriously an independent foreign policy, neither pro-Washington nor pro-Moscow," wrote a Chinese political science scholar visiting the United States. "And this is the general course Chinese foreign policy is likely to follow in the years ahead." [18]

Search for Peace, Stability in East Asia

China's effort to maintain a peaceful and stable atmosphere in East Asia has reduced tensions between China and its noncommunist neighbors in the region. In particular, bilateral relations with Japan have enjoyed a rare period of respite from centuries of strife. Like Peking, Tokyo worries about increasing Soviet military intervention in East Asia. Japan is particularly vulnerable to any threat to shut down the sea lanes from the Middle East; it is almost totally dependent on Arab oil to fuel its highly industrialized economy. Recent Soviet-Japanese talks

---

[16] Deputy Assistant Secretary of State William A. Brown, testifying Oct. 19, 1983, before the House Foreign Affairs Committee on the Soviet role in Asia.

[17] Bialer, director of the Research Institute on International Change at Columbia University, writing in *The Christian Science Monitor*, Jan. 27, 1984.

[18] Edmund Lee (a pseudonym), "Beijing's Balancing Act," *Foreign Policy*, summer 1983, p. 28.

over a proposed bilateral peace and cooperation treaty ended without compromise on Japan's demands that Moscow reduce its forces in East Asia and return the Kuril Islands it seized following Japan's defeat in World War II.

Japan has become China's largest trading partner since the two countries established diplomatic relations in 1973. Trade between the two countries has ranged between $8.6 billion and $10.1 billion over the past four years. During a recent visit to Peking, Japanese Prime Minister Yasuhiro Nakasone offered China a $2 billion loan for energy, transportation and tele-communications projects. Japan also agreed to export equipment to be used in China's first nuclear power plant, due to go into operation in Qingshan (Zhejiang province) by 1988.

China also has encouraged the opening of reconciliation talks between North and South Korea with the aim of neutralizing a source of recurring turmoil in East Asia. Peking remains closely allied with North Korea where it vies for influence with the Soviet Union. Although it withheld comment on the October 1983 killing of 17 South Korean officials in Rangoon, Burma, widely attributed to North Korea, China recently signaled its desire to improve relations with South Korea, which it does not formally recognize, by hosting a tennis match between South Korean and Chinese teams.

China also acted as the messenger of North Korea's recent initiative to open reconciliation talks with South Korea. Premier Zhao conveyed to Reagan North Korea's invitation to join tripartite talks to pacify the peninsula. North Korea had previously insisted on dealing exclusively with the U.S. government because it, not South Korea, had signed the 1953 armistice ending the Korean War. While the administration has not rejected the proposal out of hand, it has expressed its preference for direct North-South discussions. "If others are to be involved," explained an American official, "both we and the South Korean government have made known our preference for a four-party format, in which China would join ourselves and the two Koreas at a conference table." [19] Neither North Korea nor China, however, has shown interest in four-party negotiations.

Reunification for Hong Kong, Taiwan

A matter of primary importance to Peking is reunification with Hong Kong and Taiwan. To reduce opposition to its plans, both by the indigenous populations of these highly successful capitalist enclaves and by foreign powers acting on their behalf, the Chinese government has proposed transforming them upon

[19] Assistant Secretary of State for East Asian and Pacific Affairs Paul Wolfowitz, speaking Jan. 31, 1984, before the Asia Society, New York.

reunification into "special administrative zones," where their present economic and social conditions could be maintained.

China and Britain since September 1982 have been negotiating the status of Hong Kong after 1997, when Britain's 99-year lease on the territory is due to expire. According to press reports, Britain may be ready to agree to relinquish all control over the territory to China at that time in exchange for Peking's promise to allow Hong Kong's 5.5 million inhabitants to keep their economic and social systems for 50 years. During that time Peking would limit its role to defense and foreign policy matters. The territory is China's second-largest trading partner and promises to contribute greatly to the country's economic development. For this reason, many observers believe Peking will honor its pledge to let Hong Kong operate under its own system, despite the periodic panics on the colony's stock market as the negotiations draw near their September 1984 deadline.

China hopes that a peaceful transfer of power in Hong Kong will further its plans for reunification with Taiwan. Since 1979 Peking has relaxed some barriers to contacts between the island's 18.5 million inhabitants and the mainland, still formally at war, and increased indirect bilateral trade through Hong Kong to several hundred million dollars a year. China's current reunification proposal, a nine-point program introduced in September 1981, would make Taiwan — like Hong Kong — a special administrative zone. In addition to its social and economic systems, Taiwan would be allowed to keep its armed forces, and China has offered the Nationalists "posts of leadership" in Peking after reunification.

The Nationalist government on Taiwan assigns the same priority to reunification as Peking, but on the condition that mainland China give up communism and recognize the Nationalists. Taiwan's president, Chiang Ching-kuo, son of the Nationalist leader Chiang Kai-shek, has rejected Peking's proposals as a trick to lure Taiwan into subjugation under communist rule.

With the aging of the Nationalists, Peking's chances of achieving peaceful reunification of the island hinge increasingly on the aspirations of the indigenous population. The islanders enjoy one of the highest standards of living in the region, and a growing number of native-born Taiwanese and children of the 1.5 million mainlanders who escaped there in 1949 appear not to share their elders' yearning to oust the communists in Peking or to reincorporate with the less developed "motherland." An increasing number of native-born Taiwanese, who make up 85 percent of the island's population, are finding their ways into government positions vacated by the aging mainlander elite, where they tend to focus their energies on economic issues.[20]

Potential Trouble Areas

S INCE REAGAN signed the joint communiqué of Aug. 17, 1982, the administration has played down the Taiwan issue, striving to further mutual understanding on other levels where agreement can be reached. But the question of Taiwan continues to return to the forefront, often as the result of Chinese misinterpretation of American political institutions, particularly the separation of powers. Peking considers the "Taiwan independence" movement in the United States to be a reflection of official views. Similarly, when a group of private American owners of Chinese railroad bonds issued before the People's Republic came into being sued the Chinese government for default in a U.S. federal court, Peking protested the proceeding as an officially sanctioned act of hostility against China; the State Department earlier this year persuaded the judge to set the judgment aside.

American views of China are also often colored by misunderstanding. Ironically, the most glowing American accounts of life in China appeared at the height of the now-reviled Cultural Revolution, while China's recent opening to foreign journalists and academics has produced a flow of less favorable descriptions even as China embarks on its modernization program.[21] Long-time China watcher Theodore H. White warned that "the transition regime in Peking is trying to recapture control of events . . . in its own way, by trying to re-establish some system of law rather than seek a liberty that China has never known. To impose American standards on their internal struggle is irrelevant." [22]

Internal Challenge to Peking's Leadership

More frequent and direct contacts may go a long way toward dispelling mutual misunderstanding. Meanwhile, the future of U.S.-China relations hinges on the outcome of the political transition now in progress in Peking. Deng Xiaoping's efforts to

---

[20] Lee Teng-hui, an American-educated economist, was elected Nationalist Party vice president March 22, putting him in line to be the first native Taiwanese president of the island. President Chiang Ching-kuo, 74, is in poor health, as is Premier Sun Yun-suan.

[21] See, for example, Steven W. Mosher, *Broken Earth: The Rural Chinese* (1983), for a critical view of Chinese agricultural reforms; and Ross Terrill, *The White-Boned Demon: A Biography of Madame Mao Zedong* (1984), on the role of personal relations in Chinese politics.

[22] Writing in *Time*, Sept. 26, 1983, p. 49.

China's Top Leaders

Leadership in the People's Republic of China is vested in the six-member Standing Committee of the Chinese Communist Party Politburo. Beneath the 25-member Politburo is the Central Committee, whose 210 members represent all areas of the country.

Ranging in age from 64 to 86, China's six top leaders all played important parts in national events before the Cultural Revolution. All suffered to varying degrees before regaining power under Deng Xiaoping's leadership following Mao Tse-tung's death in 1976. One of the most critical tasks on the aging leaders' agenda is to assure the transfer of power to a younger generation of Chinese political figures willing to continue the economic modernization program now under way.

The members of the Politburo Standing Committee are listed below in descending order of rank.

Hu Yaobang: Communist Party general secretary. He rose to power through the army and early established his support of Deng. At 68, Hu appears likely to play an important role in Chinese politics for the foreseeable future.

Deng Xiaoping

Ye Jianying: Central Military Commission vice chairman. The eldest of China's leaders, at 86, Ye today plays no crucial role in China's affairs and likely will be replaced soon.

Deng Xiaoping: Chairman of the Central Advisory Commission and Central Military Commission. Deng, 79, has weathered several purges over the years to surface as China's undisputed leader.

Zhao Ziyang: Premier of the State Council. As head of the government and the youngest member of the Standing Committee, Zhao, 64, appears likely to remain in a ruling position, with Hu, after the rest of the present leadership has passed from the scene.

Li Xiannian: President of the People's Republic. Li, 78, was a protégé of the late Chou En-lai. One of the least affected among the present leadership by the Cultural Revolution, Li is known to resist some of the more innovative policies being implemented to further China's economic development.

Chen Yun: First secretary, Central Discipline Inspection Commission. Chen, 78, is one of China's best-known economists. He has favored decentralization and relaxation of state controls to stimulate the nation's economy.

modernize China's economy by turning outward for investment and technology have not gone unopposed. To stem growing discontent, the government late last year launched two national campaigns. The first, against "spiritual pollution," defined as the spreading of bourgeois values and criticism of the party leadership, was aimed at "rightist" elements, mainly artists and intellectuals. Blame was placed on remaining "gang-of-four counterrevolutionary cliques" and on the very open-door policy sanctioned by the party leadership itself. "As a result of the implementation of an open-door policy in China," wrote one official, "all kinds of bourgeois ideas have taken advantage of the opportunity to force their way in. The people, sealed off for a long time, have not come into contact with these things before and have no immunity against them. The young people in particular are liable to find such things new and attractive and will be affected by their theory." [23]

This anti-bourgeois effort soon was superceded by a "party rectification" campaign, aimed instead at rooting out Maoists imbued with "erroneous leftist ideas of the past" and still entrenched in the party bureaucracy and the army. Consensus at these levels for the new economic policies is considered essential to the aging leadership's success in completing the political transition in China.

While Deng and his supporters now appear to have weathered these challenges to their authority, their ultimate success in guaranteeing a peaceful transfer of power to a new generation of party leaders sympathetic to the modernization effort is by no means assured. "Like people whistling past a graveyard in the night," wrote one recent visitor to China, "Chinese leaders are uncertainly feeling their way, and hoping that everything will work out all right." [24]

Economic Implications of a Strong China

The Reagan administration has proclaimed the Chinese leadership's plans for modernization to be in the overall interests of the United States and is encouraging greater trade and commercial involvement with the People's Republic. Treasury Secretary Donald T. Regan predicted March 20 the tax and investment treaties to be signed on Reagan's visit would provide a more favorable environment for some 25 to 30 U.S. manufacturing, agricultural, construction and electronics firms that currently are considering investing in China.

Nonetheless, the commerical ties between the two countries are still fragile. China complains about what it calls unfair

---

[23] Ministry of Culture official Zhu Muzhi, writing in *Wenyi Bao*, Jan. 7, 1984, reprinted in *FBIS*, Feb. 21, 1984, p. K 9.
[24] Orville Schell, *The New Yorker*, Jan. 23, 1984, p. 83.

quotas on textiles and other products exported to the United States and seeks even more freedom to import high technology than the Reagan administration has granted. For their part, American interests such as the textile industry object to China's dual exchange rate system, which they believe has undervalued Chinese exports. Although China has said it would make up for the grain purchases it failed to make last year under a grain purchase agreement the administration would like to renew when it expires this year, critics point to the episode as evidence of Chinese unreliability in satisfying long-term contracts.

The Chinese leadership's difficulties in rapidly modernizing the economy while avoiding the pitfalls of high inflation are reflected in the recent decision to restore central control over foreign trade, reversing the decentralization of economic decision making of the past five years. Observers see the "readjustment" as a sign of the leadership's determination to stick to its plan to develop the country's backward infrastructure — particularly energy and transportation — before allowing industrial production to grow rapidly in the 1990s.

Some observers feel the United States should do even more to spur the rate of industrial development in China. In spite of Peking's Draconian birth control policy, imposing stiff penalties against couples who have more than one child, China's 1.06 billion population continues to grow, straining the country's ability to feed itself and impeding its efforts to modernize. With decentralization of industry and the growth of the private sector, unemployment has become a problem, threatening to outpace the rate of industrialization. "A healthy economic growth must be sustained if we are to avoid a return to a more centralized, and probably more unfriendly, regime," Anderson of the State Department said in November.

But U.S. collaboration in China's development may prove to be a two-edged sword. By its very numbers, China holds the potential to become not only the world's largest consumer market and a significant importer of American products, but its largest labor market as well. With its relatively low living standards, China could become a leading exporter of inexpensive consumer goods, following in the footsteps of Japan and other Asian economies that are moving into more sophisticated sectors. In that event, the United States, whose basic manufacturing industries have already fallen prey to foreign competition, could find itself in even greater difficulty in the years ahead. The very qualities that make China so alluring to U.S. corporate interests — principally low production costs — may pose a grave threat to American workers unless a solution is found to slow the export of U.S. jobs abroad.

Selected Bibliography

Books

Barnett, A. Doak, *China and the Major Powers in East Asia*, The Brookings Institution, 1977.
——*China's Economy in Global Perspective*, The Brookings Institution, 1981.
——*U.S. Arms Sales: The China-Taiwan Tangle*, The Brookings Institution, 1982.
Bonavia, David, *The Chinese*, Lippincott & Crowell, 1980.
Butterfield, Fox, *China: Alive in the Bitter Sea*, Bantam Books, 1982.
China: U.S. Policy Since 1945, Congressional Quarterly Inc., 1980.
Mosher, Steven W., *Broken Earth: The Rural Chinese*, Macmillan, 1983.
Rawski, Thomas G., *Economic Growth and Employment in China*, Oxford University Press, 1979.
Terrill, Ross, *The White-Boned Demon: A Biography of Madame Mao Zedong*, William Morrow & Co., 1984.

Articles

"China," *Current History*, September 1983.
Cross, Charles T., "Taipei's Identity Crisis," *Foreign Policy*, summer 1983.
Foreign Broadcast Information Service, selected issues.
"The Future of Hong Kong," *Business Week*, March 15, 1984.
Lee, Edmund, "Beijing's Balancing Act," *Foreign Policy*, summer 1983.
Manning, Robert A., "Reagan's Chance Hit," *Foreign Policy*, spring 1984.
Problems of Communism, selected issues.
Schell, Orville, "A Reporter at Large: The Wind of Wanting to Go It Alone," *The New Yorker*, Jan. 23, 1984.
White, Theodore H., "China: Burnout of a Revolution," *Time*, Sept. 26, 1983.
Zagoria, Donald S., "The Moscow-Beijing Détente," *Foreign Affairs*, spring 1983.
——"China's Quiet Revolution," *Foreign Affairs*, spring 1984.

Reports and Studies

Atlantic Council of the United States, "China Policy for the Next Decade," October 1983.
Central Intelligence Agency, "China: International Trade, Second Quarter, 1983," December 1983.
Editorial Research Reports: "Trade With China," 1980 Vol. II, p. 885; "China's Opening Door," 1978 Vol. II, p. 641; "Sino-Soviet Relations," 1977 Vol. I, p. 81; "China after Mao," 1974 Vol. I, p. 101; "Future of Taiwan," 1972 Vol. I, p. 397; "Reconciliation with China," 1971 Vol. I, p. 449.
Johnson, D. Gale, "Progress of Economic Reform in the People's Republic of China," American Enterprise Institute, 1982.
The World Bank, "China: Socialist Economic Development (three volumes)," 1983.

Credits: Cover by staff artist Belle Burkhart; p. 113 photo by Mary Anne Fackelman, The White House; p. 117 map by Assistant Art Director Robert Redding; p. 125 photo courtesy of the Embassy of the People's Republic of China.

DEMOCRATIC REVIVAL IN SOUTH AMERICA

by

Richard C. Schroeder

Nov. 9
1 9 8 4

Editor's Note: As anticipated, Brazil and Uruguay have turned out their military regimes in favor of civilian rule. In Uruguay, Julio María Sanguinetti, a 48-year old attorney and leader of the centrist Colorado party, took office March 1 for a single five-year term. At his inauguration Sanguinetti said a military dictatorship "will not happen again because all Uruguayans will turn democracy into our great national cause."

Fate dealt Brazil's passage from military to civilian rule a sad and unsettling blow. As predicted, Tancredo Neves, the prime minister of Brazil before the military coup in 1964, was elected president by Brazil's electoral college, ending 21 years of military rule. But on the eve of his March 15 inauguration, Neves took gravely ill and died April 21 without ever being sworn in. His vice president, José Sarney was named interim president upon Neves' hospitalization and president upon his death. Sarney, 54, once led the Democratic Social Party that supported the military government. He resigned to head a dissident group backing Neves. Sarney does not have the personal popularity, political backing nor, some say, the political acuity, that Neves had. Neves was expected to have a difficult time leading his country through the economic crisis it confronts, and Sarney can expect even more difficulties.

DEMOCRATIC REVIVAL
IN SOUTH AMERICA

DEMOCRACY seems to rise and fall like a tide in Latin America. So closely intertwined are the politics and economies of the Latin American republics that movements toward or away from authoritarian governments in one country more often than not trigger parallel reactions in others. The democratic tide is now rising throughout the hemisphere and particularly in South America, but there is no guarantee, given the history of the region, with its chronic instability, that the trend toward civilian elected governments will be permanent or even that it will continue for a prolonged period.

Even as the generals return to their barracks, the South American governments face a challenge of unprecedented proportions in the form of a mountain of foreign debts that have been accumulated over the past decade by military and civilian regimes alike. By draining capital in huge gulps for debt repayment, slowing down the rate of economic development and depressing living standards throughout the region, the debt is a time bomb threatening to destroy not only stability in South America but the integrity of the international financial system as well. It is no exaggeration to say that resolution of the debt problem is the indispensable condition of the future well-being of the democracies of South America and indeed of all Latin America and the Third World.

Argentina will celebrate a full year of democratic rule on Dec. 10, after enduring seven and a half years of sometimes brutal and often inept military control. Uruguayans are to vote for a new government on Nov. 25 to bring to a close 11 years of de facto rule by the military. Brazil's electoral college, made up of the National Congress and officials of state governments, is due to choose a civilian president on Jan. 15, 1985. If a new president takes office March 15 as scheduled, it would mark the first time in nearly 21 years that a military man has not held the reins of power in Brasilia. Moreover, dissension within the official government party has made it highly likely that the opposition candidate, Tancredo Neves, former governor of the state of Minas Gerais and prime minister of Brazil before the military coup in 1964, will defeat the government's nominee, Paulo Maluf, former governor of Sao Paulo, Brazil's industrial heartland and its most populous state.

Elsewhere in South America, elected governments are the rule rather than the exception. Democracy has been firmly entrenched in Venezuela and Colombia for many years. Last August, Leon Febres Cordero, a conservative businessman whose political philosophy is akin to that of President Reagan, was sworn in as president of Ecuador. His administration succeeded an elected government which had served out its full five-year mandate, a rarity in Ecuadoran politics.

Peru, although deeply troubled by violence and the terrorism of the *Sendero Luminoso* (Shining Path) Maoist guerrillas, will go to the polls next year to select a successor to President Fernando Belaunde Terry, whose five-year term ends in July. Belaunde Terry returned to the presidency in 1980, ending 12 years of military rule that began with his ouster in 1968. Bolivia is ruled by an elected, albeit shaky, civilian government. In all of Spanish-speaking South America, in fact, dictatorships remain only in Chile and Paraguay, and Chile is beset by rising opposition and frequent street demonstrations against the iron-fisted, eleven-year regime of Gen. Augusto Pinochet.

Attempts to Settle Hemispheric Quarrels

Progress is also being made in easing tensions among the South American nations. Talks have begun in Bogotá, Colombia, between representatives of Chile and Bolivia, to discuss Bolivia's hundred-year quest for access to the Pacific Ocean, which Bolivia lost in a tripartite war pitting Bolivia and Peru against Chile in the 19th century. Few advances have been made in the talks, but Colombian President Belisario Betancur, under whose auspices the discussions are being held, is said to be optimistic as to the outcome.

More positive results have been achieved by the Vatican, which has been mediating a quarrel between Chile and Argentina over possession of three islands in the Beagle Channel at the southern tip of South America. A draft accord has been reached, giving sovereignty over the islands to Chile and territorial rights 12 miles to sea, while Argentina retains jurisdiction beyond the 12-mile limit. Chile has said it is ready to sign the agreement; Argentina will submit it to a popular referendum next year. In a second South Atlantic dispute, less progress has been noted in resolving the question of sovereignty over the Falkland Islands, claimed by both Argentina and Britain. The two countries went to war briefly in 1982 after Argentina invaded the British-held islands. Britain ousted the Argentines within a few weeks in fighting that took a heavy toll of Argentine soldiers and naval vessels. In recent weeks, the two countries have engaged in secret talks on the future of the Falklands, but no results have yet been made public.

Improvement in domestic political conditions is also reflected in this year's report of the Inter-American Commission on Human Rights (IACHR), to be presented to the General Assembly of the Organization of American States, which will meet in Brasilia beginning Nov. 12.[1] The commission noted advances in the human rights situations of several countries it had previously found to be in violation of international standards of

[1] *Annual Report of the Inter-American Commission on Human Rights 1983-1984*, OAS Document OEA/Ser. P, AG/doc. 1778/84, Oct. 5, 1984.

conduct. Progress had been made, the commission said, in Argentina, El Salvador, Guatemala and Uruguay, even though troubling practices persisted in some of those countries. The commission expressed concern about human rights violations in Chile, Haiti, Nicaragua and Paraguay.[2]

Menace From Enormous Foreign Debts

Democracy in South America is fragile in the best of times. What makes the current shift from military to civilian rule so tenuous is that it coincides with a virtually insoluble foreign debt problem and an economic depression worse than anything the hemisphere has experienced in half a century. For the past three years, nearly all of Latin America has teetered on the edge of bankruptcy and default. The countries have saved themselves from a final fall into ruin only by imposing extraordinarily harsh economic conditions on their people. Austerity does not enhance the popularity of governments, whether elected or not, and there is serious question as to how long South American democracies can stand up under the storms of protests that have greeted wage controls, price increases and shortages.

Latin America's output of goods and services fell by more than 3 percent last year, after declining by 1 percent the year before. Because of relatively high rates of population growth, the region's per capita gross product plummeted even more rapidly, by 6 percent in 1983. The per capita output, which is a reasonably accurate measure of living standards, has fallen to about the level of 1976.[3] The main cause of the decline, according to the Inter-American Development Bank (IDB), was the debt crisis, which began in 1982 although its full effects were felt only in 1983.

"The worst possible scenario of default by one or more countries," the IDB said, "was avoided through severe domestic adjustments that had high social costs in terms of unemployment, inflation and overall deterioration of living conditions...."[4] About half the Third World debt of more than $700 billion is owed by Latin American countries. Two-thirds of their debt has been contracted with commercial banks at floating, or variable, rates of interest. Although interest rates have declined modestly in recent weeks, they still impose a severe strain. Each percentage point of interest costs the debtor countries some $5.4 billion a year in debt service.[5]

---

[2] For background, see "Human Rights Policy," *E.R.R.*, 1979 Vol. I, pp. 361-380.
[3] *The World Bank Annual Report 1984*, p. 112.
[4] *Economic and Social Progress in Latin America, 1984 Report*, Inter-American Development Bank, October 1984, p. 183.
[5] "Rethinking Debt Strategy," *Vision Letter*, June 1, 1984. *Vision Letter* is a fortnightly newsletter on Latin American politics and economics, published in English by *Vision*, a leading Latin American Spanish-language news magazine. The author is chief of the magazine's Washington bureau.

One expert, Professor Riordan Roett, observes: "To generate the foreign exchange required to service the interest on the private bank debt alone, Latin America has had to mortgage a higher and higher share of its export earnings. . . . This is at a time when the world recession has cut the demand for the region's exports; merchandise exports in 1983 were estimated at about $87 billion compared to $97 billion in 1981. . . ." [6] Another expert, L. Ronald Scheman, notes that the debt crisis has forced Latin America into the unenviable position of becoming a net exporter of capital to the industrialized countries. In 1983, almost $30 billion more flowed out of Latin America than came into the region — and its debt still rose by over $20 billion.[7]

Economic Causes of Political Instability

The debt crisis is not in itself the cause of South American political instability, which has roots extending far back into history. It greatly intensifies the problem, however, and makes solutions much more difficult to reach. The size of the Latin American debt, variously estimated at between $350 billion and $400 billion, is without precedent. The speed with which it has grown is truly awesome. In Argentina, for example, the total public and private debt in 1976, the time of the last military takeover, was $6.4 billion. "It grew modestly, in the first two years, then began its steep climb," writes journalist Edward Schumacher. "From $9.8 billion in 1978, it quadrupled in just four years to $38 billion in 1982. The Argentina economy was hemorrhaging, yet the banks continued to pour money into it, often lending through state companies to cover deficits, on the theory that a sovereign power never goes bankrupt.[8]

There are numerous explanations of how the debt seemingly took on a life of its own and became a cancer on the South American body politic. Corruption and mismanagement by government officials are frequently cited. Mexican President Miguel de la Madrid, who took office in December 1982, was so appalled by the monumental graft of previous Mexican administrations that he promised to "moralize" Mexican political life. Billions of dollars had reportedly disappeared from the coffers of government-owned corporations and several officials of former administrations are now awaiting trial on malfeasance.

Significantly, one of the first moves by Argentine President Raul Alfonsin was to begin to strip the military of control over a

---

[6] Riordan Roett, "Democracy and Debt in South America: A Continent's Dilemma," *Foreign Affairs* (Special Issue on America and the World 1983), p. 697. Roett is director of the Latin American Studies Program at the Johns Hopkins School of Advanced International Studies in Washington, D.C.

[7] Quoted in *Vision Letter,* March 15, 1984. Scheman is a Washington-based attorney who served as assistant secretary for management of the Organization of American States from 1975 to 1983.

[8] Edward Schumacher, "Argentina and Democracy," *Foreign Affairs,* summer 1974, p. 1077. Schumacher is *The New York Times* bureau chief in Buenos Aires.

vast network of public companies that were notorious money-
losers and the source of a substantial portion of the public-
sector debt. The largest of these was
Fabricaciones Militares, a military-
industrial complex that produces
everything from farm machinery to
munitions. The corporation accounts for 2.5 percent of Argentina's gross national product, and has
been run by military officers for 50
years. Moreover, journalist Martin
Andersen has reported, "military
officers, both retired and active, sat
on the boards of directors of or ran
nearly all the country's most important businesses...." [9]

But corruption alone is not
enough to explain the current crisis.
The huge debt burden stems from

President Alfonsin

unwise lending practices of the commercial banks, from world
economic events over which individual governments had no
control and, paradoxically, from the fervor for development that
has overtaken Third World countries in the past two decades.

After a period of sustained growth and favorable trade and
payments balances in the 1960s, South American countries saw
a weakening in international markets for their basic commodities. The economic downturn in the industrialized world reduced the demand (and prices) for everything from cocoa beans
to copper. Oil was a special case. A series of "oil shocks" in the
1970s had run the price of oil to well over $30 a barrel. In the
1980s, the market softened and prices fell back. The decline in
petroleum prices caught many economic planners off balance.
The pinch was most severe in an oil giant like Venezuela, but it
was also felt in smaller producing countries such as Ecuador and
Peru. On the other hand, the benefits realized from lower oil
prices were minimal in the oil-importing countries, notably
Brazil, and proved of little advantage to Argentina, which is
virtually self-sufficient in energy.

When oil prices were rising and petrodollars flowed freely, the
big international commercial banks were in fierce competition
to lend money to the developing countries. Little analysis was
made of the countries' real needs and abilities to repay. Money
was used not only to keep up the momentum of development
but also to paper over balance-of-payment deficits. The banks
sharply reduced their lending when the petrodollars stopped

[9] Martin Andersen, "Dateline Argentina: Hello, Democracy," *Foreign Policy,* summer
1984, p. 157. Andersen reports for *Newsweek* from Uruguay and Argentina.

flowing, and cut it off entirely for some countries when repayment problems began to appear.

Over the long run, the crises of South American countries and other Third World nations reveal a paradox. The very success of Third World development efforts during the past few decades has saddled those countries with a massive debt burden that — bankers now recognize with perfect hindsight — can be serviced only in the best of economic times. Third World economies have been growing at a faster rate than those of the industrialized countries for many years, and Latin America has been a leader in Third World growth. Most of the South American countries have reached a stage 'of development characterized as "middle level," and Argentina and Brazil are classified as "newly industrialized countries." South America is at a point where it is not yet rich, but, in most instances, no longer very poor.

Social Consequences of Economic Drop

South America's return to a democratic way of life will not be smooth. As the quality of life has deteriorated, labor unrest, street demonstrations, strikes and violence have been growing. The rigid austerity measures insisted on by the International Monetary Fund (IMF) as the price for renegotiation of payment terms on the debt have hit hardest at the working classes and the poor. Currency devaluations have spurred inflation to new heights, reducing the purchasing power of all segments of the population, but impacting most heavily on lower income groups. Argentina's current inflation rate — approaching 700 percent a year — evokes echoes of the runaway price spiral that debilitated the German Weimar Republic in 1923-24.

Urban unemployment has reached double-digit figures in many South American cities. The countryside has fared even worse. Agricultural unemployment exceeds 35 percent of the economically active population in Brazil, Colombia, Ecuador, Peru, Bolivia and Paraguay. In Argentina, the blue-collar work force has declined from 1.8 million to 1.3 million since the military takeover in 1976. The country's overall jobless rate is more than 15 percent.

Argentine trade unions have called several one-day strikes, shutting down rail lines in and around Buenos Aires. Peru and Bolivia have also been plagued by recurrent strikes which have shut down not just transportation but other public services as well. Political strife has left more than 100 people dead in Chile in the past year and a half. In Brazil, riots and looting swept through Sao Paulo in April 1983 and Rio de Janeiro a few months later. Still, the continent has not yet erupted in the kind of violence and internal conflict that plagues Central America. *The Economist* magazine observed in a recent issue that South

America is surprisingly quiescent, given the magnitude of its economic problems. "One reason for this relative calm," the London-based magazine declared, "is that, apart from the booming 1970s, when the region lived on borrowed money, Latin Americans have always been poor. Many people accept the austerity of the 1980s as a return to normal." [10]

But Professor Roett believes that it is precisely the contrast with the 1970s that makes the current situation so volatile. The economic crisis is "ominous," he writes, because "it has come so drastically and suddenly after years of relatively good economic growth in the 1960s and 1970s." He recalled that "political danger may be the greatest not when an economy remains stagnant, but when it has turned upward and then become disappointing." [11]

Military Involvement

I N THE minds of many Americans, the words "Latin American dictator" evoke a stereotyped image of corruption and a lust for political power. In truth, the military establishments of South American countries differ widely from one another and show evidence of considerable internal diversity as well. In most cases, the South American military sees itself as a "court of last resort," which takes power reluctantly only when the civilian political process breaks down. The military may surprise the world — and itself — by holding onto power for prolonged periods once installed, as in Brazil and Chile, and especially in Paraguay, where Gen. Alfredo Stroessner has been president since 1954. But initially, at least, the motive for a coup is usually despair over the sad state to which civilians have brought the country.

The Argentina military may come closest to the stereotype, but it is well to remember that the first military coup in modern Argentine history took place only a little over a half a century ago, in 1930.[12] Since 1955, when the military overthrew Juan Domingo Peron, the overriding preoccupation of the generals in Buenos Aires has been to keep the Peronists out of power. In 1974 Peron did return to Argentina and was elected president, with his wife Isabel, a former cabaret dancer, as vice president. She succeeded him upon his death a year later but governed for less than two years, under chaotic conditions. Terrorism of both

[10] "Latin America: Why It's So Quiet," *The Economist*, Sept. 8, 1984, p. 34.
[11] Roett, p. 701.
[12] For background, see "Argentina's Political Instability," *E.R.R.*, 1972 Vol. II, pp. 725-744.

the right and left mushroomed and the economy turned sour. By March 1976, when the coup occurred, inflation had reached the staggering rate of 1,000 percent a year. Argentines as a whole welcomed the military takeover as needed relief.

For the next several years, the military pursued a so-called "dirty war" against terrorism, in which thousands of Argentines suspected of subversive connections simply disappeared, presumably killed or kidnapped. The government made some progress in combating inflation and began to restructure the economy along free-market lines, permitting the peso to become overvalued and lifting restraints on imports. Boom times ensued until 1981, when the speculative bubble collapsed. The peso tumbled by 400 percent almost overnight; there was a run on Argentine banks, and the foreign debt crisis was born.

In what some observers see as an attempt to divert attention from economic problems, the military leadership launched its disastrous attack on the Falkland Islands, which Argentina had long claimed, on April 2, 1982. Within 11 weeks, the British had retaken the islands and the military establishment stood in disgrace. Bowing to the inevitable, the president, Gen. Reynaldo Bignone, scheduled elections for Oct. 30, 1983, and agreed to the installation of a new government ahead of schedule on Dec. 10.

The election of Raul Alfonsin, long a stalwart of the Radical Civic Union (UCR) party, destroyed the myth of Peronist political superiority in Argentina as effectively as the generals destroyed the credibility of the military establishment as the savior of the Argentine nation. Some analysts profess to see in Alfonsin's election the end of military intervention in Argentine politics. Others doubt that the era has been ended. Just before Alfonsin's inauguration, Mariano Grondona, a noted Argentine political commentator, said: "Two to three years down the road, Argentina will probably fall once again into a cyclical depression when the new government is unable to meet all the hopes it has raised. By that time, it is also likely that the armed forces will have re-established their internal discipline and morale and will be able, once again, to re-enter the political fray." [13]

Brazil's Alliance: Generals, Technocrats

The Brazilian military has a long tradition of intervening in the affairs of state. It dates from the ouster of the country's second and last emperor, Pedro II, in 1889. But until 1964, the military leaders also had a penchant for relatively short periods in power. The precept was, "Put the house in order and let the civilians try again." Aside from replacing the empire with a republican form of government after the fall of Pedro II, the military has seldom left any permanent stamp on the country's political or economic directions.

---

[13] Quoted in *Vision Letter*, Dec. 1, 1983.

The 1964 coup had its origins in a historical quirk. In a climate of high inflation and mounting economic confusion, Janio Quadros, a former governor of Sao Paulo, had been elected president in 1960 on a promise to sweep out corruption and inefficiency. It had been building up since Getulio Vargas, the "father" of modern Brazil, came to power three decades earlier. Installed as president in January 1961, Quadros suddenly — almost whimsically — resigned by the following August. He was succeeded by Joao Goulart, minister of labor in the Vargas government and vice president under Quadros.

Goulart's leftist tendencies were anathema to the Brazilian military, and he was permitted to assume the presidency only after agreeing to a compromise that introduced parliamentary government to Brazil, greatly reducing the powers of the president. The prime minister during the brief parliamentary experiment was Tancredo Neves, currently the opposition candidate for president. The arrangement handicapped all branches of government; inflation continued unchecked and corruption mounted, extending even to the president himself who managed to accumulate 1.5 million acres of prime farmland on a salary of just $350 a month.[14]

The military removed Goulart from office in April 1964 and, deciding the time had come for a thorough economic and political housecleaning, settled in for what was to become more than two decades of uninterrupted rule. Every president in the inter-

---

[14] See "Brazil: Awakening Giant," *E.R.R.*, 1972 Vol. I, pp. 271-290.

vening period has vowed to return the country to civilian control, a process the Brazilians refer to as *abertura,* or opening. But none has kept the promise, and, until the current president, Joao Batista Figueiredo, turns over the office to a civilian successor on March 15, no one can be sure that the process of *abertura* will be completed this time.

One reason for the unaccustomed longevity of the current military government is that the generals early on formed an alliance with Brazil's economic technocrats, U.S.- and European-trained economists and financiers, who forged a truly remarkable record of growth and development through the 1960s and 1970s. Until the beginning of the present decade, Brazil had one of the fastest-growing economies in the developing world. Brazilian exports became so competitive in foreign markets that the United States removed several Brazilian products from the U.S. Generalized System of Preferences, which provides duty-free entry into the United States for an array of goods from Third World countries.[15]

The world recession and the debt crisis took much of the steam out of Brazil's economic miracle, and may have influenced the generals' decision to retire to the barracks. The country's foreign debt is estimated to be as much as $98 billion, the highest in the developing world.[16] Several times in recent years Brazil has reached agreements with the IMF on adjustment measures, and the country is currently negotiating rescheduling arrangements with commercial banks.

Unrest Under Chile's 11-Year Dictatorship

Until 1973, Chile's army was a rarity in Latin America: wholly apolitical and dedicated to the support and defense of constitutional government. The nation underwent a brief period of military adventurism in the 1920s, culminating in a coup that sent the dictator Carlos Ibanez into exile in 1931. After that, though, the army resolutely withdrew from the political scene for more than four decades, even refraining from moving against a left-wing "Popular Front" government that held power from 1938 to 1942.[17]

The army's forbearance began to recede with the election in 1970 of Salvador Allende at the head of a communist-socialist coalition. Allende was the first avowed Marxist to be freely elected as president of a country in the Western Hemisphere, and he entered office with a vow to "put Chile on the path to socialism." He proceeded to do just that, at a pace that sur-

---

[15] See "U.S. Pares Down GSP Duty-Free List," *OAS/CECON Trade News,* April 1984. *Trade News* is a monthly bulletin on inter-American trade published by the Organization of American States.

[16] But still well below the U.S. federal budget deficit of $175 billion in fiscal year 1984.

[17] See "Chile's Embattled Democracy," *E.R.R.,* 1970 Vol. II, pp. 773-792.

prised even his own supporters. During his first year in office, Allende nationalized 1,400 of Chile's largest farms, expropriated five U.S.-owned copper mines, and refused to pay compensation for the seizures. He established relations with Cuba and gave a hero's welcome to Fidel Castro when the Cuban leader visited Chile late in 1971.

Allende took over privately owned publishing houses, newspapers and magazines, turning them into organs of state propaganda. In the process, he even transformed familiar children's tales into vehicles of socialist realism. Puss 'n' Boots became a rogue who was finally caught and censured by the peasants he had deceived. Sleeping Beauty laughed at the prince who had awakened her for thinking that one little kiss entitled him to marry her.[18]

Under Allende, Chilean politics quickly became a class struggle, with the nation polarized into extremes of left and right. As the economic situation deteriorated and basic foodstuffs and other items became scarce, throngs of housewives took to the streets, beating pots and pans and chanting slogans against the government. When they were challenged by Allende supporters, the demonstrations turned violent. The army's patience wore thin, and on Sept. 11, 1973, troops stormed La Moneda, the government palace. In the ensuing confusion, Allende was shot to death, but it has never been clear whether he took his own life or was cut down by soldiers.[19] What is clear is that in the following weeks and months, thousands of Allende supporters, or those suspected of left-wing leanings, were arrested, killed or sent into exile. Chile entered into a reign of state-sponsored terror the like of which it had never before experienced.

In the early days after the revolt, a military junta ruled the country but on June 26, 1974, Gen. Augusto Pinochet was named head of state. Pinochet proceeded to remodel the Chilean economy along free enterprise lines, eliminating all vestiges of Allende's socialist institutions. Milton Freedman, a conservative economist from the University of Chicago, became an adviser to the government, and several Chileans who had studied under him were appointed to Cabinet and sub-Cabinet posts. The experiment worked well throughout the 1970s. The country showed outward signs of prosperity. Businessmen and bankers amassed huge fortunes. Political opposition, when it

---

[18] "Cultural Revolution Changing Chilean Reading Habits," Nathan A. Haverstock and Richard C. Schroeder, *Latin American Service,* Dec. 8, 1971.

[19] The U.S. Central Intelligence Agency (CIA) worked against Allende's election and aided his opponents after he took office. The Senate Select Committee on Intelligence, under the chairmanship of Sen. Frank Church (D-Idaho), determined in 1976 that the CIA had spent $1 million in attempting to prevent Allende's victory and was authorized to spend $7 million during his tenure for opposition activities. No evidence of direct CIA involvement in the 1973 coup and death was presented to the committees, however. See "Intelligence Agencies Under Fire," *E.R.R.,* 1979 Vol. II, pp. 941-962.

appeared, was ruthlessly suppressed, and deportations of political foes continued to mount. In 1978, the junta's Air Force representative, Gen. Gustavo Leigh Guzman, was ousted after calling for a swift return to democracy. In 1980, a national referendum endorsed a new constitution drafted by Pinochet that assures him control of the Chilean government until 1999. Congressional elections will not be held until 1989.

As in the rest of South America, the Chilean economy crumbled under the impact of the debt crisis in 1982. Inflation and unemployment increased apace. The first large-scale protests against Pinochet began in mid-1983 and have increased in size and fury ever since. In August 1983, opposition politicians defied a ban against organized political activity and formed the Democratic Alliance, composed of Chile's center-left parties, demanding a return to democracy by 1985. Pinochet bent only slightly, appointing a civilian-dominated Cabinet and agreeing to permit the return of thousands of Chileans in exile, but refusing to change his timetable for turning control of the government over to civilians. All 16 Cabinet members resigned Nov. 5, apparently over Pinochet's handling of the unrest, which had claimed 14 lives in the preceding week. The next day he declared a state of siege throughout the country for the first time since 1978. The situation in Chile is considered to be the most volatile in South America.

Uruguayan Election; Situation Elsewhere

The Uruguayan military has displayed much less intransigence than its Chilean counterpart. In power since a coup on June 27, 1973, the high command has set Nov. 25 for the election of a civilian president and a new congress. The generals have promised to hand over power March 1, 1985.

Unlike Pinochet, who solidified his position in the 1980 constitutional referendum, Uruguayan military leaders received a rude shock when their plebiscite, offering limited democracy and a new constitution in exchange for a perpetuation of the military regime, was soundly rejected by the voters the same year. Six months of silence and political confusion followed the plebiscite, but as the economy began to decline, the generals agreed to restore the country to civilian control. Official data show that Uruguayan inflation hit 51 percent in the first nine months of 1984. Foreign indebtedness now exceeds $5 billion. The per capita foreign debt of Uruguay, which has slightly fewer than three million people, is higher than that of either Argentina or Brazil. The country's gross domestic product has fallen by 2.4 percent in the past six months, while unemployment and underemployment have risen above 30 percent.

Three major parties will contest the November election — the first to be held in Uruguay since 1971. These are the Colorados, the country's traditional conservative grouping; the National Party, formerly called the Blancos, a traditional center-left unit; and the Frente Amplio, or Broad Front, a coalition of socialists, Christian democrats, communists, and independents. As an indication that the military is uneasy about giving up its political power, the candidate of the National Party, Wilson Ferreira Aldunate, was arrested and put in a military prison when he returned from exile last May.

Elsewhere in South America, the military establishments are relatively quiescent. Venezuela's last military dictator, Gen. Marcos Perez Jimenez, was toppled in 1958. In every election since 1968, the party in power has been defeated by its opposition. The presidency has alternated between the Democratic Action Party and COPEI, a Christian democratic grouping. The pattern was repeated in December 1983, when Jaime Lusinchi of Democratic Action, a U.S.-trained physician, trounced Rafael Caldera of COPEI, a former president of Venezuela.

Gen. Gustavo Rojas Pinilla was thrown out of the presidency of Colombia in 1957. After a year under an interim military junta, Colombia has alternated between Conservative and Liberal presidential administrations. The current president, Belisario Betancur, a Conservative, was elected in May 1982. Between April and August of this year, Betancur negotiated a truce with guerrilla groups representing 90 percent of the armed opposition, which has been battling government forces for the past three decades. The largest of the guerrilla groups, the Revolutionary Armed Forces of Colombia (FARC), announced in October that it had converted itself into a political party and would participate in future elections.

Ecuadoran democracy, restored in 1979, proved its resilience in 1981 when President Jaime Roldos was killed in a plane crash and Vice President Osvaldo Hurtado assumed the presidential office in a smooth transition supported by the military. Hurtado handed power over to a democratically elected successor, Leon Febres Cordero, in August of this year. A similar transition is scheduled to take place in Peru next year at the end of the five-year term of President Fernando Belaunde Terry.

In Bolivia, however, democracy has only a tenuous hold. The elected government of President Hernan Siles Zuaso, a veteran leftist politician and one of the leaders of the 1952 revolution,[20] is under sharp attack for its handling of Bolivia's faltering economy. Bolivia has endured nearly 200 coups and uprisings in 157 years of independence. The average government has lasted

---

[20] The reform-minded National Revolutionary Movement seized power and carried out a thoroughgoing political and social revolution under Victor Pas Estenssaro and Siles Zuaso.

just 10 months and the military is once again showing signs of restlessness. No such uncertainty is to be found in Paraguay, on the other hand, where General Stroessner has run a well-oiled dictatorship for the past 30 years and gives no indication of relaxing his grip.

The three other political entities in South America — Guyana, Suriname and French Guiana — are more akin to the Caribbean area than to Latin America. Guyana, a former British colony, became an independent member of the Commonwealth in 1966 and in 1970 declared itself a "cooperative republic," reflecting the socialist views of Forbes Burnham, whose People's National Congress had led Guyana since 1964. Suriname, independent of the Netherlands since 1975, has been under military rule — in fact if not always in name — since 1980. French Guiana has been a territory of France since 1816.

Economic Perils Ahead

VIRTUALLY all observers agree that the nascent democratic movement on the continent has little chance for survival unless the enormous social and economic pressures generated by massive debt repayments are relieved. At the annual meetings of the World Bank and the IMF in Washington, D.C., Sept. 24-27, financial experts expressed the view that the Latin American debt problem has passed through a first critical phase and was now entering a second phase in which the international community can look beyond immediate crises. "Phase one" was the mad scramble over the past several months to devise new repayment schedules to permit the beleaguered debtor countries to honor their commitments, at least in a minimal way. "Phase two" is far more difficult; it entails a search for creative ways to stop the flow of capital pouring out of Latin America and other parts of the Third World, and to restart the engine of economic growth in the developing nations.

Signs of economic improvement were visible at the Bank and Fund meetings. Mexico and Brazil, with IMF approval, had previously reached agreement with their creditor banks on rescheduling their payments. During the week of the meetings, Venezuela, without the IMF imprimatur, signed a rescheduling package with the commercial banks. And as the meetings drew to a close, Argentina came to terms on an economic program with the IMF that will pave the way for Argentina to begin negotiating with lenders on easier repayment terms. As frosting on the cake, several U.S. banks cut their prime lending rate during the week and made further cuts during October.

The debt problem has been the focus of attention at the Bank and Fund meetings in recent years, but this year concern about the strength of the American dollar eclipsed the debt. The view that an overvalued dollar is sucking foreign capital out of Europe and other countries, weakening investment, dominated a meeting of the "Group of Five" — the finance ministers of Germany, Britain, Japan and France, and the U.S. secretary of the Treasury. Privately, the European ministers said they were pessimistic about the possibility of a rapid change in the situation because the dollar's value is tied so closely to high U.S. interest rates.

Partly to allay such fear, Treasury Secretary Donald Regan made a surprise proposal during the meetings for the convocation of a global conference on world economic problems, especially the Third World debt, development and trade problems. The United States had previously been reluctant to "multilateralize" discussions of Third World debt, preferring instead to support bilateral talks between debtors and lenders.

Just before the meetings, finance ministers of 11 Latin American countries met at Mar del Plata in Argentina and issued an invitation to the industrialized countries for a "political dialogue" in the first half of 1985 to discuss the regional economic crisis. The Mar del Plata invitation echoed an earlier consensus reached by the Latin American governments in Cartagena, Colombia. Regan's proposal, however, fell considerably short of what the Latin American countries want. U.S. Treasury officials emphasized that Regan was not calling for a new "Bretton Woods" — a reference to the 1944 meeting that created the World Bank and the IMF.[21]

Instead, the officials said, Regan was suggesting a joint conference of the World Bank and the IMF to coincide with the regular spring meeting of the IMF's Interim Committee and the IMF-Bank Development Committee. Regan's plan was praised by some of the central bankers and finance ministers, but others called it a "political ploy" to cover up U.S. opposition to proposals to expand the capacity of both the Bank and the Fund to lend money to Third World debtor countries.

Trade's Major Role in Future Recovery

One of the far-reaching proposals for attacking the Latin American debt problem was put forth last May by Martin Feldstein, who was then chairman of the White House Council of Economic Advisers.[22] Speaking to the Council of the Americas, a prestigious business group made up of executives of corporations that account for 80 percent of all trade between

---

[21] See "Bretton Woods: Forty Years Later," *E.R.R.*, 1984 Vol. I, pp. 449-468.
[22] Feldstein left his White House post on July 10 to return to his professorship at Harvard University.

Marketplace at Guayaquil, Ecuador   Port of Santos, Brazil

Traditional and Industrial Latin America

the United States and Latin America, Feldstein said: "Although the current strategy has been successful in dealing with the initial stage of the financial crisis, the time has come to shift from crisis management to a policy of promoting Latin American growth. . . . The only way for debtor nations to pay interest on their existing debt . . . is by maintaining an appropriate trade surplus with the rest of the world."

Latin American countries have increased their trade surplus significantly in the past few years, Feldstein observed, but they have done so largely by reducing their imports. Brazil, for example, reduced its imports by 32 percent between 1980 and 1983, and Argentina by 57 percent. "Reduced imports of materials, machinery and spare parts have already depressed productive capacity and economic activity," he said, adding that the key to export growth is a "real devaluation" of Latin American currencies. The industrialized countries, in turn, "must guarantee that markets . . . will be open in the years ahead."

Feldstein's call for expansion of Latin American exports flies in the face of mounting pressures for protectionism in the United States and other developed countries. The Reagan administration faces increasing demands from basic industries that are feeling the pinch of competition from foreign suppliers. In two landmark decisions, the president recently turned down import relief for U.S. producers of copper — an important export for Chile and Peru — but agreed to negotiate restraint agreements with Third World exporters of steel, including Argentina and Brazil. There may be a growing consensus on the need to get Latin America back on a growth and expansion cycle, but the political will to do so is yet to be developed.

Selected Bibliography

Books

Baer, Werner, *The Brazilian Economy: Its Growth and Development,* Grid Publishing Inc., 1979.

Burns, E. Bradford, *A History of Brazil* (2nd ed.), Columbia University Press, 1980.

Decker, David R., *The Political, Economic and Labor Climate in Argentina,* University of Pennsylvania, Wharton School, 1983.

Enders, Thomas O. and Richard P. Mattione, *Latin America: The Crisis of Debt and Growth,* Brookings Institution, 1984.

Keen, Benjamin and Mark Wasserman, *A Short History of Latin America* (2nd ed.), Houghton Mifflin, 1984.

Lernoux, Penny, *Cry of the People,* Doubleday, 1980.

—— *In Banks We Trust,* Anchor Press/Doubleday, 1984.

Levine, Daniel H., *Religion and Politics in Latin America,* Princeton University Press, 1981.

Articles

Andersen, Martin, "Dateline Argentina: Hello, Democracy," *Foreign Policiy,* summer 1984.

Kuczynski, Pedro Pablo, "Latin American Debt," *Foreign Affairs,* winter 1982-83.

—— "Latin American Debt: Act Two," *Foreign Affairs,* fall 1983, pp. 17-38.

OAS/CECON Trade News, selected issues.

Roett, Riordan, "Democracy and Debt in Latin America," *Foreign Affairs,* special issue on America and the World 1983.

Schumacher, Edward, "Argentina and Democracy," *Foreign Affairs,* summer 1984.

Vision Letter, selected issues.

Reports and Studies

Editorial Research Reports: "Strong Dollar's Return," 1983 Vol. II, p. 761; "World Debt Crisis," 1983 Vol. I, p. 45; "Trade Talks and Protectionism," 1979 Vol. I, p. 1; "Brazil: Awakening Giant," 1972 Vol. I, p. 271; "Argentina's Political Instability," 1972 Vol. II, p. 725; "Chile's Embattled Democracy," 1970 Vol. II, p. 773.

Inter-American Development Bank, "Economic and Social Progress in Latin America," 1984 Report.

—— External Debt and Economic Development in Latin America, Background and Prospects," January 1984.

International Monetary Fund, "Annual Report 1984," Aug. 13, 1984.

Organization of American States, "Annual Report of the Inter-American Commission on Human Rights," 1983-84, OEA/Ser. P, AG/doc. 1778/84, Oct. 5, 1984.

World Bank, "Annual Report 1984," September 1984.

—— "World Debt Tables," 1983-84 edition, January 1984.

—— "World Development Report 1984," July 1984.

Graphics: Maps by Assistant Art Director Robert Redding; photos, p. 136 from Argentine government, and p. 147 from World Bank.

CARIBBEAN
BASIN
REVISITED

by

Nicholas Raymond

**Feb. 1
1 9 8 5**

CARIBBEAN BASIN REVISITED

NO NEWS story during President Reagan's first term occupied the American press so continuously or troubled the American people more than the bloody fighting in Central America. Increased American involvement there, together with the invasion of Grenada, raised the specter of "another Vietnam." An official response was slowly shaped that would define a region of special U.S. interest, the "Caribbean Basin," and new policies to deal with it. These would combine a much-increased military presence and a new regionwide program of Amerian economic assistance to be called the "Caribbean Basin Initiative" (CBI), now just a year old. Many believed both the military and economic thrusts were inevitable. In this region, wrote Robert W. Tucker in *Foreign Affairs*, "our pride is engaged as it cannot possibly be engaged in Africa or Southeast Asia." [1]

When Reagan took office in 1981, Nicaragua's Sandinista government was well into its second year and appeared to be slipping steadily into a Marxist format, while Cuban-sympathizing governments had taken power by coups in Grenada in the Caribbean and Suriname on the South American mainland. El Salvador was reeling under the so-called "final offensive" by leftist guerrillas and was losing the public relations battle in the United States. The killing of three nuns and a Catholic lay worker in 1979 had underscored the brutality of the country's right-wing goons and death squads, while unproven charges of guerrilla atrocities were written off as propaganda. To the north, Guatemala was in the throes of a guerrilla war of its own, and for the first time in history leftist agitation appeared to be penetrating that country's normally apolitical Indian masses.

Rightly or wrongly, President Reagan and Secretary of State Alexander M. Haig saw a planned regional pattern of Soviet-Cuban subversion and takeover that directly threatened the United States "in its own back yard." [2] A year later *The Economist*, the London-based magazine, would write: "The fires in Nicaragua, El Salvador and Guatemala did not ignite in swift

[1] Robert W. Tucker, "The Purposes of American Power," *Foreign Affairs*, winter 1981-82.
[2] For background, see "Latin American Challenges," *E.R.R.*, 1981 Vol. I, pp. 269-288.

succession by accident. . . . They seem to be flowing together in a single isthmus-wide conflagration." [3]

Almost immediately, the new administration moved to isolate Nicaragua and step up support for the Salvadoran junta then running the country. A Gallup Poll in March 1981 indicated that American opinion for these measures was sharply divided, but with an overwhelming majority opposed to any use of American troops. Congressional critics, and there were many in the president's own party, argued that Haig's Cold War rhetoric, in particular, was frightening the American people as well as America's allies, while the roots of the Caribbean's problems could be laid more to poverty than subversion.

Indeed, within a year the president embraced a more balanced approach. On Feb. 24, 1982, he went before the Organization of American States (OAS) in Washington to propose the Caribbean Basin Initiative to upgrade the region's crippled economies. His proposal set off a debate, which still continues, over whether the initiative's true goal is economic development or a cover for pouring more money into tottering Central American governments.

Reagan's speech was in fact two in one: the velvet glove of aid and trade benefits, but still the mailed fist of anti-communism. "Guerrillas, armed and supported by and through Cuba, are attempting to impose a Marxist-Leninist dictatorship on the people of El Salvador as part of a larger imperialistic plan," he said. Nonetheless, most of the address was oriented to economic assistance, and it was received with a sigh of relief in Latin America and Congress. "Reagan," said *Time* magazine, "finally seemed to be on the track with a sensible and well-rounded policy initiative." [4]

Through it all, however, there was a startling similarity to the U.S. shock and response after the victory of Fidel Castro in Cuba in 1959. Then the hostility to a communist presence in the Western Hemisphere encouraged the creation of the Alliance for Progress.[5] Although the success or failure of the Alliance is still debated, stability in the region was restored for the better part of two decades by military threat and economic support.

By the time of President Reagan's second inaugural, the question of whether that approach would work again was still in doubt. Progress had been agonizingly slow, but the crisis at-

---

[3] *The Economist*, March 27, 1982, p. 7.
[4] *Time*, March 8, 1982, p. 14.
[5] The Alliance for Progress was an aid program to provide economic relief in Latin American countries. The agreement was signed by the United States and participating Latin American nations at Punta del Este, Uruguay, Aug. 17, 1961.

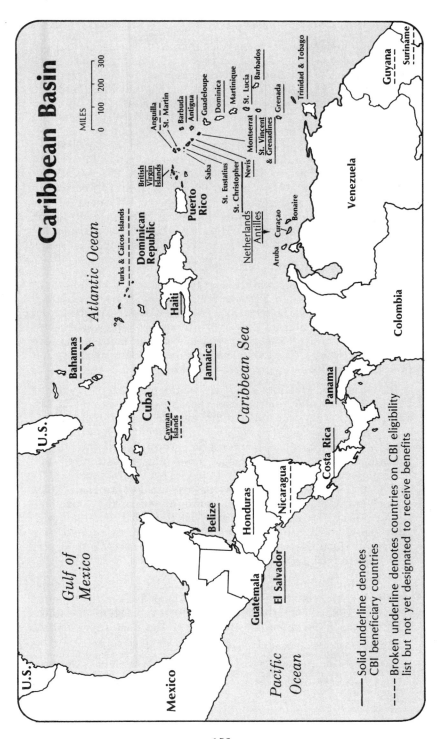

Caribbean Basin

U.S.

Gulf of
Mexico

Pacific
Ocean

Mexico

Guatemala

El Salvador

Belize

Honduras

Nicaragua

Costa Rica

Panama

Cuba

Cayman
Islands

Jamaica

Caribbean Sea

Bahamas

U.S.

Atlantic Ocean

Turks & Caicos Islands

Dominican
Republic

Haiti

Puerto
Rico

British
Virgin
Islands

Saba

St. Eustatius

St. Christopher

Nevis

Netherlands
Antilles

Aruba   Curaçao

Bonaire

Anguilla

St. Martin

Barbuda

Antigua

Guadeloupe

Dominica

Martinique

St. Lucia

Barbados

Montserrat

St. Vincent
& Grenadines

Grenada

Trinidad & Tobago

Colombia

Venezuela

Guyana

Suriname

MILES

0   100   200   300

—— Solid underline denotes
CBI beneficiary countries

----- Broken underline denotes countries on CBI eligibility
list but not yet designated to receive benefits

153

mosphere had dissipated in Washington. Although still fluid and dangerous, the political situation in Central America appeared to be stabilizing. Christian Democrat José Napoleón Duarte had been elected president in El Salvador, and the rightist elements grouped around Maj. Roberto D'Aubuisson were in retreat. A constituent assembly had been elected in Guatemala with centrists in control, holding out the prospect for return to civilian rule this year. Fears of a war between Nicaragua and Honduras, with the obvious potential for full-scale U.S. intervention, were much diminished. The leftist government in Grenada was toppled by a U.S. military invasion in November 1983, and replaced by a new government of the center that was elected overwhelmingly in December 1984. Col. Desi Bouterse, Suriname's strongman, had been alarmed by events in Grenada and sent home most of his Cuban advisers.

First-Year Results From Economic Plan

Hopeful signs also could be seen for most of the economies of the region. The Inter-American Development Bank reported they were slowly returning to a growth pattern in 1984, and exports were starting to revive with the end of the world recession. The Caribbean Basin Initiative, its main trade provisions finally passed by Congress in the Caribbean Basin Recovery Act of 1983, was also showing signs of taking hold.

In December, business and government leaders from the Caribbean, Central America and the United States met in Miami to weigh first-year CBI results and prospects for the future. The conference itself, the eighth annual event of its kind to be organized by a private promotional group called Caribbean/Central American Action,[6] was an important indication of growing interest in the region. The first C/CAA conference in 1977 had just 150 participants; this one attracted more than 2,000, including the majority of the prime ministers of the Caribbean island states, President Duarte of El Salvador, Cabinet ministers from most other Central American countries, and Secretary of State George P. Shultz. Honduras sent 70 delegates and Britain 34.

Shultz, in a speech to the conference Dec. 8, happily compared statistics for the first eight months of 1984 with the same period in 1983 showing economic gains in the region.[7] Business investments reported in the press over the past year seem to

---

[6] It is based in Washington, at 1333 New Hampshire Ave. N.W., 20036.

[7] Among the statistics he cited: U.S. imports from CBI countries, excluding oil, increased by almost 34 percent, and exports to the United States soared in Grenada (114 percent), Belize (91), Jamaica (83) and Barbados (78). Shultz said further that the Overseas Private Investment Corporation (OPIC) had approved 43 projects in the area in 1984 and the Commerce Department was receiving 100 inquiries a day. Barbados, he added, had generated 2,000 new jobs through joint ventures with high-tech industries and Jamaica had approved some 300 investment projects. Finally, he said that during President Reagan's first term, U.S. aid to the Caribbean Basin nearly tripled.

bear out Shultz's optimism. Dozens of American companies have started or expanded activities in the region — to make basketballs and stuffed toys in Haiti, ship fruits and vegetables from Costa Rica, package spices in Grenada, export shrimp and crab from the Dominican Republic and orange juice concentrate from Honduras, make costume jewelry in Barbados and assemble electronic components nearly everywhere.

Nor have CBI possibilities been lost on other countries. British and German companies are setting up in Barbados to ship hospital supplies and agricultural pesticides, and an Israeli company is growing cantaloupes in the Dominican Republic for the off-season U.S. market. South

Secretary Shultz

Korean embassies have sprouted throughout the region. Foreign companies are standing in line to rent "factory shells" in industrial free-trade zones. Taiwan reportedly has given Costa Rica $3 million to help it build a new industrial park on the country's Pacific coast. Miami-based shipping lines report their business has increased substantially in the past year and are looking for still greater growth in 1985. For all the good news, however, there was also bad.

Corporate Closings Among the Islands

In the space of a few short months, several countries in the Caribbean have been hit with devastating news that could undermine their recoveries and spark social tensions as well. Late in 1984 the Exxon subsidiary Esso-America announced it would close its huge Lago oil refinery in Aruba in March, and *The Wall Street Journal* warned on Dec. 10 that a number of other oil companies around the Caribbean were following suit. Underscoring the small size and fragility of the region's economies, the Lago closing alone could wipe out up to a fourth of the Netherlands Antilles' foreign income.

On Curacao, one of that group of islands, the Royal Dutch/Shell Group's refinery has also been losing money and cutting staff for years, and is asking the government to buy half the venture. A Shell official said the refinery there would probably close in two or three years if it did not get help.[8] Meanwhile, Trinidad & Tobago has agreed to buy the Texaco refinery in Trinidad — another losing venture — as the only way to protect the installation's 3,400 jobs.

---

[8] All persons quoted in this report were interviewed by the author unless otherwise noted.

Other older refineries in the Bahamas and the U.S. Virgin Islands are rumored to be on the way out and a Big Oil exodus from the entire region may be under way. Venezuela and Mexico have set up their own refining capacity and new offshore oil unloading facilities in the Gulf of Mexico have undercut U.S. need for Caribbean refineries, many of which were built during World War II.[9]

In January, in another blow to regional recovery, the United Brands Co. announced it would phase out its massive banana operations on the Pacific coast of Costa Rica, despite what *The Washington Post* termed "hand-wringing in Washington." Although the company's other operations in Costa Rica won't be affected, an estimated 50,000 people depend on the company's Pacific plantations, which earn debt-ridden Costa Rica about $40 million a year. Officials in San José, according to the *Post* story by Joanne Omang, fear that shutting down the operation "could lead to leftist-inspired riots over the sudden unemployment and to economic disintegration from the loss of income." [10]

Prime Minister Seaga

On the same day the Costa Rican story appeared, riots were spreading through Kingston and other Jamaican cities after the government of Prime Minister Edward Seaga imposed a 20 percent increase in kerosene and gasoline prices. Seaga, one of the intellectual authors of the CBI and the first foreign dignitary to visit the Reagan White House in 1981, has vowed that he will not yield "one blade of grass or one inch of ground" in the harsh economic recovery program he imposed in order to obtain loans from the International Monetary Fund (IMF). P. J. Parsons, chairman of the opposition People's National Party (PNP), was quoted as saying the riots were "a clear sign that the economic policies have failed."

Despite the opposition party's demand for new national elections, Seaga does not have to go back to the polls until 1988. But the riots dealt a bitter blow to the country's tourist trade, only slowly being rebuilt after the strident anti-Americanism of the 1970s under PNP Prime Minister Michael Manley. Jamaica's tourist promotion campaign in the U.S. pleads, "Come back to

---

[9] These refineries came into operation near harbors deep enough to berth big oil tankers. From these deepwater ports, plentiful in the Caribbean but lacking on the U.S. mainland, crude oil is taken from the tankers and refined for shipment to the United States aboard smaller vessels.

[10] *The Washington Post,* Jan. 16, 1985.

Jamaica again." Jamaica's tourist arrivals jumped 30 percent in 1983 and climbed again in 1984. Most international flights and thousands of tourist bookings were canceled during the riots.

Over the past year, a *CBI Business Bulletin* published by the Department of Commerce has been announcing a steady growth in Caribbean exports to the United States. They probably climbed back in 1984 to the record level of $10.3 billion in 1979, before the world recession. But CBI-related growth will have to make enormous strides if it is to make up for losses in oil products or any downturn in the important tourist business. The biggest exporters in the region are the Netherlands Antilles, Trinidad & Tobago and the Bahamas. Most of their foreign earnings come from oil.

Congressional Compromise Over the CBI

Even without these shocks, however, the results of the CBI's first year were more mixed than Shultz' rosy picture would indicate. Caribbean leaders attribute the reason mostly to changes Congress made in the president's original proposal. Between the time of Reagan's address to the OAS and the CBI start-up — officially Jan. 1, 1984 — two important years were lost and some of the key features of the plan were changed or discarded entirely.

The CBI plan was introduced in Congress in March 1982 with three basic components: (1) A one-time request for $350 million in direct supplemental economic aid to the Caribbean states; (2) 12 years of duty-free access to the U.S. market for all Caribbean exports except textiles; and (3) a five-year U.S. tax credit of 10 percent to American companies on the cost of their investment in plant and equipment in the beneficiary countries. Each of these components faced a shifting constituency of interests, pro and con, and each fared differently.

With relatively little fuss, Congress passed the supplemental aid bill the following September, adding to the $474 million it had already allocated to the region in the 1982 budget, to tide over cash-short countries. The lawmakers made only one major change, giving El Salvador $70 million rather than the requested $128 million. Some liberals argued that the CBI was an elaborate disguise to increase aid to El Salvador.

Nearly all the more serious debate came over the second component — one-way free trade. The AFL-CIO, later strengthened by the addition of 26 Democratic seats in the House in the 1982 elections, was the most vociferous antagonist. It argued that in the midst of a recession and high unemployment it was a poor time to open the country to a new wave of low-wage imports.

157

Organized labor was not alone in the fight. Other opponents included domestic sugar producers, threatened manufacturing industries, representatives of Puerto Rico who feared the loss of its existing advantages as a U.S. commonwealth,[11] many prestigious Washington "think tanks" that questioned the value as well as the motive of the plan, and a variety of citizen organizations which saw the CBI as a Reagan payoff to multinational corporations and a new form of covert economic imperialism.

Hearings continued in the House into the fall and had hardly begun in the Senate, causing speculation that the plan was dead. When a House vote finally came on Dec. 17, Majority Leader Jim Wright, D-Texas, made an impassioned speech in support of the bill, drawing a standing ovation from his colleagues, many of whom had obviously been swayed by his recounting of a history of U.S. relations with Latin America "mottled by recurrent broken promises and benign neglect, raising hopes that were then dashed." The bill was passed on a vote of 260 to 142.

Other important support for the bill came from Rep. Dan Rostenkowski, D-Ill., chairman of the Ways and Means Committee. He had visited Central America on a White House-arranged tour during Congress' fall recess. Frightened by what he saw and heard, he changed from a lukewarm to a fervent CBI supporter. To gain House passage, however, Rostenkowski had to agree to lengthen the list of exemptions from CBI trade benefits and jettison the entire third component, the tax credit. The Senate still could not act before the 97th Congress ended and the bill had to be reintroduced in 1983 in the new 98th Congress. But no real attempt was made to restore the tax-credit provision in either house that year.

The Caribbean Basin Recovery Act received final passage July 28, 1983, with drastically reduced trade benefits and no tax incentive. Products exempted from duty-free entry included canned tuna, textiles and apparel, petroleum and petroleum products, footwear, work gloves, luggage, handbags, flat leather goods such as wallets, and leather wearing apparel. Despite strong objections from Puerto Rico, rum was not exempted.[12]

Mixed Reaction of Basin Political Leaders

Even CBI boosters concede that most of the export gains by the beneficiary countries in 1984 could be laid to an expanding U.S. economy, but they also argue that one year is hardly

---

[11] Under its commonwealth status, granted in 1952, Puerto Rico has received many of the duty-free and tax-incentive benefits now being accorded its neighbors under CBI.
[12] For an overview of the bill's legislative history, see Congressional Quarterly *1982 Almanac*, pp. 54-55, and *1983 Almanac*, pp. 252-253.

CBI's Promotional Push

The U.S. government has undertaken an enormous promotion campaign to encourage business participation in the CBI. Federal agencies have brought together thousands of U.S., Central American and Caribbean business executives through workshops, seminars, trade fairs and trips. Commerce Department seminars, for example, drew 780 company representatives to San José, Costa Rica, and 300 to San Pedro Sula, Honduras. These were among 20 CBI-related seminars that Commerce alone sponsored last year. There were others, funded by the Agency for International Development (AID) and the Agriculture Department. C/CAA, with AID backing, organized private tours of Basin countries.

enough time to measure the impact of a program that counts heavily on a host of separate private business decisions. Early in 1984, with the trade provisions finally in place, the Puerto Rican monthly *Caribbean Business* offered the following puckish quiz: "The Caribbean Basin Initiative is: (a) a tremendous opportunity to create jobs and commerce; (b) a political sideshow signifying nothing; or (c) both of the above. If you answered a, b or c, you could be right. Only time will tell."

From the outset, the main reason why CBI's detractors were answering "b" was simply that 87 percent of the region's exports already entered the United States duty free under the Generalized System of Preferences offered to all Third World countries by the non-communist industrial nations. U.S. trade officials do not accept the GSP argument. William Cavitt, director of the Commerce Department's Central America office, recently told *The Washington Times* that while the duty-free status was extended only from 87 to 94 percent of the traditional products, "the list of products is going from around 2,400 to around 3,800." Cavitt also maintained that CBI countries are much less vulnerable than under the GSP to having their exports removed from the duty-free list in response to hardship petitions from American companies. Trade officials also note that a central purpose of the CBI is to get the region into new kinds of exports.

However, U.S. officials admit that exemptions pinch badly, and Caribbean leaders who met in Miami in December repeatedly called for their removal. "Exclusion in any shape or form is a detriment to the CBI and seriously reduces its effectiveness," Prime Minister Kennedy Simmonds of St. Christopher-Nevis told the conference. And, after noting that he had traveled frequently to Washington to urge the program's adoption, Simmonds added, "Up to now the CBI as presently constituted has produced absolutely nothing for St. Kitts [St. Christopher-Nevis]." More plaintively, Maryse Dominique, commercial attaché at Haiti's Embassy in Washington, recently said that "to identify new products takes a lot of time and we aren't very sophisticated.... If they would give us the opportunity to manufacture things we know how to export, such as textiles, it would be a bigger help." [13]

Not all the reactions in the beneficiary countries are negative. Prime Minister Seaga told the Miami meeting that Jamaica was enjoying "the biggest investment boom in its history." President Duarte of El Salvador was another strong supporter. Most observers were more cautious. "The consensus of the meeting seemed to be that the results are mixed," according to Richard C. Schroeder, Washington correspondent for the Latin American news magazine *Visión*. "There are encouraging signs . . . but over time the CBI is likely to be hampered by some fundamental flaws that crept into the program during its stormy passage through the U.S. Congress." [14]

Contours of the Caribbean

THE CARIBBEAN Basin encompasses a vast area, stretching 2,000 miles north and south from the Bahamas to Suriname and 2,500 miles east and west from Barbados to El Salvador. Its identification as a single, unified region (basin with a capital B) is not new in defense terms, but had never before been set out in an economic and geopolitical context and, to geographers as well as a reluctant Congress, took some swallowing. Most awkwardly, it lumped together the predominantly English-speaking islands of the Caribbean Sea with the six Spanish-speaking countries of the Central American isthmus, two previously distinct regions with little common history, culture, trade or even contact.

Other contradictions abound. The CBI includes El Salvador, which does not border the Caribbean Sea, but excludes Colombia, Venezuela and Mexico, all with long Caribbean coastlines and history. It includes the remaining British and Dutch dependencies without inviting Britain and the Netherlands into the program. But it excludes Martinique, Guadeloupe and French Guiana, although it can be assumed that this was at France's behest. It excludes Cuba, because it is communist; but Nicaragua, which routinely is accused of communist leanings, is a potential beneficiary, although it has not qualified for aid.

---

[13] Cavitt and Dominique were quoted in *The Washington Times,* Sept. 4, 1984.
[14] *Visión,* Jan. 14, 1985.

But the basin concept has as many justifications as short-comings. All of the potential 27 CBI beneficiaries *(see p. 163)* are underdeveloped, poor and too small to create self-sustaining internal economies. Nearly all are overpopulated; their surplus labor drifts steadily into the United States either legally or illegally. All but three — Haiti, Guatemala and Suriname — have elected governments, and Guatemala appears likely to return to democratic rule soon. All of the independent countries belong to the OAS, the Inter-American Development Bank or some other regional body and have ties to their immediate neighbors. All except Nicaragua count heavily on U.S. trade and are eager to attract U.S. investment. All the CBI countries seem willing to belong, but no country has publicly complained of its exclusion.

Overriding these considerations is the simple fact that all 27 are in a region which the United States believes is vital to its strategic interests and, in the words of the Reagan administration, this country's "natural sphere of influence." Strategic interests and spheres of influence are contentious terms which raise memories of "gunboat diplomacy" and the "Big Stick" policies of President Theodore Roosevelt, but rightly or wrongly they have guided Washington thinking since the Monroe Doctrine in 1823 declared the primacy of American interests in this hemisphere.

Three more dates are of equal significance: the Spanish-American War in 1898, with the resulting U.S. occupation of Cuba and Puerto Rico; 1914, with the opening of the Panama Canal; and 1959, with the coming to power of Fidel Castro in Cuba and the fear of communism, as expressed in the popular phrase, "just 90 miles off our shores."

Strategic Importance to the United States

The strategic importance of the Caribbean is impossible to question. More than 25 percent of the crude oil and 50 percent of all refined petroleum products in world trade are loaded or unloaded in the region.[15] Much of the supplies destined for U.S. and Allies' armies in World War II went out through the Straits of Florida. Nearly two-thirds of all cargo passing through the Panama Canal goes to or comes from the United States, while a big share of U.S. grain and industrial exports flow down the Mississippi River through the Gulf of Mexico.

The degree of Soviet and Cuban involvement in the region has long been in dispute. The Reagan administration obviously believes that Castro has never given up exporting revolution —

---

[15] For background, see Thomas J. Anderson's *Geopolitics of the Caribbean,* Hoover Institution Series (1983).

to Nicaragua, Grenada, El Salvador or wherever else he finds the opportunity. And while Cuban support of guerrilla movements may be political Washington's primary concern, Pentagon planners take the protection of the Caribbean and Panama sea lanes in deadly earnest.

Soviet submarines and even sometimes surface vessels now routinely patrol the region from Cuban refueling stations, and the Cuban air force is reported to have about 200 combat aircraft.[16] In his book *Geopolitics of the Caribbean,* geographer Thomas D. Anderson includes a map showing the entire basin is within range of such aircraft operating from bases in Cuba, Nicaragua and Grenada. That official Washington takes such dangers seriously is evidenced by the 1983 U.S. invasion of Grenada, where an airport was being built under the leftist government of Maurice Bishop. There was also a U.S. warning to Moscow that the United States will not tolerate the introduction of MiGs in Nicaragua, where another air base construction program is reported to be well advanced.

The proliferation of mini-states in the Caribbean, especially since the British withdrawal in the mid-1960s, has become another source of strategic concern.[17] In 1967 two journalists asked Errol Barrow, the prime minister of Barbados, "Who will send the troops in the future?" He replied testily, "The United States is not so crazy as to intervene in a [British] Commonwealth nation." [18] But in the invasion of Grenada, Barrows' successor, Prime Minister Tom Adams, sent in a contingent of his Barbadian forces with the American troops. As nothing else possibly could, the invasion of Grenada underscored U.S. primacy in a region where European powers had vied for control over the past centuries.

How the Regional Economies Crumbled

At least a part of the carping about the CBI can be attributed not so much to the program itself, but to the extreme economic distress felt throughout the Caribbean even as the rest of the world comes out of recession. Also, although it might be forgotten, most of today's Caribbean business and political leaders grew up in an era of economic growth, and only in the past half dozen years have they had to cope with the strains of hard times.

Average annual growth rates in domestic products in the re-

---

[16] *The Almanac of World Military Power,* published by Presidio Press in San Rafael, Calif., lists 210; other sources vary somewhat.

[17] For background, see "Caribbean Security," *E.R.R.*, 1980 Vol. I, pp. 21-40.

[18] Interview by Winthrop P. Carty and Nicholas Raymond, published in *The Reporter* magazine, March 1967. Carty and Raymond wrote: "A vacuum has been created that, ready or not, the United States will be forced to fill."

CBI Eligible Countries

(Those not yet designated to receive benefits are in italics)

Country	Population (add 000)	Per capita GNP (in dollars)	1983 Trade U.S. Exports	1983 Trade U.S. Imports
Anguilla (a)	7	n.a.	(b)	(b)
Antigua & Barbuda	79	1,740	(b)	(b)
The Bahamas	223	6,643	443.9	1,676.4
Barbados	251	2,753	192.5	202.0
Belize	154	1,080	33.4	27.3
British Virgin Islands (a)	13	n.a.	(b)	(b)
Cayman Islands (a)	20	n.a.	64.4	8.6
Costa Rica	2,624	1,466	378.5	386.5
Dominica	74	710	(b)	(b)
Dominican Republic	6,248	1,212	622.8	806.5
El Salvador	4,685	632	338.1	358.9
Grenada	111	760	(b)	(b)
Guatemala	7,714	1,235	310.5	374.7
Guyana	833	711	35.4	67.3
Haiti	5,690	310	356.9	337.5
Honduras	4,276	665	279.3	364.7
Jamaica	2,335	1,714	444.5	262.4
Montserrat (a)	12	n.a.	(b)	(b)
Netherlands Antilles (a)	247	n.a.	531.8	2,274.5
Nicaragua	2,812	1,088	129.8	99.0
Panama	2,058	2,159	732.2	336.1
St. Christopher-Nevis	45	750	(b)	(b)
St. Lucia	119	720	(b)	(b)
St. Vincent and the Grenadines	134	620	(b)	(b)
Suriname	363	2,336	115.5	63.1
Trinidad & Tobago	1,211	3,011	708.2	1,317.5
Turks and Caicos Islands (a)	8	n.a.	11.7	4.0

(a) Dependencies; all others are independent states

(b) British Virgin Islands and Eastern Caribbean states taken together show U.S. exports of $159.2 million and U.S. imports of $38.8 million.

Sources: Population statistics from the U.S. Bureau of the Census; GNP statistics from World Bank for 1982 or 1983; trade statistics from U.S. Department of Commerce.

gion as a whole grew more than 5 percent in the 1950s, then 7 percent in the 1960s and nearly 8 percent in the first half of the 1970s.[19] By 1978, according to the World Bank, per capita GNP averaged about $1,000 a year, ranging from Haiti's rock-bottom $300 to the Bahamas' oil-swollen $6,600. While it is also true that income distribution was generally badly skewed toward the

---

[19] Figures cited by William H. Bolin, "Central America: Real Economic Help is Workable Now," *Foreign Affairs*, summer 1984, pp. 1096-1106. Bolin, a retired vice president of the Bank of America, is a senior fellow at the Latin American Center at the University of California at Los Angeles.

rich in most countries, there was visible improvement everywhere.

Those who look to extreme poverty as a harbinger of political unrest might also note that the Caribbean region is not dirt poor in world terms. Measures of health, education and nutrition — though very bad in comparison with developed countries — all show the region better off than most of Africa or Asia or even some parts of South America. Of 26 countries labeled "least developed" by the United Nations, Haiti is the only one in the Western Hemisphere.

Impressive growth rates over nearly 30 years reflect an expanding world economy and trade that provided markets and reasonable prices for the region's commodity exports. But another important engine of growth, particularly for Central America, was regional integration. The Central American Common Market was created in 1960 as a free-trade zone with a common external tariff. Internal trade among the five member countries — Costa Rica, El Salvador, Guatemala, Honduras and Nicaragua — immediately boomed as regional products were substituted for goods formerly imported. Trade expanded by a factor of 10 between 1950 and 1980 to reach a value of $2.2 billion, nearly all of it in manufactures. Exports to countries outside the region also took off, growing from $250 million in 1950 to $3.2 billion in 1978.[20]

In the Caribbean, similar growth was taking place. Although manufacturing played less of a role, despite the stimulus of the Caribbean Common Market for 13 English-speaking countries,[21] even smaller islands had a steady source of income from tropical products, tourism and light manufacture. Trinidad had oil, and Jamaica and Guyana bauxite.

High Oil Prices and Burdensome Debts

Progress began to slow after the first world oil shock in 1973-74 and the roof fell in after the second shock in 1979-80 and the world recession that followed. During the years of growth, the Central American and larger Caribbean economies had changed character, more modern in one sense but more fragile in another. Traditionally, basic commodities had been sold abroad and consumer goods bought in exchange. If income from commodities fell off, it was fairly painless to cut back imports. But new manufacturing industries, in need of imported equipment and some materials, and with a more complex financial struc-

---

[20] Statistics cited by Bolin. For background, also see "Central America and the U.S.A.," *E.R.R.*, 1978 Vol. I, pp. 321-340, and "Common Market for Latin America," *E.R.R.*, 1965 Vol. II, pp. 759-778.
[21] Antigua & Barbuda, Belize, the Bahamas, Barbados, Dominica, Grenada, Jamaica, Montserrat, St. Christopher-Nevis, St. Lucia, St. Vincent and the Grenadines, Trinidad & Tobago.

ture, could not retrench in the same way. Energy costs were another big problem, although oil-producing Venezuela and Mexico generously offered concessionary prices to cushion the shock. Meanwhile, world prices for commodity exports such as coffee and sugar plunged, while the import-substitution drive began to slow.

In response, all the countries began to borrow heavily from commercial banks to finance industry and trade and from governments to continue development programs. By the end of 1983, total debt of the region was estimated at $28 billion, only $21 billion of which was publicly held and guaranteed. Total external debt was more than 10 times the level of 1970. Service costs have risen even faster. For example, Jamaican-born economist Robert Enriques Girling said in 1983 "several countries are forced to devote more than a fifth of their export earnings to debt service." Guyana's debt service, he said, was bigger than its export earnings.[22]

While Brazil and Mexico draw "debt crisis" attention, the situation is also acute in the Caribbean, though on a smaller scale. The $350 million in emergency loans under the CBI "provided less than 10 percent of the external resources needed to cover the region's balance of payments shortfalls, and the disbursal of new CBI monies will not halt the decline," according to a study published in *Caribbean Review*.[23]

Official Visions of the Future

C ONCERNED with the continuing congressional and public debate over his Central American policies, President Reagan in mid-1983 named a high-level, bipartisan commission headed by former Secretary of State Henry A. Kissinger to study U.S. options in the region. The Report of the National Bipartisan Commission on Central America (Kissinger commission) was released under the president's seal in January 1984, and, not unsurprisingly, found U.S. policies to be on the right track. It concluded: "Our task now, as a nation, is to transform the crisis in Central America into an opportunity: to seize the impetus it provides, and to use this to help our neighbors not

---

[22] Quoted in the *International Herald Tribune* supplement on the Caribbean Basin, Dec. 2, 1983.

[23] By Richard D. Feinberg, Richard Newfarmer and Bernadette Orr, spring 1983 edition. *Caribbean Review* is published quarterly by Caribbean Review Inc. at Florida International University at Miami.

only to secure their freedom from aggression and violence, but also to set in place the policies, processes and institutions that will make them both prosperous and free."

To achieve this happy result, the commission proposed a number of short, medium and long-term measures and $8 billion in aid over the next five years. And while the program would have a definite CBI tilt toward strengthening the private business and trade sectors, it would also "promote the development of Central America in all its dimensions — economic prosperity, social change, political modernization and peace." It was, in short, vintage Alliance for Progress, and rather than still the debate the commission report probably added to it.

Jeffrey E. Garten, a former deputy director of the State Department's Policy Planning Staff who became a vice president of the Wall Street firm of Lehman Brothers Kuhn Loeb Inc., wrote in *The New York Times Magazine:* "In 30 years of experience in Asia, Africa and Latin America . . . the lesson has not been learned. Once again advocates of massive economic assistance, this time to Central America, overestimate the benefits to the recipient countries and to the United States. In expending such huge sums in the expectation of counteracting leftist rebellion and nourishing democracy . . . we are setting ourselves up for a bitter disappointment [which] could lead to a political backlash and eventual abndonment of the whole region." [24]

The debate continues into 1985. Is U.S. policy in the region to be based on business incentives and free trade, leaving the beneficiary countries to profit from their "natural advantage" of low-wage surplus labor, or is it to be a plan of social and political as well as economic transformation? Is the United States going back on President Carter's promotion of human rights by support for El Salvador?

And, finally, can the region absorb the amounts of aid the Kissinger commission envisaged? According to a study prepared by Richard E. Feinberg and Robert A. Pastor for the Carnegie Endowment for International Peace, "The sums contemplated could reach 10 percent of Central America's GNP [gross national product] over the next five years. This compares with the 3 percent of European GNP accounted for by the Marshall Plan."[25] Secretary Shultz told his Miami audience last December, "We are committed to the assistance levels called for by the

[24] Jeffrey E. Garten, "Aid in the Eighties," *The New York Times Magazine*, March 25, 1984.

[25] The Marshall Plan, named for Gen. George C. Marshall, President Truman's secretary of state after World War II, made large amounts of American aid available to war-torn Europe for the rebuilding of its industrial base.

[Kissinger] commission." But Congress has not yet shown that it shares that big a commitment.

Shultz' View of Industrial Development

There is a separate issue, however, that is more pertinent to the Caribbean Basin states themselves: whether the whole premise of the CBI is valid. If it is to work, at least the larger countries in the region will have to recast past economic and development theories and fully open up their economies to imports and foreign investment while reorienting their own industries and investment plans to export-led growth.

Shultz put the CBI doctrine forcefully to the Caribbean leaders. Noting that the Inter-American Development Bank had estimated that $47 billion a year in net capital inflows into the region would be necessary to sustain a 5 percent annual growth rate, Shultz warned that external borrowing and foreign aid could not come close to that level in the foreseeable future. Even if it could, he said, it would lift the region's debt to $620 billion by the end of the decade — up from the present $28 billion — making debt service unsupportable. Then came the message:

> I am calling here [Shultz said] for the reversal of state ownership and anti-import policies. These policies have placed stifling controls on private agriculture and industry. They have made them dependent on restricted markets. They have built costly protectionist barriers at national frontiers. And they have produced inefficient state enterprises that divert resources from more productive activities.

To reverse course, Shultz called for: (1) government policies to strengthen internal private investment; (2) equal treatment of foreign and domestic investment; (3) domestic savings to be stressed above foreign aid and debt; and (4) trade as the engine of development. In short, the basin countries are being asked to emulate the policies that led to the success of the "newly industrialized countries" (NICs) of East Asia — Taiwan, South Korea, Hong Kong and Singapore. In return, the United States will offer a market for the goods produced on terms equal to or better than those enjoyed by Asia, and will encourage the private investment flow to make it possible.

"To put the question dramatically," writes Boston University sociologist Peter Berger in *Caribbean Review,* "What are Jamaica's chances of becoming another Taiwan?" Berger cites Jamaica because Prime Minister Seaga is the region's greatest CBI booster, but the issue is the same for any other CBI beneficiary. Apart from the steps advocated by Shultz, Berger and other analysts mention other difficulties: well-organized unions in most Caribbean countries, so that while wages remain very low strikes are frequent; a lack of capital and risk-taking history among entrepreneurs; a strong tendency, particularly among the Spanish-speaking countries, toward state organization and controls; poor electrical power systems and high transport costs; irresponsible political parties and a high level of political tension; and lack of a strong work ethic. To most observers, the "NIC trick" will take some doing.

Selected Bibliography

Books

Anderson, Thomas D., *Geopolitics of the Caribbean: Ministates in a Wider World,* Hoover Institution Series, Praeger, 1984.

Trouble in Our Backyard, collection of essays edited by Martin Diskin, Pantheon Books, 1983.

Wiarda, Howard J., *In Search of Policy: the United States and Latin America,* American Enterprise Institute Studies in Foreign Policy, 1984

Articles

Bolin, William H., Central America: "Real Economic Help is Workable Now," summer 1984.

Carty, Winthrop P., and Nicholas Raymond, "The New Mini-States of the Caribbean," *The Reporter,* March 9, 1967.

Feinberg, Richard E., et al., "The Battle Over the CBI," *Caribbean Review,* spring 1983.

Garten, Jeffrey E., "Aid in the Eighties," *The New York Times Magazine,* March 25, 1984.

Tucker, Robert W., "The Purposes of American Power," *Foreign Affairs,* winter 1981-82

Reports and Studies

Editorial Research Reports: "Caribbean Basin Policy," 1984 Vol. I, p. 21; "Caribbean Security," 1978 Vol. I, p. 21; "Central America and the U.S.A.," 1978 Vol. I, p. 321.

Inter-American Development Bank, *Annual Report 1984.*

Lamar, Harry, "Trade and Employment Effects of the CBI" (pamphlet prepared for Caribbean/Central American Action), May 1983.

"Report of the National Bipartisan Commission on Central America," January 1984, U.S. Government Printing Office.

World Bank, *Development Report 1984.*

Graphics: Map by Assistant Art Director Robert Redding; cover photo by Paul Conklin for World Bank of hydroelectric plant in El Salvador; p. 155 photo by Ken Heinen and p. 156 photo from Jamaican government.

CANADA'S TIME OF CHANGE

by

Andrew Cohen

Mar. 8
1 9 8 5

CANADA'S TIME OF CHANGE

T HIS is a time of change in Canada. The country has come
out of its worst recession since the 1930s seeking ways to
sustain the affluence it has known since World War II. The
economy, more than the new constitution (*see p. 179*), dominates the national agenda. Regionalism and Quebec separatism,
though still a strain on the fabric of Confederation, have re-
ceded in the public mind. According to opinion polls and pun-
dits, Canadians are more confident about the prospects for
national unity than at any time in recent memory. Some say the
national mood has not been as buoyant and assertive since 1967,
the 100th anniversary of independence.[1]

As the national agenda has changed, so have the leaders. An
era ended last June with the departure of Pierre Elliott Trudeau, the acerbic, charismatic intellectual who with but one
brief interruption had been Canada's prime minister since 1968.
Soon after he stepped down, turning the Liberal Party and the
prime ministership over to John Turner, the momentum for
change quickened. In parliamentary elections on Sept. 4, Brian
Mulroney led the Progressive Conservative ("Tory") Party to a
sweeping national victory, winning a popular majority and un-
challenged control of the House of Commons.[2]

Mulroney, a lawyer from Quebec, leads the most broadly
representative government in a quarter-century. While it is
uncertain if the election will mark an enduring political realignment, several things have become clear during Mulroney's first
six months in office. One is that he has cast aside Trudeau's
economic nationalism and put out the welcome mat to foreign
investment, to the delight of American business and the White
House. President Reagan, who has expressed admiration for
Mulroney, will visit him in Quebec City on March 17-18.
Mulroney has twice called on Reagan in Washington, first as a
leader of the opposition last June and again three weeks after
the September election. He returned to the United States in
December to tell the Economic Club of New York: "Canada is
open for business again."

---

[1] See "A Confident Nation Speaks Up," *Maclean's*, Jan. 7, 1985.
[2] The other house of Parliament, the Senate, commands far less power than the House of
Commons; its 104 members are appointed by the prime minister and may serve until age 75
— some for life. Because of the long years of Liberal rule, most (currently 72) of the
senators are Liberals. Conservatives have recently charged them with obstructing
legislation.

While Mulroney's Tories attempt to consolidate their massive victory, the defeated Liberals are engaging in a review and reappraisal, much like Democrats in the United States.[3] Elections could bring new governments this year in the two largest provinces, Ontario and Quebec. In Quebec, where the uncertain national aspirations of the French-speaking majority have long been a national obsession, the separatist forces are in retreat. Sovereignty for Quebec is fading. The Progressive Conservative Party in Ontario, which has governed Canada's most populous province since 1943, has chosen a leader (Frank Miller) whose immoderate views could jeopardize its control. Elsewhere, the provinces are looking forward to better relations with the federal government — a relationship that has been marked by bitter quarrels, especially in the West.

Canada faces critical decisions in social policy. The universality of social welfare programs, for years considered sacrosanct, is being questioned. Capital punishment, which was abolished in 1976, may be restored. Abortion is being challenged in the courts. New laws on divorce and prostitution will be introduced this year. Much of the impetus for change will come from the judiciary, which is beginning to interpret the nation's Charter of Rights and Freedoms, a key element of constitutional reform enacted in 1982 after years of national debate.[4] Challenges to old laws are beginning to reshape the legal system. Now, in effect, the courts will begin to make law, and their judgments will touch every aspect of life.

Directions of a New Tory Government

As old problems are being met with new policies and politicians, there is less pessimism and self-doubt. Much of the surge of self-confidence is attributed to the change of government, bringing to office a party with broad electoral support. After six months in office, the Conservatives still enjoy widespread popularity, though there are signs the honeymoon is coming to an end. The government has moved decisively in some areas, but its general approach has been cautious and deliberate. There have been no grand designs, few initiatives, and little bloodletting in the civil service. The Conservatives, still finding their feet after years in opposition, have been reluctant to chart a new course.

In its early months, the government has been listening and studying. Consultation has become the byword in Ottawa, giving new flavor to the maxim: "When in doubt, consult." Studies, inquiries and task forces have been launched on several issues,

---

[3] See "Post-1984 Political Landscape," *E.R.R.*, 1985 Vol. I, pp. 21-40.
[4] For background on the constitution and the political and historic forces that shaped it, see "Canada's Political Conflicts," *E.R.R.*, 1981 Vol. II, pp. 957-980.

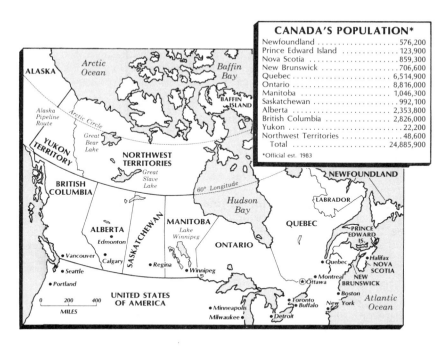

including tax reform, free trade, foreign policy, day care, social security and government spending. To underscore its commitment to cooperation, a national meeting of business, labor and interest groups will convene this month to discuss the economy. It follows a meeting between Mulroney and premiers of the 10 provinces in mid-February.

Jeffrey Simpson, a leading political columnist, wrote[5] that the government leaders simply have not made up their mind on anything: "Uncertain of where they want to take Canada, unwilling as yet to make hard decisions, determined to massage rather than challenge voters, trapped by the intellectual unreality of their campaign, the Mulroney ministers are leading by following public opinion."

Still, Mulroney has used his first six months to sketch his objectives. In the Speech from the Throne[6] on Nov. 5 opening Canada's 33rd Parliament and unveiling the government's legislative program, there was the promise of less government, a stronger economy, better relations with the United States, cooperation with the provinces, and assistance for women, pensioners, and "native people" (Indians and Inuits). The speech held few surprises. More telling was the composition of

---

[5] In the Toronto *Globe and Mail*, Jan. 31, 1985.

[6] The Speech from the Throne is comparable to an American president's State of the Union address to Congress. However, the prime minister does not make the speech, although it reflects his aims. In keeping with tradition and Canada's British past, the governor general (currently Jeanne Sauvé), acting on behalf of the absent monarch, delivers the address.

the new House of Commons. Almost half of the members, 134 of 282, were new. It had more women and more businessmen than before, and the average age had dropped from 49 to 45. The new faces best symbolized the change in Ottawa.

Mulroney called his mandate a "historic opportunity to overcome past divisions in the country and to purge the spirit of confrontation from the conduct of the nation's affairs." The message, a mixture of conservatism and pragmatism, reflected the new prime minister's background (*see p. 180*). For a country in need of balm, he offered a soothing statement of purpose. Predictably, the opposition was not impressed. "It offers only mediation, contemplation, rumination, and most of all, hesitation," scoffed Liberal leader John Turner. On most questions, the approach has been moderate. The new Cabinet has regional and ideological balance. All major appointments have been widely applauded.[7]

Retreat From Past Economic Nationalism

The government has been less vague on the economy, which represents its greatest challenge. During the election campaign, Mulroney promised less interventionism, a freer market, deregulation, more jobs and, most of all, smaller deficits. While his hope for economic growth is based on lower interest rates and a flood of foreign investments, both matters depend greatly on decisions — governmental and corporate — that are made in America. By early 1985 the Canadian dollar remained weak against its American counterpart and unemployment was still in double figures. Moreover, interest rates had begun to rise.[8]

Perhaps the greatest impediment to economic recovery is an accumulated national debt of $190 billion. The deficit for the current fiscal year is expected to be $34.5 billion and for the one beginning April 1 some $37.1 billion[9] — comparable to the U.S. federal budget deficit for a country with a population of about 25 million, only slightly more than one-tenth of America's.[10] It would amount to about 8 percent of Canada's projected $422 billion gross national product, the total value of the goods and services the country produces. It is one of the highest deficit-GNP ratios among Western industrial nations.

---

[7] For example, Mulroney named Stephen Lewis, a former leader of the New Democratic Party in Ontario, ambassador to the United Nations; Douglas Roche, a former Conservative member of Parliament and passionate advocate of arms control, as disarmament ambassador; and Gerald LaForest, a distinguished legal scholar, to the Supreme Court of Canada.

[8] The Canadian dollar was valued at only about 72 U.S. cents on international money markets early in March; In January, unemployment amounted to 11.2 percent of the work force, down only slightly from 12.8 percent in 1982 at the depth of the recession. Inflation, in contrast, was running at about 3.8 percent, down from a high mark of 12.5 percent in 1981.

[9] Figures cited by Finance Minister Michael Wilson, Nov. 8, 1984. All financial figures in this report are expressed in terms of Canadian dollars unless otherwise noted.

[10] The U.S. population is currently estimated at about 237 million and the fiscal 1985 deficit at $215 billion (U.S. dollars).

Canada's Time of Change

In his first economic statement to Parliament, Finance Minister Michael Wilson reaffirmed his commitment to reducing the deficit. He promptly cut $3.2 billion from the budget. For Wilson, a former investment dealer from Toronto, reducing the deficit is an article of faith. He worries that the debt robs the government of control of its spending priorities, drives up interest rates and leads foreigners to question the reliability of Canada as a place to invest. By instituting a review of federal spending, closing loopholes in the tax system, and selling Crown (state-owned) corporations, he hopes to make a modest reduction. But as his predecessors have discovered, there is little discretionary spending in the budget. In the $105.4 billion budget roughly one-third goes to service the debt, another third in transfer payments to the provinces for health care and education, and a final third for social service entitlement programs. Defense spending accounts for $9.4 billion.

Wilson, realizing his predicament, ordered a review of old-age pensions, family allowances and baby bonuses. But the prospect of examining social security — which the Conservatives pledged not to touch — caused an uproar in Parliament. Under heavy criticism from the opposition, the government retreated. Mulroney overruled his finance minister and declared he would look only at ways to redistribute benefits, not use savings to reduce the deficit. Wilson lost the battle over social spending and appeared to be losing the war on the deficit as well.

The problem with the economy, however, runs deeper than the deficit. This summer a blue-ribbon commission will issue a final report after a two-year study. It is likely to recommend that Canada liberalize its trading practices with other nations, stop subsidizing unprofitable industries, and switch its emphasis from natural resources to high technology. The process has been under way for years; the question now is whether the new government will make a new industrial strategy its top priority. The commission has already stimulated a national debate on the future of the economy.[11]

In the short term the government wants to stimulate the economy by invigorating the private sector. It has already decontrolled natural gas prices, which means that for the first time since 1975 the prices are set by buyers and sellers, not the government.[12] It has also promised to modify the National

---

[11] See "Challenges and Choices," preliminary report of the Royal Commission on the Economic Union and Development Prospects of Canada, Minister of Supply and Services, Ottawa, 1984.

[12] *The Wall Street Journal* reported Feb. 15, 1985, that the average price of Canada's natural gas sales to the United States had declined by 20 percent since November. America's growing imports of Canadian energy, especially oil and gas, accounted for 70 percent of Canada's trade surplus with the United States. After Mexico, Canada is America's biggest foreign supplier of petroleum.

Energy Program (NEP) which Trudeau instituted in 1980, sell public corporations valued at $6 billion and relax rules on foreign investments. While the business community has applauded these changes, their impact is uncertain. Canada's economy is so dependent on the United States that all hopes for a durable recovery inevitably turn on lower interest rates and continued prosperity south of the border.

Closer U.S. Relations Under Mulroney

The new government has made improved U.S. relations a priority. Mulroney talks of renewing "the special relationship" — a term used to describe the relationship in the 1960s, before both Canada and the United States began to assert their economic interests more aggressively. Nearly half of the manufacturing in Canada is foreign-owned, and four-fifths of the foreign ownership is American. The Economist of London has observed that "no other industrial country is as dependent on foreign capital as Canada." [13] Seven of its 12 biggest companies are owned or run from outside the country.

In promising changes on energy policy, Mulroney hopes to eliminate a lingering source of friction. A particularly sore point with American petroleum investors is a provision which retroactively gives the Canadian government a 25 percent share of oil and gas discoveries that private companies make on lands they lease from the government. Wall Street, especially, cheered Mulroney's plan to abolish the Foreign Investment Review Agency (FIRA), established under Trudeau to screen foreign investment, and replace it with a promotion-minded body called Investment Canada. [14]

Problems remain in Canadian-U.S. relations despite the new harmony. Canada is worried about acid rain and frustrated that Washington does not act to alleviate it by curbing pollutants arising from smokestack industries in the upper Midwest. Canada also perceives a rising threat of protectionism among American industries and sees it as a threat to its access to American markets. Each country is the other's biggest trading partner, but the trade is of far greater importance to Canada's smaller economy. [15] Trade is likely to be high on the agenda when Mulroney and Reagan meet in Quebec City, and is certain

[13] "Canada counts on other people's money," *The Economist*, Nov. 3, 1984, p. 88.

[14] For American business views of new investment opportunities in Canada, see "Canada Warms Up to U.S. Business," by Rod McQueen, in *Fortune*, March 4, 1985, pp. 114-120.

[15] While about three-fourths of Canada's exports go to the United States, only about a fifth of America's exports go to Canada. During the first nine months last year, for which official U.S. figures are available, the United States exported $34.9 billion in goods to Canada and imported $49.4 billion (amounts expressed in U.S. dollars). This trade amounted to 21.5 percent of all U.S. exports and 20.0 percent of all U.S. imports during that period. Canada's trade surplus with the United States is usually offset by a net outflow to the United States on dividends, interest and tourism.

Canada and Free Trade

In 1911, the Liberal Party campaigned for re-election on a platform of free trade with the United States. The proposal rejected the National Policy implemented by Sir John A. Macdonald, Canada's first prime minister, which erected a high tariff wall to protect infant industry from foreign competition. The Tories, urging "no truck or trade with the Yankees," routed the Liberals. The election defined Canada's economic structure for years to come. Only recently has the idea of free trade — the movement of goods across national borders without restrictive tariffs, duties and quotas — become attractive again.

The country rejected free trade, or trade reciprocity as it was called in 1911, because it feared its political sovereignty would be compromised in an emerging economic union. Yet slowly, almost imperceptibly, the high tariff walls have fallen. By 1987, three-quarters of Canada's trade with the United States — which now totals around $150 billion a year — will be duty-free.* Increasingly, free trade is seen as the best way for Canada to secure markets for its exports in a more competitive world.

Trade is critical to Canada. Exports are the engine of economic growth. Canada had a trade surplus of $20 billion in 1984, up from $17 billion in 1983. Exports grew by a third.

In a discussion paper issued in February, the government proposed four options in forging a new trading relationship with the United States: the status quo, sectoral free trade, full free trade, and a framework agreement to promote trade between the two countries. It appeared to favor the last proposal, which would mean determining how to ease trade barriers between the countries, a process the government could initiate before it decides how far to go in pursuing free trade.

The call for free trade has been building in Canada for the past decade. A Senate committee, the Economic Council of Canada and several leading economists and business organizations have urged the government to seek an agreement on free trade in one form or another. A royal commission on the economy is likely to make a similar recommendation in its final report later this year. The Liberal government began negotiations with the United States on free trade in several sectors. Canada already has sectoral free trade in automobiles and defense products. The talks lapsed, however, after the Conservatives were elected.

*Under terms of the international General Agreement on Tariffs and Trade (GATT). See "Global Recession and U.S. Trade," E.R.R., 1983 Vol. I, pp. 169-188.

to dominate the Canadian-U.S. relationship in the near future. The two governments now appear ready to begin in serious negotiations of a new, and possibly historic, agreement.

In a country whose size and proximity to America has always fed an undercurrent of nationalism, Mulroney's embrace of the United States has drawn criticism. "Mr. Mulroney went down to New York to say that, hey, Canada is open for business again," John Turner commented. "I say to Mr. Mulroney — maybe, but Canada is not for sale." Jean Chrétién, Turner's former minister of external affairs, recently told an audience at Harvard University: "A partnership between equals is one thing. A master-servant relationship is quite another." [16]

Dealing With Separatism and the West

In matters of federal-provincial relations there is a new vitality. Quebec's governing Parti Québécois, in a stunning reversal of policy, decided in January to remove independence from its election platform. To many of the party's supporters, the struggle for independence was its only reason for existence. The decision split the party and threatened to bring down the provincial government.

This turn of events will not douse the fires of nationalism, or the desire of Mulroney to accommodate his home province. Premier René Lévesque, unable to reach a deal with Trudeau, seems inclined to open negotiations with Mulroney to restore Quebec's historic veto over many national matters, which it lost in constitutional negotiations in 1981. It is uncertain whether there will be time to strike a deal before Quebec's next election, expected in June. If Lévesque and his Parti Québécois are defeated by the province's Liberal Party, the rejuvenated Quebec Liberals can be expected to deal with Ottawa. One way or another, the province is expected to find common ground for a settlement of some immediate grievances.

All provincial governments are in Conservative hands except in Quebec, British Columbia (Social Credit Party) and Manitoba (New Democratic Party). As if to symbolize Ottawa's desire to court the provinces and usher in a new era of cooperation, the prime minister and premiers met in February for an "economic summit" at Regina, Saskatchewan — the first that was not held in Ottawa. All the provinces have their grievances: Alberta wants changes in the National Energy Program; Saskatchewan wants better water management; British Columbia wants protection for its critical forest industries; industrial Ontario wants job creation. Accommodating their diverse and often conflicting aspirations will test Mulroney's capacity for compromise. Conflict between the central government and the provinces is as old as Canada itself. It inheres in the structure of government, and is unlikely to fade under Conservative rule. But for now the mood is sunny.

---

[16] Chrétién was quoted in the *Toronto Star*, Dec. 3, 1984, and Lewis in *Maclean's*, Oct. 8, 1984.

Political Realignment

FOR nearly 16 years Pierre Elliott Trudeau dominated Canadian politics. From the time he swept into office on a wave of "Trudeaumania" in 1968, this enigmatic Quebecer evoked strong emotions. At one time he represented the idealistic, bilingual Canadian, the image of what many Canadians aspired to be. He won four elections (1968, 1972, 1974, 1980), made bilingualism the law of the land, forged a new constitution, and established an international reputation. He entered politics to pursue his vision of a united, tolerant country that could accommodate two cultures and two languages. He left a charter of rights but an ailing economy and a disenchanted people.

Trudeau's Liberals were narrowly defeated in May 1979 by a Conservative Party led by Joe Clark, a young Albertan whose vision of the country differed sharply from Trudeau's. But Clark faltered and an election the following February returned Trudeau to office with the biggest Liberal majority in the House of Commons since 1968. Trudeau resolved to make the most of his remarkable political return. He knew he would have one last chance to pursue a lifelong goal to bring home ("patriate") the British North American Act, the nation's founding charter which had resided in London since the Confederation of Canada was created by an act of the British Parliament in 1867.

Trudeau not only wanted to erase his country's last vestige of colonialism, he sought a Charter of Rights and Freedoms guaranteeing basic human rights. His proposals sparked an acrimonious struggle between the federal government and eight provinces (Ontario and New Brunswick sided with the federal government) which raged for two years. On April 17, 1982, the new constitution was finally proclaimed. Though less comprehensive than the one Trudeau had sought, it did have an amending formula. Canada could now change its constitution without asking Britain. The new constitution was widely hailed as an exercise in nation-building, helping to define the Canadian identity.

While the government was preoccupied with the constitution, the economy went bad. Interest rates, unemployment and inflation soared. Determined to defeat inflation, the government imposed an austerity program limiting wages and prices in federally regulated sectors. By 1983 the recovery had taken hold but the Liberals remained out of favor. Long unpopular in western Canada, where they held only two seats in the House of Commons, they also found themselves in trouble in Ontario and in the Atlantic provinces. Many Liberals hoped Trudeau would step down.

But he had unfinished business. In 1983, he set off on a personal mission to gather international support for renewed disarmament talks between the United States and the Soviet Union. His crusade took him around the world for meetings with heads of state and government, including Reagan and Soviet Premier Yuri V. Andropov. While Trudeau, by now a senior statesman, was welcomed as a voice of moderation, his proposals — including a five-power summit meeting and a ban on the militarization of space — yielded few results. But Canadians suspended their growing distaste for the prime minister and embraced his mission enthusiastically. By the time Trudeau reported to Parliament in February 1984 the Liberals and Conservatives were running neck and neck in the opinion polls.

Then on Feb. 29 Trudeau went for a walk in a snowstorm, contemplated his future, and announced he was quitting politics. Within a few days, the race for the leadership of the Liberal Party began. Amid a crowded field of Cabinet ministers, two stood out: Jean Chrétién, a folksy Quebecer whose candor and pugnacity characterized his 21 years in politics; and John Turner, a handsome, urbane lawyer-businessman from Toronto who had previously served in Parliament and Trudeau's Cabinet. Turner had the support of the party establishment while Chrétién inspired emotion and affection among ordinary Liberals. Turner won at the party's leadership convention in Ottawa in June. He was sworn in as prime minister on July 1, Canada Day, and, confident of his lead in the polls, soon called an election for Sept. 4

Conservative Party's Sweeping Mandate

While the Liberals were picking a leader, the Tories were preparing for an election. In Brian Mulroney, they saw the prospect for their first majority government since 1958. The Conservative Party had never forgiven Joe Clark for losing power after only nine months in office. When the Tories returned to the opposition, a move to unseat Clark was already afoot. He failed to win more than two-thirds support at his party's biennial convention in Winnipeg in February 1983 and, seeking a new mandate, called a leadership convention for the following June. The winner was Mulroney, the man Clark defeated for the same job in 1976.

Mulroney, who turns 46 on March 20, was born in the remote, paper-mill town of Baie Comeau on the St. Lawrence River 265 miles north of Quebec City. He grew up speaking English at home and French with his playmates, becoming fluently bi-lingual. He attended St. Francis Xavier University in Nova Scotia, where he became active in the Conservative Party. Upon graduating in 1964 from the Laval University Law School in Quebec City, he joined a prestigious Montreal law firm and specialized in labor litigation on behalf of management. Later he became president of the Iron Ore Co. of Canada, an American subsidiary.

Brian Mulroney

While Mulroney worked for the Tories in Quebec and established a reputation as being energetic and charming, he never ran for office. When he sought the party's leader-ship position in 1976, he was criti-cized as being too young, too smooth and too inexperienced. But when he ran in 1984, he won largely because he persuaded the Conservatives that he would strengthen the party in Quebec, the Liberal bastion. He repeatedly reminded that 112 mem-bers of the House of Commons represented ridings (election districts) in which at least 10 percent of the voters were French-speaking ("francophone"), but the Tories held only two of them. To form a majority government, they would have to do better.

Turner's decision to call an election within weeks of becoming prime minister — his mandate ran until February 1985 — turned out to be politically fatal. The Liberal Party was ex-hausted from its convention and ill-prepared to fight an elec-tion. Turner undermined the image of freshness by making few changes in the Cabinet he inherited from Trudeau and by rewarding longtime Liberals with patronage posts. The Tories gleefully exploited the issue. Midway through the campaign, Turner fired his campaign manager and replaced him with a veteran strategist who had engineered two decades of Liberal victories. For a beleaguered Turner, it was too late.

While Turner stumbled, plagued by poor television appear-ances, Mulroney was leading a united party. On Sept. 4, the Tories won 211 of the 282 seats in the House of Commons, the most by any party in Canadian history.[17] The Liberals fell to 40 seats from 147, and the left-of-center New Democratic Party won 30, only one less than it held in the previous Parliament. The Conservatives took 55 percent of the popular vote and a

---

[17] The Conservatives won a greater percentage of the seats (208 of 265) in 1958, when the House of Commons had a smaller membership.

majority of the seats in every province. Most astounding was the breakthrough in Quebec. In a province where the Liberals had held 74 of 75 seats, the Conservatives won 58.

New Contours of the Political Landscape

The Conservative victory, so sweeping in its size, could mark a realignment of Canada's three-party system. Already the Conservatives are attempting to occupy the political center which the Liberals had held. The Tories will attempt to consolidate their base, especially in Quebec, through the kind of middle-of-the-road politics they have demonstrated in their first six months in office. With an eye on public opinion, they are tailoring their appeal to the broad middle class and to women and ethnic groups, three traditional areas of Liberal strength.

Conservatives well remember squandering the electoral majority they won in 1958. Led by John Diefenbaker, a populist from the Prairies, they captured 208 seats that year. But they made enough mistakes to enable the Liberals to regain power in 1963.[18] Accordingly, Mulroney has moved quickly to keep his large following intact. He is widely regarded as a consummate politician, sensitive to shifts in popular opinion. At his first Cabinet meeting, he reportedly told his ministers: "Ladies and gentlemen, the campaign for re-election begins today."

For the Liberals, the picture is far less sanguine. Reduced to little more than a rump, skeptical of their leader and uncertain of their ideology, they face the task of reviving what was one of the most formidable political parties in the Western world. The Liberals had called themselves Canada's natural governing party. They had governed with only one brief interruption since 1963 and had been out of office only twice in the last half-century. Their past leaders — Wilfrid Laurier, Mackenzie King, Louis St. Laurent, Lester B. Pearson and Trudeau — are leading figures in Canadian history. In alternating between English-speaking and French-speaking leaders, appealing to public opinion, co-opting the ideas of their adversaries, and running a well-financed electoral machine, they fashioned a long string of successes.[19]

The task of rebuilding the party will fall to John Turner. Many doubt that he can do it. He has often been derided as "yesterday's man" — a reference to a view of the world formed in the 1960s when he entered politics. Ironically, during his years of political self-exile in Toronto he was widely considered the heir apparent to Trudeau, the crown prince who could best

---

[18] For background on the Diefenbaker years, see Peter C. Newman's *Renegade in Power* (1965).
[19] For background, see *Grits, an Intimate Portrait of the Liberal Party* by Christina McCall-Newman (1982). The book was a best-seller in Canada.

preserve the dynasty. Turner was born in British Columbia June 7, 1929, and later moved to Ottawa. He was a Rhodes scholar at Oxford before entering law practice in Montreal in 1962. He held a succession of Cabinet posts, including minister of finance, before resigning in 1975 over a personality conflict with Trudeau. Turner, who led a life blessed with success, now faces simmering dissension. If he cannot narrow the Tory lead in the polls, he will have trouble winning the confidence of his party when it reviews his leadership next year.

What most frightens the Liberals is the strength of the New Democratic Party, which sees their weakness as an opportunity to broaden its base. The NDP, a quasi-socialist party, ultimately would like to displace the Liberals in a new two-party system. It would occupy the liberal left, leaving the Tories on the conservative right. Already the party is considering the softening of some of the more controversial elements in its platform — such as calling for Canada's withdrawal from the North Atlantic Treaty Organization (NATO) and nationalizing the banks. The NDP's leftist image holds its share of the popular vote to about 20 percent, which comes mainly from Ontario and the western provinces. As the party surveys it future, it sees a respected leader (Ed Broadbent) and an experienced parliamentary caucus, loyal partisans including organized labor, and a strong organization in provincial politics.

Shifting Fortunes of Quebec Separatism

All parties look longingly at Quebec, the most unpredictable of the provinces. The Tories want to consolidate their base while the Liberals want to restore theirs. The New Democrats simply want to establish a beachhead. Over the next five years, all three parties will try to strengthen their presence in the province, Canada's second most-populous (after Ontario) and the home of six million French-speaking Canadians.

Like the rest of Canada, Quebec is breaking with the past. It has been retreating from militant separatism since a referendum in 1980, when Quebec voters refused to give the provincial government a mandate to negotiate "sovereignty-association" with the federal government. The plan envisioned political independence but a loose economic association with Canada. Three timely, carefully crafted speeches by Trudeau, coupled with misjudgments by the Parti Québécois and its leader, Premier Lévesque, are largely credited with turning the tide. The proposal was defeated by a 60-40 margin.

Still, the Parti Québécois, which won power in a stunning election upset in 1976, clung to the dream of an independent Quebec. Last June it voted to make independence the central

People Who Speak . . .

	English only	French only	Both	Neither
Alberta	92.4%	0.2%	6.4%	1.0%
British Columbia	92.8	0.1	5.7	1.4
Manitoba	90.3	0.3	7.9	1.5
New Brunswick	60.5	13.0	26.5	0.1
Newfoundland	97.6	0.0	2.3	0.1
Northwest Territories	79.9	0.1	6.0	13.9
Nova Scotia	92.3	0.2	7.4	0.1
Ontario	86.7	0.7	10.8	1.7
Prince Edward Island	91.7	0.2	8.1	0.0
Quebec	6.7	60.1	32.4	0.8
Saskatchewan	94.6	0.1	4.6	0.8
Yukon Territory	79.9	0.0	7.9	0.2
Total	67.0	16.6	15.3	1.2

Source: Statistics Canada, 1981 census

issue in the next provincial election even though polls indicated that fewer than 20 percent of the Quebecers supported it. Lévesque, the emotional, chain-smoking journalist who founded the party in 1967, never agreed that it should make independence the centerpiece of its election platform. With the election of Mulroney, he saw an opportunity for a new constitutional agreement to restore Quebec's historic veto. His decision to ask the party to reverse its commitment to independence shocked its militants. Some ministers in his Cabinet left, including some of his most trusted confidants. The government's majority in the 122-member legislative Assembly has been reduced to three. Lévesque is likely to call an election later this year, though it can be held as late as next March.

Why the decline in separatism? One reason is mentioned often. For years Quebec was driven to strengthen its French culture and language because it feared losing them in English-speaking North America. Now those fears have subsided. Quebec has preserved its language. Bilingualism is the law in Canada and one-third of the public service is French-speaking. Federal services are available in most places in Canada in both languages. Quebecers spend their everyday lives, speaking their ancestral tongue. Many now feel they can advance their social and cultural interests within the Confederation.

Even before the Parti Québécois jettisoned independence from its election platform, it was losing support. Its image as a social democratic government was eroded when it rolled back the salaries of provincial employees and halted labor negotiations in the public sector. It was further weakened when the courts struck down key parts of its sweeping language legislation, called Bill 101, which forbade the use of English in the legislature and on public signs. Since the party buried its independence option, its popularity has risen. While a year ago its prospects of re-election were minimal, it is now given an even chance. The leader of the Liberal opposition is Robert Bourassa who served as premier in 1970-76 and returned after his successor, Claude Ryan, lost to Lévesque in 1981.

Setting the Agenda

A S MUCH as bringing Quebec into the constitutional accord is an aim of the new government in Ottawa, so is improving the climate of federal-provincial relations. The four western provinces — British Columbia, Alberta, Saskatchewan and Manitoba — are likely to gain special attention. Under the Liberals, who had no representation at either the federal or provincial level of government west of Manitoba, the West felt neglected. Historically, it has always resented the dominance of central Canada. It has complained that the cost of shipping its raw materials east was too high and the prices it received for them, particularly for oil and gas, were too low. The new Conservative government is well represented in the four provinces, holding 58 of their 77 seats in the House of Commons. Understandably, it has promised to address western concerns.

But how it will soothe the region's deep-seated grievances is uncertain. The new question of Canadian politics in the 1980s may ask what the West wants, just as in the 1960s the question was what Quebec wanted. All the provinces have their shopping lists. The government may be able to protect the forestry industry in British Columbia and please the oil industry in Alberta, but a far greater task will be renegotiating cost-sharing agreements which expire next year. If the government attempts to cut its share of payments for postsecondary education, manpower training and health, it can expect the kind of conflict that marked the Trudeau years.

Trudeau saw federalism as a balance of power between two levels of government and praised its creative tension. He feared and fought the devolution of power from the center because, in his words, it would make "Ottawa the headwaiter for the provinces." Mulroney talks about a greater role for the provinces and his promise of conciliation and compromise is attractive, but he believes in a strong central government far more than western Tories do. He may offer the premiers a role in shaping national economic policy, but he is unlikely to allow a significant realignment of power in a country which is already one of the most decentralized in the world.

Divisive Social Questions; Defining Rights

Several social issues are crowding the national agenda. The most pressing is capital punishment. Although Canada abolished the death penalty in 1976,[20] the murders of several policemen in recent months have renewed calls to restore hanging, which was last used in 1962. While Mulroney personally opposes capital punishment, public opinion and his party's parliamentary caucus are against him. Mulroney appears to be trying to keep the issue from coming before Parliament until the public mood has time to cool.

Abortion is also an emotional question in Canada. Abortion is legal if a committee of three doctors in a certified hospital determines that a woman's life or health is in danger. Usually the approval is a formality. The law has been in place for several years but critics say it is inequitable because only 271 of the country's 1,348 hospitals have abortion committees. Henry Morgentaler, a Montreal doctor, has been opening clinics in Ontario and challenging the law. A jury recently acquitted him of running an illegal clinic, and the government of Ontario is appealing the decision. All sides want the law clarified, but many believe the law is the best compromise on an issue that offers no workable consensus.

Through revisions of Canada's body of criminal laws, prostitution is likely to come under greater control. The government, besieged by complaints from angry city dwellers, will introduce legislation to outlaw soliciting on the street. Under current law, it must be "pressing and persistent," a criterion which police found impossible to prove. The government will not outlaw prostitution, but it will drive it off the streets. It also expressed its intention to liberalize divorce laws.

While some believe the election of the Conservatives signals a swing to the right, it is not reflected in social policy. Legislation on prostitution is likely to be stricter but not draconian. The abortion question will probably go unresolved, and capital punishment has yet to come to a vote. In Canada, a nation with a history of moderation and absence of extremes, governments are most comfortable occupying the center.

Challenges to many laws — on Sunday shopping, provincial movie censorship, and rights of the accused — are coming before the Supreme Court. Hundreds of cases invoking the Charter of Rights and Freedoms have been heard in the lower

---

[20] In 1967 Canada outlawed the death penalty for all but persons convicted of murdering prison guards or policemen. Then in 1976, upon Trudeau's impassioned plea, all capital punishment was abolished, though by a close vote in Parliament.

courts Among those that have reached the Supreme Court, it recently struck down a federal law for the first time. The charter seems destined to change the nature of the Supreme Court, which until now has been restricted to interpreting laws enacted by Parliament — unlike in the United States where the judiciary has long been a separate and equal branch of government with a tradition of passing on a law's constitutionality. Under the leadership of Chief Justice Brian Dickson, a cautiously liberal jurist from Manitoba, the Canadian Supreme Court is moving from a musty, often remote, institution to one that may rival Parliament. When he was sworn in last year as chief justice, Dickson offered this assessment of the court's responsibility: "We are going to have a much more important function as an umpire between the state and the individual to make sure the individual rights are protected."

Post-Trudeau Conduct of Foreign Policy

With Trudeau's departure, Canada lost its most eloquent spokesman on the international stage. The Trudeau years marked a change in foreign policy from the style of diplomacy practiced by the man he succeeded, Lester Pearson, a career diplomat who won the Nobel Peace Prize for negotiating a cease-fire in the 1956 Arab-Israeli War. Under Trudeau, Canada withdrew from its traditional role as "honest broker" and peacemaker, and began to pursue its national interests more vigorously.

Mulroney has none of Trudeau's international credentials. His intellectual interest in foreign affairs is unlikely to match Trudeau's. Still, he has said foreign policy will be a priority for his government. That in itself is revealing. In Canada, a middle power of modest capabilities, foreign policy attracts little attention in the legislative process. Within weeks of entering office, Mulroney ordered a review of foreign policy. Joe Clark, the former prime minister, became secretary of state for external affairs (foreign minister), and promised that Canada would continue to emphasize its role as a trading nation.

In public pronouncements, the government says peace and disarmament are its main objectives. It has promised to play a leading role in the search for peace. "We believe the nuclear buildup threatens the life of every Canadian, and the existence of human society," Clark said in an address to the U.N. General Assembly on Sept. 25. "Countries like our own must use our influence to reverse that buildup and reduce the danger of destruction." The question is, of course, whether Canada wields enough influence in the councils of the world to make a difference. That, like so many other lofty goals of the government, is uncertain.

Selected Bibliography

Books

Cahill, Jack, *John Turner*, McClelland and Stewart, 1984.

Canadian Almanac and Directory, Clark Copp Pittman Ltd., 1984.

Clarkson, Stephen, *Canada and the Reagan Challenge*, Canadian Institute of Economic Policy, 1981.

Doran, Charles, *Forgotten Partnership: U.S.-Canada Relations Today*, Johns Hopkins University Press, 1984.

Fried, Edward F., *U.S.-Canadian Economic Relations*, Brookings Institution, 1984.

Gwyn, Richard, *The Northern Magus* , McClelland and Stewart, 1980.

McCall-Newman, Christina, *Grits, An Intimate Portrait of the Liberal Party*, Macmillan of Canada, 1982.

Martin, Lawrence, *The Presidents and the Prime Ministers: Washington and Ottawa Face to Face: The Myth of Bilateral Bliss, 1867-1982*, Doubleday, 1983.

Martin, Patrick, et al., *Contenders: The Tory Quest for Power*, Prentice-Hall of Canada, 1983.

MacDonald, L. Ian, *Mulroney: The Making of the Prime Minister*, McClelland and Stewart, 1984.

Morton, Desmond, *A Short History of Canada*, Hurtig Publishers, 1983.

Simpson, Jeffrey, *Discipline of Power: The Conservative Interlude and the Liberal Restoration*, Personal Library (publisher), 1980.

Articles

Current History, May 1984 issue devoted to Canadian affairs.

McQueen, Rod, "Canada Warms Up to U.S. Business," *Fortune*, March 4, 1985.

Newman, Peter C., "A Confident Nation Speaks Up," *Maclean's*, Jan. 8, 1965.

Wilson-Smith, Anthony, "The Eclipse of Separatism," *Maclean's*, Jan. 21, 1985.

Reports and Studies

"Canada and the United States," 68th American Assembly, (American) Council on Foreign Relations, 1984.

"Challenges and Choices," preliminary report of the Royal Commission on the Economic Union and Development Prospects for Canada," 1984.

Editorial Research Reports: "Canada's Political Conflicts," 1981 Vol. II, p. 957; "Quebec Separatism," 1977 Vol. II, p. 825; "Canadian-American Relations," 1976 Vol. II, p. 807.

"Looking Outward," the Economic Council (Ottawa), 1975.

McKercher, William R., ed., "The U.S. Bill of Rights and the Canadian Charter of Rights and Freedoms, Ontario Economic Council, 1983.

"Report on the Nation," *The Financial Post* (Toronto), winter 1984-85.

"Statements and Speeches," Department of External Affairs, 1980-85.

Graphics: Map and cover illustration by Staff Artist Kathleen Ossenfort; Canadian government photo, p. 181.

CAMBODIA:
A NATION
IN TURMOIL

by

Marc Leepson

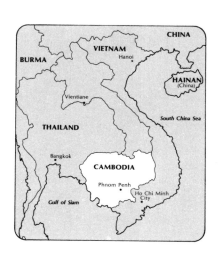

**Apr. 5
1 9 8 5**

CAMBODIA:
A NATION IN TURMOIL

"WHEN ELEPHANTS FIGHT," an ancient Asian saying has it, "the grass gets trampled." Nowhere has that adage been more true in recent years than in the small Southeast Asian nation of Cambodia. The country's troubles began in earnest in 1970 when Cambodian communist troops, known as the Khmer Rouge, stepped up their war to gain control of the country from the newly installed, U.S.-backed Cambodian government led by Gen. Lon Nol. Hundreds of thousands of Cambodians died in that civil war as well as in the American bombing of Vietnamese communist sanctuaries in Cambodia.

The Khmer Rouge triumph came a decade ago, two years after U.S. troops had left Indochina and just two weeks before the South Vietnamese government surrendered to North Vietnam. On April 17, 1975, the Khmer Rouge marched into the Cambodian capital of Phnom Penh and set up a communist regime with Pol Pot at its head. That government proceeded to put Cambodia through a hell as brutal and terrifying as any of history's great atrocities. Millions were forcibly removed from the cities and sent to do forced manual labor in rural villages. Schools, libraries and banks were burned. Soldiers, government workers, scientists, doctors, other professionals and their families were systematically murdered.

The Khmer Rouge's holocaust against its own people, in which it is believed as many as two million died, ended when Soviet-backed Vietnam invaded Cambodia on Christmas Day 1978. The Vietnamese took over the country in January, installing a puppet government headed by Heng Samrin, a defector from the Khmer Rouge army. Cambodians initially greeted their Vietnamese "liberators" with relief. But tens of thousands soon perished due to a famine, caused primarily because the invasion prevented the planting of the annual rice crop. "All told, these calamities killed somewhere between two and three million Cambodians from 1970 to 1980, which was between 20 and 35 percent of the pre-war population," said Cambodian expert Stephen J. Morris.[1]

---

[1] Stephen J. Morris, "Vietnam's Vietnam," *The Atlantic,* January 1985, p. 71. Morris, an Australian, is a researcher at the Institute of East Asian Studies at the University of California, Berkeley. He visited Cambodia in 1983 and 1984. Population figures for Cambodia are uncertain at best. There has never been a census, and the exact number of deaths attributable to the civil war and the Vietnamese invasion is disputed.

The nation's troubles continue today. The economy has been battered from 15 years of war and political and social instability. Basic services, such as electricity and medical care, are severely limited. Intermittent food shortages, widespread malnutrition and outbreaks of infectious disease continue. The current communist government is by most accounts extremely authoritarian, with little regard for human rights.

Aggravating day-to-day life is an ongoing guerrilla war against the 160,000-to-200,000 Vietnamese troops stationed on Cambodian soil. The three-pronged resistance movement consists of 25,000-40,000 Khmer Rouge troops and two non-communist groups: the Sihanouk National Army, a force of about 10,000 led by former Cambodian leader, Prince Norodom Sihanouk, and the 16,000-strong Khmer People's National Liberation Front led by Son Sann, a prime minister under Sihanouk in the 1960s. The three groups have formed the Coalition Government of Democratic Kampuchea (CGDK), headed by Prince Sihanouk. The CGDK represents Cambodia in the United Nations and has been recognized by 90 countries including the United States *(see p. 203)*.

Located primarily along the 450-mile Thai border, the resistance forces never have been strong enough to threaten seriously Vietnam's power in Cambodia. Nevertheless, every year during the November-to-May dry season, Vietnam has tried to crush the resistance groups by attacking their camps. The 1984-85 Vietnamese offensive has been particularly rough on the rebels; by mid-March the Vietnamese had overrun or forced the evacuation of all the main guerrilla camps, which also serve as refugee camps for families of the rebels and others uprooted by the war. Following the guerrillas into Thailand, Vietnamese units even engaged Thai government forces in battle.

Despite the apparent success of the Vietnamese offensive, it appears as if the resistance movement will still be able to harass the Vietnamese — especially after the rainy season begins in May. The Vietnamese "haven't done any serious, long-term damage" to the resistance forces, said Lyall Breckon, director of the State Department's Office of Vietnam, Laos and Cambodia Affairs. "On the whole, all they've done is to concentrate a numerically superior force and a force superior in terms of equipment against lightly armed guerrilla forces and civilians and made them move." [2] Most of the Khmer Rouge seem to have taken up new positions within the interior of Cambodia. Most of the non-communist fighters — who are not as well equipped as the Khmer Rouge — have retreated across the Thai border. The Vietnamese actions also forced about 250,000

---

[2] Breckon and others quoted in this report were interviewed by the author, unless otherwise indicated.

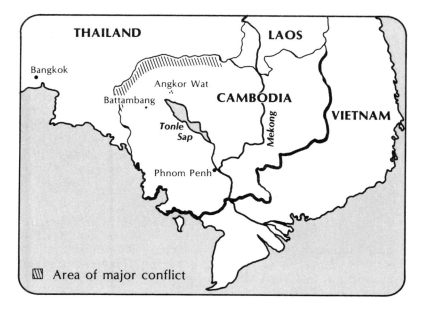

THAILAND

LAOS

Bangkok

Angkor Wat

Battambang

CAMBODIA

Tonle Sap

Mekong

VIETNAM

Phnom Penh

Ⓜ Area of major conflict

Cambodian civilians to flee the western part of their country and seek sanctuary in overcrowded and ill-equipped refugee camps in Thailand.

Motives Behind the Vietnamese Occupation

Western analysts disagree about the exact reasons behind Vietnam's occupation of Cambodia and its goals in that country. But there is near unanimous agreement in the West that the reasons put forward by Vietnam are, in the words of former U.S. Representative to the United Nations Jeane J. Kirkpatrick, "a transparent deception."[3] Vietnam's Prime Minister Pham Van Dong, in an interview published last year in *Newsweek* magazine, said his government "could not stand by in good conscience and watch the Pol Pot clique butcher millions of innocent Kampucheans in cold blood."[4] The evidence shows, however, that Vietnam knew of the Khmer Rouge terror for years prior to the invasion. "Hanoi showed not the slightest concern for the fate of the Cambodian people while most of the killing was actually going on," Morris said. "On the contrary, Vietnamese Communist Party and government statements were lush in their praise of Pol Pot and his regime."[5]

Some believe that Vietnam invaded Cambodia because it felt threatened by an aggressive and unfriendly Khmer Rouge government, which launched raids into Vietnam late in 1978. "The first thing that drives the Vietnamese is their own security

---

[3] Statement before the U.N. General Assembly, Oct. 30, 1984. Kirkpatrick resigned her post effective March 31.
[4] Quoted in *Newsweek*, May 14, 1984, p. 40.
[5] Morris, *op. cit.*, p. 76.

concerns," said Linda Hiebert, co-director of the Center for International Policy's Indochina Project.[6] "They would like to see a very close relationship between the three countries of Indochina [Cambodia, Laos and Vietnam] because that will maintain security on many levels — military, economic, et cetera." Arnold Isaacs, author of *Without Honor: Defeat in Vietnam and Cambodia* (1983), agreed. "What is uppermost in the Vietnamese minds is their own security," said Isaacs, who was a war correspondent for the Baltimore *Sun* in Indochina in 1972-75. "They feel they should be the dominant power in the region and ... the governments of Laos and Cambodia should be friendly and not a threat. . . ."

There may be another factor behind the invasion: Vietnam's desire to rid Cambodia of a government that was closely aligned with Vietnam's longtime enemy, China. "The major national security concerns of Vietnam's present leadership are to successfully weather Chinese pressures and to consolidate all the nations of Indochina into an alliance structure," said Southeast Asia expert Carlyle A. Thayer.[7] Stanley Karnow, a journalist and former Vietnam war correspondent, agreed with that assessment. The "real reason" behind the invasion, Karnow wrote in *Vietnam: A History,* was Vietnam's "concern that Pol Pot's forces, underwritten by China, intended to embark on a campaign to annex the Mekong Delta and other parts of Vietnam that had formally belonged to the Cambodian empire. 'When we look at Cambodia,' a Vietnamese official in Hanoi told me, 'we see China, China, China.' "[8]

Some analysts dismiss this argument. Despite centuries of antagonism between the two countries, they note, China was a strong supporter of Vietnam in its wars against France, the United States and South Vietnam. "Without the Chinese, the Vietnamese probably couldn't have 'won' the war against the United States," one expert who asked not to be identified told Editorial Research Reports. "That nullifies allegations that the Chinese represent a threat to the Vietnamese." China stopped sending military aid to the Vietnamese communists when they defeated South Vietnam in 1975, but continued to support Vietnam economically until June 1978 when Vietnam joined Comecon, the Soviet-dominated Council for Mutual Economic Assistance.

---

[6] The Washington-based Center for International Policy is a non-profit education and research organization concerned with U.S. policy toward the Third World and the impact on human rights and needs.

[7] Carlyle A. Thayer, "Vietnamese Perspectives on International Security . . ." in Donald Hugh McMillen, ed., *Asian Perspectives on International Security* (1984), p. 72. Thayer is a lecturer in Southeast Asian politics in the Faculty of Military Studies at the University of New South Wales, Royal Military College-Duntroon in Australia.

[8] Stanley Karnow, *Vietnam: A History* (1983), p. 45.

Cambodia or Kampuchea?

Until 1975, the land of the Khmer people in Southeast Asia had been known as Cambodia. When the communist Khmer Rouge took control a decade ago they changed the country's official name to Democratic Kampuchea. When the Vietnamese overthrew the Khmer Rouge late in 1979, they installed a new government officially called the People's Republic of Kampuchea. Today, the forces fighting the Vietnamese-backed regime are known collectively as the Coalition Government of Democratic Kampuchea. This is the government recognized by the United States and most of the non-communist world.

The United States, which does not recognize the People's Republic of Kampuchea, officially refers to the country as Cambodia. The non-communist nationalist organizations fighting the Vietnamese-backed regime also call their country Cambodia, except when acting with the Khmer Rouge in the coalition government. This report uses the word Cambodia.

"Until mid-1978 China was Vietnam's second-biggest benefactor [behind the Soviet Union]," Morris said. "China showed public signs of hostility toward Vietnam only after Vietnam began to persecute and drive out its ethnic Chinese minority in the first months of 1978." [9] In February 1979, only a few weeks after Vietnam's successful takeover in Cambodia, Chinese troops engaged Vietnam in a brief but fierce border skirmish, which China described as a "lesson." [10] The two nations have been enemies ever since.

Some historians believe that the Vietnamese communists had long planned to bring Cambodia and neighboring Laos under its control *(see box, p. 205).* "Ever since they started the Indochinese Communist Party in the 1920s, [the Vietnamese] have had a goal of being the suzerain over the whole of Indochina," said Allan Goodman, associate dean of Georgetown University's School of Foreign Service. Arnold Isaacs agreed. "The Vietnamese regard themselves as sort of the older brother of the revolution that encompasses all of Indochina," he said. "The attitude goes back to the 1930s. . . . Certainly the Vietnamese operated on an assumption that they would be the dominant party. They have no intention of seeing an unfriendly regime in Laos or Cambodia."

Colonization Debate; Question of Thailand

There is some evidence that Vietnam's long-range goal is to colonize Cambodia — to subjugate the Khmer people. Journal-

---

[9] Morris, *op. cit.,* p. 77.
[10] China, which supplies the Khmer Rouge rebels with much of their military needs, has warned that the latest Vietnamese offensive in Cambodia could bring about a second Chinese "lesson," but many Western analysts are skeptical that this will take place.

ist Jack Wheeler, who visited Thailand and Cambodia in July 1984, said that some 700,000 Vietnamese farmers, fishermen, merchants, technicians, mechanics and others have been brought into Cambodia as settlers since the 1978 invasion. The settlers, Wheeler said, have "appropriated much of the best land" and gained control over commercial fishing operations in the Tonle Sap (the Great Lake), a large and bountiful fishing ground in the center of the country.[11] A significant number of jobs in urban areas have been taken by Vietnamese settlers, many of whom do not speak the Khmer language. "At least half the people in Phnom Penh who do mechanical work and the trades ... are Vietnamese," a Cambodian analyst told Editorial Research Reports. "The Vietnamese have taught Cambodians the Vietnamese language. So colonization is real, no question about that. . . ."

Vietnam claims that the settlers are former Vietnamese residents of Cambodia who fled that nation during periods of anti-Vietnamese sentiment in the 1960s and 1970s. But that appears to tell only part of the story. The settlers include "what they call 'Old Vietnamese' — people who lived there before the Pol Pot era ...," said Linda Hiebert. But there also are "New Vietnamese," who have not previously lived in Cambodia. "These people are young — often draft resisters from Ho Chi Minh City [formerly Saigon] — or people who simply find it much easier to make a living being small entrepreneurs inside Cambodia," Hiebert said. "There are apparently more restrictions on that kind of activity in Vietnam than in Cambodia." Hiebert, who visited Vietnam and Cambodia in 1984, does not believe that Vietnam is out to colonize Cambodia.

Vietnam's long-term goals also might involve Thailand, a staunch U.S. ally that basically has escaped the last four decades of war and turmoil in neighboring Indochina. Some believe that if conditions were ripe — if Thailand were politically and socially unstable, for example, or if Thai communist rebels gained popular support — then Vietnam might move against Thailand. "I don't think [Vietnam] has an imminent intention of invading Thailand," said Rep. Stephen J. Solarz, D-N.Y., chairman of the House Foreign Affairs Subcommittee on Asian and Pacific Affairs. "But I would not preclude the possibility that if [the Vietnamese] could consolidate their position in Cambodia, they would then attempt to support communist revolutionary forces in Thailand, particularly in the provinces adjacent to Laos that might, with assistance, have a better prospect of succeeding."

Morris believes that Vietnamese nationalism is traditionally

---

[11] Jack Wheeler, "The Khmer in Cambodia," *Reason*, February 1985, p. 28.

expansionist and that "communist revolutionary values" shape Vietnam's foreign policy. Still, he said, it is unlikely the Vietnamese would try to take Thai territory because "the Vietnamese army, occupying Laos as well as Cambodia, and pinned down by China to the north, cannot escalate much further."[12] Then, too, Thailand has a security treaty with the United States. Any large-scale Vietnamese movement into Thailand risks war with this country, as well as with China, which has said it would fight to stop Vietnamese expansion outside Indochina.

Finally, there are historic factors that buttress the argument that Vietnam has no interest in expanding its influence beyond Laos and Cambodia. Vietnam's domination of Cambodia and Laos, Allan Goodman said, "is much more consistent historically with what the Vietnamese have seen as their patrimony and their sphere of influence, and is not an 'opening wedge' in an effort to export their revolution throughout Southeast Asia. They own Indochina and they want to make sure they do."

Historical Influences

THE FIRST STATE established in what is now Cambodia is known by the Chinese name Funan and came into existence around A.D. 100. The Funan empire began expanding under the leadership of a warrior-king, Fan Shih-man, known as Fan Man, who ruled during the first two decades of the third century. Ancient Chinese texts refer to Fan Man as the "Great King" who conquered 10 kingdoms and built a powerful fleet. It is believed that at its zenith, the Funan empire occupied most of the Mekong Delta in present day southern Cambodia and southern Vietnam.

The Funan empire lasted until the middle of the 6th century when it was conquered by its northern neighbor, a rival state called Chenla that was inhabited by the Khmer people. However, the Khmers were unable to consolidate their rule for two centuries. King Jayavarman II is credited with stabilizing the situation and founding what became known as the Angkor Monarchy in the early ninth century, probably in 802. Yasovarman I was the Khmer ruler (889-900) who set up the capital at Angkor. For the next 550 years the Khmers were the dominant power in Southeast Asia. At times Khmer emperors ruled all of modern

---

[12] Morris, *op. cit.*, p. 82

Cambodia as well as sections of Vietnam, Laos, Thailand, Burma and the Malay Peninsula.

Using slave labor, the Khmers built cities, reservoirs, canals and dams throughout Cambodia, but are best known for their architecture and sculpture, especially the large "temple-mountains" built to honor their god-king rulers. The most famous example of Khmer architecture — Angkor Wat, a mammoth, ornate temple that consisted of a 130-foot-high central building surrounded by towers and colonnades — was constructed during the reign of Suryavarman II (1113-50).

The last three centuries of the Khmer empire were characterized by repeated wars against the neighboring Annamese and Chams (in north and central Vietnam) and the Siamese (in Thailand). The Siamese took Angkor in 1431, which, historian D. G. E. Hall noted, "ended finally the great period of Khmer civilization. The Khmers were not to repeat elsewhere the wonderful works of art and architecture ... which they had wrought at Ankgor in the days of its glory." [13]

For the next 400 years Cambodia was pushed and pulled between its stronger neighbors to the east and west, the Vietnamese and Thais. "Like an Asian Poland," Arnold Isaacs wrote, Cambodia "faced partition between two expanding neighbors." [14] Religious and cultural similarities ameliorated Khmer-Siamese relations somewhat, but relations between Vietnam and Cambodia were brutal and bitter. There was a "sharp cultural clash," British journalist William Shawcross wrote, "between Cambodia's Indian-influenced and Vietnam's Chinese-dominated views of society. . . . Unlike the Siamese, the Vietnamese regarded the Cambodians as 'barbarians' and attempted to eradicate Cambodian customs in the areas they seized." [15] There also was an element of racism in the Vietnamese attitude toward Cambodians, which continues today. Some Vietnamese look down on the marginally darker-skinned Cambodians, referring to them as "the black people."

The French Protectorate and Independence

In the mid-19th century France appeared on the scene. The French captured Saigon in 1859 and soon took control of all of Vietnam, turning it into the colony of Cochin China. In 1861 the French began a campaign to give Cambodian King Norodom "protection" against the Thais, who were then dominant in Cambodia. Norodom vacillated between accepting French protection and remaining under Siamese control. Then, in

---

[13] D. G. E. Hall, *A History of South-East Asia,* 2nd ed. (1964), p. 123.
[14] Arnold R. Isaacs, *Without Honor: Defeat in Vietnam and Cambodia,* (1983), p. 192.
[15] William Shawcross, *Sideshow* (1979), p. 41. Shawcross covered the war in Indochina for the *Sunday Times* of London.

Cambodia's Governments, 1941-1985

1941 - Prince Norodom Sihanouk crowned King of French-controlled Cambodia.

1953 - Cambodia achieves full independence under Sihanouk.

1955 - Sihanouk abdicates; his father, Norodom Suramarit, becomes king; Sihanouk wins election as Cambodia's first premier.

1970 - Sihanouk ousted in bloodless coup by his prime minister, Gen. Lon Nol, who is named president of the Khmer Republic.

1975 - Communist Khmer Rouge ousts Lon Nol; Khieu Samphan and Pol Pot become leaders of Democratic Kampuchea.

1979 - Vietnamese-backed communists, many of them Khmer Rouge defectors, overthrow Khmer Rouge. Former Khmer Rouge division commander, Heng Samrin, named head of state of People's Republic of Kampuchea.

1982 - Coalition Government of Democratic Kampuchea is formed in exile in Kuala Lumpur and headed by Sihanouk. Wins diplomatic recognition from United States, China and most non-communist nations.

March 1864, French troops occupied Norodom's palace while he was en route to Bangkok. Norodom returned to Cambodia to find a "treaty establishing a French protectorate over his kingdom awaiting him ... duly signed by the Emperor Napoleon [III]," Professor Hall wrote. "There was nothing to be done but accept the inevitable...." [16] Cambodia officially became a French protectorate on April 17, 1864. Cambodian kings and their courts continued to exist, but French administrators ran all affairs of state.

France treated Vietnam and Cambodia differently, concentrating most of its economic activity in Vietnam, which had the status of a full colony. Cambodia, regarded as a buffer between Vietnam and Thailand, which was allied with Britain, remained a more backward protectorate without an extensive colonial administration. France "tended to push the Vietnamese borders northward and westward at the expense of Cambodia," Shawcross noted. "Constant minor changes in the frontier took place; maps were always out of date, or ambiguously drawn, or both." [17]

During World War II Japan controlled all of French Indochina, but permitted the Nazi-controlled Vichy French government to run day-to-day affairs there. In 1941 the French placed Prince Norodom Sihanouk, whom they viewed as pliant and

---

[16] Hall, *op. cit.,* p. 615.
[17] Shawcross, *op. cit.,* p. 43.

weak, on the Cambodian throne. In March 1945, during the waning months of the war, the Japanese overthrew the Vichy French and proclaimed an end to French Indochina. Sihanouk then issued a declaration of independence, as did the Vietnamese emperor and the king of Laos. Independence was short-lived, however. French troops reoccupied Indochina soon after the war ended in August 1945. Sihanouk then embarked on a campaign for independence, which was achieved in November 1953 while the French were losing their war against Ho Chi Minh's communist forces in Vietnam. The Geneva Peace Conference of 1954, which partitioned Vietnam into north and south, also recognized Cambodia's neutrality and called for internationally supervised elections to select a government.

Sihanouk's Neutrality; Lon Nol's Coup

Sihanouk won the first election in 1955 and, primarily because of his extreme popularity among the peasantry who regarded him as a god-king, remained head of Cambodia for 15 more years, gradually assuming more and more autocratic control. Sihanouk's central political philosophy was neutrality. "I had to balance the influences of the West and the East and I had to walk on a tightrope," Sihanouk said in a recent interview published in *The New York Review of Books*.[18] Throughout the 1960s Sihanouk managed to play his neighbors, as well as the superpowers, against each other. He would condemn Chinese or Soviet communism, for example, and then denounce American intervention in Vietnam. At the same time that he received American military assistance to fight the small Cambodian communist movement — which he referred to in French as the *Khmers Rouges* ("Red Khmers") — Sihanouk permitted North Vietnam and the Viet Cong to use Cambodia's northeast provinces as staging and supply areas in their war against South Vietnam and the United States.

Sihanouk generally succeeded in managing the difficult neutralist stance — until the war in Vietnam heated up in the late 1960s. On March 18, 1969, the United States began to bomb suspected North Vietnamese sanctuaries in Cambodia. Sihanouk agreed to the bombing, but believed that political pressure was the best way to persuade the Vietnamese communists to leave Cambodian territory. Other Cambodian leaders — including Sihanouk's prime minister, Lon Nol, and deputy prime minister, Sirik Matak — wanted to mount a joint U.S.-Cambodian military effort against the Vietnamese. On March 18, 1970, while Sihanouk was in Moscow asking the Soviet Union to influence the Vietnamese to quit Cambodia, Lon Nol and Sirik Matak ousted the prince in a bloodless coup. The United

---

[18] " 'The Lesser Evil,' An Interview with Norodom Sihanouk," *The New York Review of Books,* March 14, 1985, p. 21.

States strongly supported Lon Nol and distrusted Sihanouk, but it appears unlikely that this country engineered the coup. "Allegations to the contrary, there is no firm evidence to substantiate the speculation that CIA agents encouraged [Lon Nol and Sirik Matak] — though contacts with American operatives may have inspired their wishful thinking that the United States favored a *coup d'etat*," Karnow said.[19]

"With Sihanouk's fall," Arnold Isaacs noted, "the Vietnam War fell on his helpless country like a collapsing brick wall."[20] South Vietnamese units attacked North Vietnamese troops inside Cambodia in late March. The North Vietnamese responded with a counteroffensive.

Then, in late April, 20,000 U.S. and South Vietnamese troops moved into Cambodia in what President Nixon, in announcing the action April 30, termed an "incursion." The operation was designed to wipe out

Sihanouk

Viet Cong and North Vietnamese headquarters in Cambodia, to assist the militarily weak Cambodian government and to show American resolve in fighting communism. The U.S. action brought a barrage of domestic protest, especially on college campuses and in Congress. Critics claimed that Nixon was illegally expanding the Vietnam War into neutralist Cambodia and backing away from his pledge to pursue peace in Vietnam. American troops withdrew from Cambodia on June 30, 1970. But South Vietnamese troops remained, and the war against the communists continued, with American bombing support.

During the next five years the U.S.-backed Cambodian forces fought the North Vietnamese, Viet Cong and increasing numbers of Khmer Rouge, who gained adherents when Prince Sihanouk gave them his support following the Lon Nol coup.[21] Pol

---

[19] Karnow, *op. cit.*, pp. 604-605.
[20] Isaacs, *op. cit.*, p. 199.
[21] Explaining his decision to support the Khmer Rouge, Sihanouk said in the *New York Review of Books* interview: "I, and Cambodians inside Kampuchea at that time, had not love, but esteem for the Khmer Rouge. Nobody could imagine that they might be the monsters they were after taking power. At that time everybody, even my compatriots in Phnom Penh under the leadership of Lon Nol, believed sincerely that the Khmer Rouge, although communists, were also non-corrupt, good democrats and dedicated people. They wished that the Khmer Rouge would take power because they were very disappointed with Lon Nol, Sirik Matak and that very corrupt regime...."

Pot led the Khmer Rouge, many of whom were trained and armed in North Vietnam and China.

Although U.S. forces officially withdrew from the Vietnam War on Jan. 27, 1973, U.S. military support to the Lon Nol government continued until Aug. 15, when funding for such operations was barred by Congress. By that time the Khmer Rouge had taken over the brunt of the fighting from the Vietnamese communists.

The final Khmer Rouge dry-season offensive, which began Jan. 1, 1975, overwhelmed the Lon Nol forces. Lon Nol fled Cambodia on April 1. Sixteen days later the Khmer Rouge seized the capital Phnom Penh, and Pol Pot took over the country. The reign of terror began.[22]

Debating Responsibility for Khmer Rouge

In his 1979 book, *Sideshow: Kissinger, Nixon and the Destruction of Cambodia,* British journalist William Shawcross argued that American policy was primarily responsible for Pol Pot's takeover. "Whatever Nixon and [Secretary of State Henry A.] Kissinger intended for Cambodia," Shawcross said, "their efforts created catastrophe." The bombing, the U.S. incursion in 1970 and American support of the Lon Nol government "did much to create" the holocaust inflicted on Cambodia by the Khmer Rouge. "Cambodia was not a mistake," Shawcross concluded, "it was a crime." [23]

Answering those charges in his 1982 memoir, *Years of Upheaval,* Kissinger said American actions were intended solely to save Cambodia and Vietnam from communism. The party to blame, "the master architect of [the Khmer Rouge] disaster," Kissinger contended, was North Vietnam. "It was Hanoi ... if it was anyone, that brought the war to Cambodia and made possible the genocide by the Khmer Rouge." [24]

Others say the responsibility for the Khmer Rouge holocaust lies largely with the Khmer Rouge themselves. "We have partial responsibility, but by no means exclusive responsibility," said Rep. Solarz. "The fact that Sihanouk joined forces with the Khmer Rouge gave Pol Pot an opportunity to recruit much more effectively among the peasantry because he could recruit in the name of the prince. My guess is that had as much if not more to do with the ultimate success of the Khmer Rouge than the American bombing."

---

[22] The Khmer Rouge atrocities have been forcefully described by, among others, Sydney Schanberg, a journalist for *The New York Times* who was one of the last Americans to leave Phnom Penh in 1975. Schanberg's account of the survival of his Cambodian aide, Dith Pran, during the Khmer Rouge reign is the subject of the movie "The Killing Fields."

[23] Shawcross, *op. cit.,* p. 396.

[24] Henry A. Kissinger, *Years of Upheaval* (1982), p. 337.

Finding a Solution

IN AUGUST 1967, five non-communist Southeast Asian nations — Indonesia, Malaysia, Philippines, Singapore and Thailand — formed a multinational cooperative organization, the Association of Southeast Asian Nations (ASEAN). In the last five years ASEAN, which now also includes the small nation of Brunei on the island of Borneo, has taken an active role in trying to solve the Cambodian problem.

In July 1981 the United Nations International Conference on Kampuchea adopted a resolution, which was a compromise between the ASEAN position and that of China, calling for a U.N. peacekeeping force to enforce a cease-fire and the withdrawal of all the factions fighting in Cambodia as well as to monitor open elections to restore Cambodian sovereignty. The U. N. General Assembly overwhelmingly has endorsed the resolution annually since 1981. China and the United States vote with the majority in favor of the proposals. Vietnam, the Soviet Union and its closest allies vote against them.

The positions of China, the Soviet Union and the United States on the ASEAN-sponsored proposals illustrate the geopolitical nature of the Cambodian situation. "China views Vietnam as the eastern link in the Soviet stranglehold on its periphery," Bangkok-based journalist Paul Quinn-Judge said. "Hanoi views China as the spearhead of the 'China-ASEAN-U.S. axis.' " [25]

China has supplied the Khmer Rouge resistance fighters in Cambodia with virtually all their armaments and made it clear that it will intervene militarily if Vietnam attacks Thailand. Vietnam says it will not withdraw until the Chinese stop supporting the Khmer Rouge.

[25] Paul Quinn-Judge, "The Vietnam-China Split: Old Ties Remain," *Indochina Issues* (published by the Center for International Policy, in Washington, D.C.), January 1985, p. 1.

The Soviet Union appears to view Vietnam's occupation of Cambodia as a way both to strengthen Moscow's position and counter Chinese influence in the region. The Soviet Union is underwriting the Vietnamese military in Cambodia and gives Vietnam economic assistance. Moscow has also increased its military presence in Vietnam, setting up what has been described as a major air and naval base at the former American military installation at Cam Ranh Bay.

American officials have consistently attacked the Vietnamese occupation of Cambodia as an illegal act of aggression against the Khmer people. The official U.S. position is that this country will not move toward normalizing diplomatic relations with Vietnam until Vietnamese troops are withdrawn from Cambodia and until Vietnam shows a willingness to cooperate fully in accounting for the nearly 2,500 Americans who are missing in action in Vietnam.[26]

The United States has worked through the United Nations and other international organizations to support the two non-communist Cambodian resistance groups. "The basic U.S. interest in Cambodia has to do with the regional stability and security of the ASEAN countries, especially Thailand," said the State Department's Lyall Breckon. "Their interest and well-being is threatened by the Vietnamese occupation of Cambodia and the presence of Vietnamese military forces as occupying power in that country and up against the Thai border." The United States contributes humanitarian aid to the international organizations that work with Cambodian refugees along the Thai-Cambodian border. In fiscal 1984 those contributions totaled $15.1 million. The United States has also stepped up its military aid and arms sales to Thailand.

So far the United States has not provided any direct military assistance to the resistance forces, despite increasing pressure from ASEAN. However, on March 20 the House Foreign Affairs Subcommittee on Asian and Pacific Affairs voted to give Thailand $5 million to be turned over to the non-communist resistance groups in Cambodia. The Reagan administration had not requested the aid and has not endorsed the subcommittee provision. But Secretary of State George P. Shultz agreed to meet privately in Washington D. C., April 10 with Son Sann of the Khmer People's National Liberation Front and Sihanouk's son, Prince Norodom Ranariddh, who are expected to lobby for the aid. Although the purpose of the proposed aid has been left unclear, State Department spokesman Bernard Kalb said the administration opposed funneling military aid to the two rebel groups. "U.S. supply of weapons to the resistance could create

[26] See "MIAs: Decade of Frustration," *E.R.R.*, 1983 Vol. II, pp. 821-840.

Laos

The second jewel in Vietnam's Indochina crown is Laos, one of the poorest countries in the world. Around three million people live in Laos, which is smaller in size than Oregon. Until the late 19th century Laos was dominated by its larger and more powerful neighbors, Thailand and Vietnam. Then, in 1890, France annexed Laos, and the country remained under French control until it was granted full independence in 1953 — the same year that France gave Cambodia its independence.

For the next 20 years Laos was the scene of intermittent civil warfare between the Royal Lao government and pro-communist Pathet Lao guerrillas, and was a secondary battlefield in the Vietnam War. In 1965 the United States launched a massive aerial bombardment of suspected North Vietnamese supply routes in Laos. The U.S. air war, which continued until the United States left Vietnam in 1973, is thought to be the longest sustained bombing campaign in military history.

In February 1973 the Lao combatants declared a cease-fire, and a coalition government was formed in April 1974. By late 1975, however, the Pathet Lao gained control of the country, abolished the monarchy and on Dec. 2 declared the formation of the People's Democratic Republic of Laos.

The Pathet Lao have long been subservient to the Vietnamese communists. Between 40,000 and 45,000 Vietnamese troops are stationed in Laos. Even though there is a separate Lao government, most of the world regards Laos as little more than a colony of Vietnam.

difficulties in reaching a negotiated settlement and in sustaining international support for the Cambodian cause by highlighting Cambodia as a U.S.-Vietnam conflict," Kalb said April 1.

Dim Prospects for Vietnamese Withdrawal

Despite the desires of the ASEAN countries, the United States and China, prospects for a Vietnamese withdrawal from Cambodia in the near future are dim. For one thing, the recent offensive against the guerrillas has given Vietnam its strongest military position in Cambodia since the 1978 invasion. The Vietnamese army is expected to fortify its positions in western Cambodia to try to keep most of the guerrillas — and the refugees that follow them — bottled up inside Thailand.

And there is evidence suggesting that the United States places a relatively low priority on solving the Cambodian problem. The Reagan administration is heavily involved in other, more demanding international issues, especially the arms control negotiations with the Soviet Union and the campaign to help Central American allies in their fights against leftists.

Some foreign policy analysts say that for the present this country is content to let the ASEAN nations and China take the lead in working on the Cambodian problem.

Finally, there is the thorny issue of the Khmer Rouge. In the months following Vietnam's invasion, the United States found itself in the awkward position of politically supporting the communist rebels, who were then the only forces resisting the Vietnamese. Today, the United States supports the two non-communist Cambodian resistance forces and tries to distance itself from the Khmer Rouge, with which they are allied.[27] As for Prince Sihanouk, he has said that his alliance with the Khmer Rouge makes him "very uncomfortable.... I have lost five children, fourteen grandchildren at the hands of the Khmer Rouge. So many innocent people died." He entered the alliance, he said, because "there is the danger of Vietnamese expansionism and Soviet hegemonism and non-democratic, very anti-free people governments and states. Those states are very dangerous; we cannot allow them to go further." [28]

Recently, Khmer Rouge leaders announced changes in their political philosophy, emphasizing "nationalist rather than revolutionary themes," Morris said. "Religion, formerly banned, is now tolerated ... in areas controlled by the Khmer Rouge.... Premarital sex is no longer punished by executions. And private commerce ... is now tolerated in the form of the black market." [29] Few people believe that the announced changes are anything more than cosmetic. "The Khmer Rouge haven't changed a bit," one Washington analyst said. "They may have changed their tactics, but they have not changed their spots."

Hints About Wanting Diplomatic Relations

In the final analysis, it is Vietnam that will determine the future of Cambodia. Some argue that the Vietnamese might consider quitting Cambodia if Vietnam's serious economic troubles continue. One of the poorest nations in the world, Vietnam is burdened with a huge foreign debt and high unemployment and inflation. "Vietnam desperately needs aid of all kinds, from medical supplies to developmental assistance," said journalist William Broyles Jr., who recently visited the country.[30] "But the

---

[27] Former Ambassador Kirkpatrick, for example, said in her Oct. 30 U.N. speech that the non-communist resistance forces "are the true embodiment of Khmer nationalism and the hopes of Cambodians for a future which is neither Khmer Rouge nor Vietnamese." More recently, Paul D. Wolfowitz, assistant secretary of state for East Asian and Pacific Affairs, told the *Los Angeles Times*, Feb. 28, that while the United States provides only humanitarian assistance to the non-communist forces, we "do not provide any assistance of any kind to the Khmer Rouge, whose atrocities we abhor."

[28] *The New York Review of Books, op. cit.,* p. 26

[29] Morris, *op. cit.,* p. 73.

[30] William Broyles Jr., "The Road to Hill 10," *The Atlantic,* April 1985, p. 100. Broyles, who served as a Marine lieutenant in Vietnam in 1969 and 1970, has been the editor in chief of *Newsweek* and *Texas Monthly.*

occupation of Cambodia has caused almost every country outside the Soviet bloc to terminate all direct aid." Vietnam could conceivably gain economic assistance from Western countries, including, perhaps the United States, if it left Cambodia.

But Vietnam has shown no indication that its economic burden will influence its Cambodian policies. And Hanoi vigorously denies that it is a puppet of the Soviet Union. The Soviet Union, Pham Van Dong said in the *Newsweek* interview, "respects our independence and has extended its hand of friendship to assist us in our defense and development. Vietnam is like a bird in the sky, flying free. It needs its flock for support and assistance — but it always remains free."

Vietnam has been hinting in recent years that it would like to normalize relations with the United States. The most recent signal came March 20 when Vietnam turned over the remains of five people believed to be American servicemen to U.S. officials. Some American analysts say that normalization might be a first step in solving the situation in Cambodia. "I feel we should have diplomatic relations with every country that exists," said Allan Goodman of Georgetown University. "That does not imply that we endorse their policies or that we are allied with them, but that we should see diplomatic relations as the normal way in which countries that are not at war carry out business with one another." The Reagan administration, however, continues to adhere to the policy that as long as Vietnamese forces occupy Cambodia this country will not undertake talks aimed at normalizing relations.[31]

What may be the best hope for a change in Vietnamese policy is the fact that nearly all of Vietnam's top leaders, known as the "old warriors," are approaching the end of their careers. Those leaders — including Party Secretary General Le Duan, Prime Minister Pham Van Dong and Gen. Nguyen Giap, a vice chairman of the Council of Ministers — are believed to be the least flexible with regard to the Cambodian issue. When the old warriors are replaced by a younger and more pragmatic group of leaders, it is possible that Vietnam will enter into serious negotiations to find a political settlement in Cambodia. That day will not come for several years — if it comes to pass at all.

---

[31] The United States and Vietnam have in recent years had sporadic meetings arranged by third parties on two humanitarian issues — accounting for Americans missing in action and the resettlement of Vietnamese political prisoners in the United States.

Selected Bibliography

Books

Barron, John, and Anthony Paul, *Murder of a Gentle Land: The Untold Story of Communist Genocide in Cambodia,* Reader's Digest Press, 1977.

Goodman, Allan E., *The Lost Peace: America's Search for a Negotiated Settlement of the Vietnam War,* Hoover Institution Press, 1978.

Hall, D. G. E., *A History of South-East Asia,* 3rd ed., Macmillan, 1968.

Isaacs, Arnold R., *Without Honor: Defeat in Vietnam and Cambodia,* Johns Hopkins University Press, 1983.

Karnow, Stanley, *Vietnam: A History,* Viking, 1983.

Kirk, Donald, *Wider War: The Struggle for Cambodia, Thailand and Laos,* Praeger, 1971.

Kissinger, Henry A., *Years of Upheaval,* Little, Brown, 1982.

Leifer, Michael, *Cambodia: The Search for Security,* Praeger, 1967.

McMillen, Donald Hugh, ed., *Asian Perspectives on International Security,* Macmillan, 1984.

Osborne, Milton, *The French Presence in Cochin-China and Cambodia,* Cornell University Press, 1969.

Ponchaud, François, *Cambodia: Year Zero,* Holt, Rinehart and Winston, 1978.

Shawcross, William, *The Quality of Mercy: Cambodia, Holocaust and Modern Conscience,* Simon & Schuster, 1984.

——, *Sideshow: Kissinger, Nixon and the Destruction of Cambodia,* Simon & Schuster, 1979.

Simon, Sheldon W., *War and Politics in Cambodia,* Duke University Press, 1974.

Smith, Roger M., *Cambodia's Foreign Policy,* Cornell University Press, 1975.

Articles

Far Eastern Economic Review, selected issues.

Indochina Issues (published by the Center for International Policy), selected issues.

Morris, Stephen J., "Vietnam's Vietnam," *The Atlantic,* January 1985.

Santoli, Al, "The New Indochina War," *The New Republic,* May 30, 1983.

" 'The Lesser Evil': An Interview With Norodom Sihanouk," *The New York Review of Books,* March 14, 1985.

Wheeler, Jack, "The Khmer in Cambodia," *Reason,* February 1985.

Reports and Studies

Editorial Research Reports: "MIAs: Decade of Frustration," 1983 Vol. II, p. 821; "Vietnam War Reconsidered," 1983 Vol. I, p. 189; "Vietnam War Legacy," 1979 Vol. II, p. 481.

Graphics: Sihanouk by Assistant Art Director Robert Redding; maps by Patrick Murphy

INDEX